Shaping Civil Litigation Using Procedur

Shaping Civil Litigation Using Procedural Agreements

Anna Nylund and Antonio Cabral (Eds.)

eleven

Published, sold and distributed by Eleven
P.O. Box 85576
2508 CG The Hague
The Netherlands
Tel.: +31 70 33 070 33
Fax: +31 70 33 070 30
e-mail: sales@elevenpub.nl
www.elevenpub.com

Sold and distributed in USA and Canada
Independent Publishers Group
814 N. Franklin Street
Chicago, IL 60610, USA
Order Placement: +1 800 888 4741
Fax: +1 312 337 5985
orders@ipgbook.com
www.ipgbook.com

Eleven is an imprint of Boom (Den Haag).

ISBN 978-90-4730-225-4
ISBN 978-94-0011-428-9 (E-book)

Table of contents

Preface

This book interrogates the potential of, and challenges associated with, procedural agreements as a tool for shaping and expediting civil proceedings. Proponents of 'contractualisation' argue that these agreements can enhance efficiency, thus benefitting both the parties involved and the justice system. However, such agreements could have repercussions on access to justice, particularly for inexperienced or vulnerable litigants. Additionally, the book explores the potential conflicts these agreements may pose with important public policies.

The practice of shaping civil litigation through procedural agreements is gaining wider acceptance. In Europe, the ELI/UNIDROIT European Model Rules of Civil Procedure Rules 57-60 represent this shift, aligning with renewed attention to the principles of cooperation and case management. Moreover, court proceedings have become more diversified in response to court dockets' growing complexity and diversity. International Commercial Courts as subdivisions within selected national courts and the rise of alternative dispute resolution are examples of this evolution. Furthermore, the implementation of special rules applicable only to specific cases, such as those involving consumer rights, further contributes to the diversification of court proceedings.

These developments raise the question of the relationship between flexibilisation, diversification and procedural agreements, such as whether flexibilisation diminishes the relevance of procedural agreements or whether, on the contrary, such agreements become valuable tools for effectively navigating complexity. Additionally, they raise questions related to the contextual elements of court proceedings, encompassing the foundations of civil procedure rules, the legal-cultural context and the extent to which courts serve as a vehicle for advancing public policies inherent in areas such as consumer or competition law.

The boundary between substantive law and procedural law is fluid. Certain agreements with tangible procedural impact, such as those on the standard of proof, fall within the realm of substantive law. Concepts from contract law and international private law are employed in interpreting and determining the effects of procedural contracts. Consequently, this book examines the degree to which concepts and tenets could and should migrate across the divide, seeking to renegotiate the boundary that separates these fields.

This book endeavours to address procedural agreements through two approaches. First, an introduction to procedural agreements is followed by an examination of selected aspects of well known procedural agreements (choice of court, evidence, litigation costs, appeals and alternative dispute resolution). The second approach involves exploring the interrelations between procedural contracts and selected developments in civil litigation, including the obligation of European courts to protect consumers against unfair terms, the rise of International Commercial Courts, the entanglements between procedural agreements, flexible procedural rules, and the increasing legal and factual complexity of litigated cases. The concluding chapter discusses the potential prospects of shaping civil proceedings using procedural agreements.

This book would not have been published without the financial support of the Nansen fund, the Meltzer fund and the University of Bergen, the insightful comments from the anonymous peer reviewers, and a smooth publication process at Eleven International Publishing.

Anna Nylund

Procedural Contracts and Agreements: An Introduction to a New Era of Party Autonomy in Litigation

Antonio Cabral

1 Introduction

Contract and litigation – the improbable encounter of the two worlds that seemed as apart as incompatible. Usually portrayed as the realm of dissensus, depicted as a game, a war or a duel,[1] litigation would always entail belligerence and repel consensual interactions among disputants to determine the formalities of court proceedings.

Furthermore, since most jurisdictions restrict self-help mechanisms (limiting one party's ability to impose unilateral determinations on others), access to justice has always been a matter of public policy. Whenever a conflict arises, the legal system would have to channel the dispute to structured organs and bodies, providing fair proceedings to solve the conflict within the rule of law. The formalities governing court procedures would thus be predetermined by imperative default rules that the parties may not modify, and judges would rule on procedural issues simply by applying statutory provisions and precedents. Based on these assumptions, many jurisdictions have consolidated an understanding of litigation as a space of public interests, and the design of court procedures reflected the choice of legislators, with no participation of the parties.

Contracts, covenants and agreements were seen as instruments of private nature, voluntary declarations driven by a logic of negotiation, flexibility and party control, mechanisms that could seldom be applied to deviate from cogent legal rules. Therefore, parties' stipulations could not determine the shape and form of court procedures. According to this line of thought, any procedural agreement, understood as a contract or consensual determination of the disputants to modify the rules of civil procedure in an actual or future litigation, would be invalid and disallowed.

1 Piero Calamandrei, 'Il processo come giuoco' in Mauro Cappelletti (ed), *Opere Giuridiche*, vol I (Morano 1965) 559.

For quite a long time, this traditional view has excited vehement opposition to party autonomy in civil procedure, reducing the protagonism of the litigants in defining procedure before state courts. Following the public nature of litigation, an agreement-based procedure would not be permissible, and parties' disposition over litigation proceedings was exceptional.[2] Then procedural agreements gradually faded away, virtually disappearing from some jurisdictions and often seen as a monstrosity, challenging to define, categorise and operate.[3]

However, attempts to implement party-driven flexibilisation of court procedures are not entirely novel. Agreements are practices as old as the law itself. The origins of concepts related to procedural agreements can be traced back to contractual forms of court proceedings observed throughout legal history.[4] Yet, a comparative analysis shows that most contemporary legal systems are familiar with at least some types of procedural contracts, such as arbitration agreements, choice of court clauses and agreements to mediate before filing a lawsuit before the judiciary.[5] Hence, this historical resistance to procedural agreements seemed to echo old practices that were hard to couple with contemporary components of civil litigation.

This perception has led to a clear pendulum swing in the past decades. Procedural agreements and contracts have been a growing trend in many jurisdictions, starting in contractual practice and slowly climbing into formal normative status. Indeed, this renewed interest in procedural contracts began as a bottom-up movement that originated in day-to-day contractual life, even if, at that point, legal scholars were not attentive to them. Despite initial scepticism towards this type of agreements, legislators and courts across the globe are steadily adopting models that favour party self-determination as to the rules of court procedures, and legal literature has begun to approach the subject from other perspectives.

This shift towards the empowerment of litigants to shape court procedures has lately acquired renewed strength and different nuances, enabling parties to contractually agree upon many procedural rules, such as those related to filing formalities, service and notifications, standing to sue and other requirements for participation in court procedures, evidence, appeals, enforcement, costs, etc. The extent to which these

2 Until the end of the 20th century, many jurisdictions only acknowledged voluntary declarations of the parties to govern procedural effects if they were unilateral, performed exclusively by way of a procedural defence (*exceptio*); cf. Arthur Nikisch, Zivilprozeßrecht (Mohr Siebeck 1950) 217-219.

3 Cf. Yvonne Muller, *Le contrat judiciaire en droit privé* (University of Paris I 1995) 4, 17, 179-182. Robson Godinho (*Negócios processuais sobre o ônus da prova no novo Código de Processo Civil* (RT 2015) 28-29, 61) has seen this as an 'epistemological trauma hard to overcome'.

4 Muller (n. 3) 11 ff; Emilio Betti, *Istituzioni di Diritto Romano*, vol I (2nd edn, Cedam 1947) 256-259; Loïc Cadiet, 'Propos introductif: faire lien' in Sandrine Chassagnard-Pinet and David Hiez (eds), *La contractualisation de la production normative* (Dalloz 2008) 170, 178.

5 Anna Nylund and Antonio Cabral, 'General Report: Contractualisation of Civil Litigation' in Anna Nylund and Antonio Cabral (eds), *Contractualisation of Civil Litigation* (Intersentia 2023) 3-5.

agreements and contracts are allowed in a given legal system varies. Still, there is certainly a movement in favour of the contractualisation of civil litigation.[6]

This introduction discusses key concepts related to contractual agreements, highlights their correlation to other aspects of contemporary civil procedure law and identifies possible future challenges. It also gives an overview of the themes and chapters of this book.

2 Procedural Contracts as Hybrid Means to Improve Access to Justice, Efficiency, Flexibilisation and Adaptation of Court Procedures

The rise of consensual dispute resolution is a tale of the search for more flexibilisation, adaptation and efficiency. It relates not only to procedural contracts but also to several connected trends of contemporary civil justice, which provide a more benign normative framework for party disposition over litigation procedures.

Undeniably, there are reasons for submitting court proceedings to a rigid and inflexible proceeding in contemporary civil procedure. Invariable formal rules protect the parties against the abusive discretion of judges, and sticking to pre-established sets of default rules might favour legal security and legal certainty while allowing courts to command litigation from filing until decision-making swiftly.

However, in many legal systems, one can observe an intense efficiency crisis in court procedures. The number of pending proceedings has skyrocketed, and the increased influx of new cases created huge backlogs and brought up problems such as excessive duration of court procedures, high costs and enforcement effectiveness deficits, which have made court administrators and policymakers struggle to provide adequate settings for dispute resolution. This frustrating scenario has provoked disillusionment and a lack of belief in litigation, which called for new strategies and different instruments to streamline, accelerate and simplify proceedings.

Therefore, in many jurisdictions, litigation shifted towards increasing flexibilisation, aiming at improving efficiency. Procedures provided for in statutory norms became defeasible, and management powers have been granted to courts to waive formalities, change deadlines, interfere in the order of the production of evidence,[7] sequence issues

6 Ibid., 36-37.

7 Emmanuel Jeuland, 'Le renouveau du principe du juge naturel et l'industrialisation de la justice' in Benoît Frydman and Emmanuel Jeuland (eds), *Le nouveau management de la justice et l'indépendence des juges* (LGDJ 2011) 98; Peter Chan and C.H. van Rhee (eds), *Civil Case Management in the Twenty-First Century: Court Structures Still Matter* (Springer 2021); C.H. van Rhee (ed), *Judicial Case Management and Efficiency in Civil Litigation* (Intersentia 2008) 11-25.

or invert stages of the proceedings,[8] set a timetable for pretrial discovery, etc.[9] This growing flexibilisation has eroded the ideal of a court procedure fully determined by constant and non-alterable default norms. The rules of court procedures are much more alterable than in the past.

Party autonomy to shape court proceedings might have also grown from the perception that statutory default norms are not optimal for governing all kinds of procedures. Arguably, the old-fashioned way of providing a fixed number of default rules, offering the parties a limited list of statutory procedures, might have indeed moved the judiciary structures smoothly with few bumps along a predictable path of pregiven curves and shapes. A smaller menu of court procedures may also decrease complexity, and a simpler display of procedural alternatives speaks in favour of more vulnerable litigants who might not always have access to sophisticated and ultra-specialised attorney services. However, pregiven legislative rules providing rigid and inflexible ordinary proceedings do not offer the parties adequate relief to solve every dispute brought before the judiciary.

Specificities of the case at hand often reveal a need not only for flexibility but also for adapting default rules. If parties are the ultimate beneficiaries of access to justice, the legal system should provide some room for party-driven flexibilisation and adaptation. Debatably, efficiency could be seen merely as a problem of the judiciary since court administration requires public expenditure and relates to budget issues. Notwithstanding this, parties might think that efficiency should be thought of from the perspective of those whose conflicts are brought to court. Therefore, the disputants should be the ones to define, if not all, at least some formalities of court procedures. After all, parties know better which proceeding suits their needs better. Therefore, they should be given some initiative to adapt proceedings to what they consider to be the most efficient framework for each case.

However, even in light of problems of low efficiency and lack of flexibility and adaptability, some legal systems have historically resisted giving the parties the power to determine court procedures, and this resistance is seen until today. So, disputants started to seek alternatives.

First, parties began to move away from the judiciary and towards alternative dispute resolution (ADR), which allows disputants to shape the procedure through contract

8 Robert Bone, 'The Process of Making Process: Court Rulemaking, Democratic Legitimacy, and the Procedural Efficacy' (1999) 87 Georgetown Law Journal 917. For the different systems regarding discretionary case management powers of the judge, see John Sorabji, 'Managing Claims – General Report' in *IAPL Tianjin Conference Papers* (2017) 38 ff.

9 Robert Bone, 'Who Decides – A Critical Look at Procedural Discretion' (2007) 28 Cardozo Law Review 1968.

as they find adequate. Indeed, arbitration agreements represent a well-known form of contractually designed procedure, although not conducted before a state judge.[10]

This movement towards ADR represented a veritable 'flight' from the courts: in the absence of suitable proceedings in litigation, the alternative extrajudicial means of dispute resolution appeared to be the only possible path.[11] However, arbitration and other kinds of ADR are not suited for every conflict (e.g. nonwaivable rights). They are often expensive dispute resolution methods, economically unfeasible for millions of people, especially in developing countries. Therefore, ADR has not entirely solved the need for adaptation and flexibilisation in dispute resolution.

The result of this complex equation is that, for a considerable number of individuals worldwide, there would be mainly two choices for dispute resolution: (i) extrajudicial alternatives such as arbitration, that is, private procedures of contractual nature where parties can model proceedings as they deem adequate, even if at high costs and (ii) litigation, less costly, more bureaucratic and with rigid and inflexible default rules of procedure, which could only be bent or adapted by decree of judges exerting case management powers. There had been no third way, no 'alternative to ADR' that would provide party-driven flexibilisation within the framework of court proceedings.[12] This lack of options has undermined access to justice. Because of the inadequacy of ordinary court proceedings for resolving certain disputes, there seem to be fewer reasons to limit the parties to only a few possible alternatives nowadays.[13]

Thus, procedural agreements appeared as an instrument to improve access to justice, fostering new settings for dispute resolution that are not framed in the 'litigation versus arbitration' duality but rather provide for intermediate and hybrid paths,[14] a way for the parties to design court proceedings (i.e. formal self-regulation) before the judiciary. Rather than 'alternative',[15] this technique could be portrayed as 'complementary', aiming at flexibilisation and adaptation but done within litigation.[16]

---

10 Loïc Cadiet, 'Le jeux du contrat et du procés' in Marie-Jeanne Campana, *Philosophie du Droit et Droit Économique: Mélanges offerts à Gérard Farjat* (LGDJ 1999) 23 ff.

11 Michelle Taruffo, 'Un'alternativa alle alternative: modelli di risoluzione dei conflitti' (2007) 152 Revista de Processo 321.

12 Sarah Rudolph Cole, 'Managerial Litigants? The Overlooked Problem of Party Autonomy in Dispute Resolution' (2000) 51 Hastings Law Journal 1233-1234.

13 Gerhard Wagner, *Prozeßverträge: Privatautonomie im Verfahrensrecht* (Mohr Siebeck 1998) 3-4.

14 Remo Caponi, 'Autonomia privata e processo civile: gli accordi processuali', (2010) 1 Civil Procedure Review 47.

15 Kevin E. Davis and Helen Hershkoff, 'Contracting for Procedure' (2011) 63 William & Mary Law Review 517.

16 Loïc Cadiet, 'Los acuerdos procesales en derecho francés: situación actual de la contractualización del proceso y de la justicia en Francia' (2012) 3 Civil Procedure Review 2.

3 Contractual Binding Determinations and Other Consensual Interplay with a Focus on Judges' Oversight

This trend of party-driven adaptation of procedural default rules has been observed in several legal systems, even in various shades and with diverse intensity.

In jurisdictions permissive of procedural contracts, parties are empowered to design many aspects of court procedures, from filing to enforcement. Their joint declarations have contractual force, are binding on judges and will be enforceable to determine the forms of court proceedings.[17] Non-performance of the agreed obligations or any action against the expected behaviour would call for dismissal, invalidity or even liability for damages, and depending on the subject matter of the procedural agreement, the contractually defined rules and formalities must be enforced by the courts against a reluctant party, either in the same judicial procedure where they are meant to produce their effects or by use of other civil actions to enforce the agreement.[18]

On the opposite end of the scale, some jurisdictions still retain a view of litigation against the backdrop of strong public policy issues. Therefore, the formalities to govern procedure must be previously determined by default rules, limiting parties' autonomy to very few types of agreements expressly provided for in legislation, such as choice of court and arbitration clauses. Court oversight or supervision over the parties' activities is understood to be necessary to maintain litigation within the boundaries of what is socially desirable. Therefore, consensual outcomes are not binding on judges; the court can simply disregard them and decide otherwise. At most, the agreement would be seen as a 'joint application' or 'joint request', so even if parties agree to a certain procedural effect, their mutual consent is not sufficient to determine the outcome. It would only produce the desired effects if the judge rules accordingly.[19] In the end, in these legal systems, the parties' agreement seems a mere fact or circumstance, only to be considered by judges, with persuasive – but not binding – effects.[20]

---

17 Antonio Cabral, 'Designing Procedure by Contract: Litigation Agreements in Contemporary Civil Procedure' (2019) 9 International Journal of Procedural Law 363; Lauranne Claus, Stefan Rutten and Gert Straetmans, 'Contractualisation of Civil Litigation in Belgium' in Nylund and Cabral (n 5); Anaïs Danet, 'La contractualisation de la procédure civile en France' in Nylund and Cabral (n 5); Remme Verkerk and Denise Walta-Jansen, 'Contractualisation of Civil Litigation in The Netherlands' in Nylund and Cabral (n 5).

18 On the possibilities and instruments to enforce procedural agreements, Peter Schlosser, *Einverständliches Parteihandeln im Zivilprozeß* (Mohr Siebeck 1968) 47 ff; Wagner (n 13) 212-237; Antonio Cabral, *Convenções processuais: teoria geral dos negócios jurídicos processuais* (4th edn, Juspodivm 2023) 294-297.

19 Slawomir Cieślak, Janusz Jankowski and Maciej Muliński, 'Contractualisation of Civil Litigation in Poland', 357-358; Miguel García Casas, 'Contractualisation of Civil Litigation in Spain' 371-375, both in Nylund and Cabral (n 5).

20 Although not binding to the judge, joint applications are another form of convergent consensual interplay by which the parties act to mould the procedure to their needs. In this sense, Robert Bone, 'Party Rulemaking: Making Procedural Rules through Party Choice' (2012) 90 Texas Law Review 1340. The most important difference between contracts, agreements and legal transactions, and other forms of bilateral conduct with legal effects is that the parties to contracts have not only the freedom to decide

Between those two extremes, many jurisdictions have moved from a total denial of party disposition over procedure towards allowing some procedural agreements, enabling the parties to deviate from statutory norms in more and more aspects of litigation. These legal systems tend to amplify party disposition to regulate court procedures differently than what was provided for by the legislator,[21] yet sometimes allowing the court to retain a high degree of oversight. In these jurisdictions, judges may often veto the procedural agreement or exert flexibilisation through case management powers instead.[22]

So, not every procedural agreement will produce direct procedural effects. Some will only softly condition or impact how the court applies procedural rules. This indicates that the 'consensualisation' of civil litigation, although related to procedural contracts, is a broader movement and entails other cooperative and participative decision-making interactions. Indeed, parties can sometimes influence the proceedings by another sort of consensual interplay without having to conclude binding and enforceable contracts.[23]

4 THE ROLE OF COURTS IN A COMPARATIVE PERSPECTIVE

Different justice systems take divergent approaches to how courts should proceed when confronted by procedural agreements. In some jurisdictions, approval or ratification of the agreement by the court is a prerequisite for any procedural contract to be valid; in others, the court has to apply the contractually defined procedure unless the agreement is invalid due to, for instance, coercion, duress, fraud, or outcomes to the detriment of weaker parties.[24]

---

whether to enter into them or not but also the ability to shape the effects that are to be derived from their consent (*Gestaltungsfreiheit*). A procedural contract would require that the judge is bound by what the parties had agreed. Joint declarations, requests or applications from the consenting parties directed to the court are connected to a related concept, 'joint procedural act' (*Gesamtakt*), which does not have any contractual binding force; cf. Johannes Emil Kuntze, 'Der Gesamtakt: ein neuer Rechtsbegriff' in *Festgabe der Leipziger Juristenfakultät für O.Müller* (Veit & Comp 1892) 40 ff; Gerhard Schiedermair, *Vereinbarungen im Zivilprozess* (L. Röhrscheid 1935) 28; Giuseppe Chiovenda, *Principii di Diritto Processuale* (Jovene 1965) 739; Loïc Cadiet, 'Les accords sur la jurisdiction dans le procès' in Pascal Ancel and Marie-Claire Rivier (dir), *Le conventionnel et le jurisdictionnel dans le règlement des différends* (Economica 2001) 39; Wagner (n 13) 15; Leo Rosenberg, Karl-Heinz Schwab and Peter Gottwald, *Zivilprozessrecht* (18th edn, C.H. Beck 2018) 357-358; Gottfried Baumgärtel, *Wesen und Begriff der Prozeßhandlung einer Partei im Zivilprozeß* (Franz Vahlen 1957) 185-186.

21 Felix Maultzsch and Stefan Klingbeil, 'Contractualisation of Civil Litigation in Germany'; Nur Bolayir, 'Contractualisation de la procédure civile en Turquie' both in Nylund and Cabral (n 5); Christoph A. Kern, 'Procedural Contracts in Germany' in Antonio Cabral and Pedro Henrique Nogueira (eds), *Negócios processuais* (3rd edn, Juspodivm 2017) 213 ff.

22 John Sorabji, 'Contractualisation of Civil Litigation in England and Wales'; Anna Nylund, Magne Strandberg and Marit Tjelmeland, 'Contractualisation of Civil Litigation in Norway', both in Nylund and Cabral (n 5).

23 Nylund and Cabral (n 5) 3-5 and 8-9.

24 Cabral (n 18) 372, 378, 380.

In some legal systems, the court only intervenes if one party invokes the contract in response to the other party having acted in breach of it. In other jurisdictions, judges may act on their own motion, depending on the type of disputed substantive rights, the circumstances of the agreement (e.g. if the clause is inserted in standard general terms) and the persons involved.[25]

Hence, the landscape of procedural agreements is not simple. This mosaic shows that legal systems differ more in emphasis than in principles. A comparative analysis does not always clarify the proximity or divergence among different jurisdictions. One cannot say, for instance, that procedural agreements are more frequently used in common law or civil law jurisdictions. Countries like the US, Brazil, Taiwan, France, Belgium and the Netherlands could be considered agreement-friendly.[26] In Europe, while Germany has a 'pro-agreement' tendency of empowering litigants to adapt court proceedings as they wish, Spain aligns with most of the Eastern European countries with former socialist jurisdictions, such as Poland, Hungary and the Czech Republic, displaying an 'anti-agreement' attitude that rejects most agreements about proceedings, with almost no party autonomy over procedure. In Latin America, where one could expect some uniformity, Brazil is agreement-friendly, and Argentina and Peru tend to expand litigants' prerogatives to dispose of procedural rules. At the same time, Chile retains an approach to flexibilisation with a focus on judges (case management).[27]

The topic goes back to the tensions of court powers vis-à-vis party autonomy. Approaches vary depending on each jurisdiction's tradition, the scope of party autonomy in civil litigation and the extent to which procedural rights can be waived. The portrait depends also on whether judges are supposed to be umpires, simply acting as facilitators of cooperative interactions among the parties, or whether the courts are considered the strong driving force of the proceedings. A comparison shows a co-variation between a larger menu of procedural agreements and a strong emphasis on the principle of party disposition, while there is less room for party autonomy where judges are the leading characters in civil procedure. Where the prevailing opinion qualifies litigation as an activity entirely or predominantly related to public policy, legal systems are more inclined to pursue inquisitorial approaches in which parties have little room for contractually defining the procedure, and judges can disregard any agreement. Nevertheless, jurisdictions with adversarial structures are keener to respect

25 Nylund and Cabral (n 5) 25-26.

26 Helen Hershkoff and Judith Resnik, 'Contractualisation of Civil Litigation in the United States' 421-437; Antonio Cabral and Pedro Henrique Nogueira, 'Contractualisation of Civil Litigation in Brazil'; Kuan-Ling Shen, 'Contractualisation of Civil Litigation in Taiwan', all in Nylund and Cabral (n 5); Danet (n 17); Verkerk and Walta-Jansen (n 17).

27 Cieślak, Jankowski and Muliński (n 19), 357-358; Petr Navrátil and Tomáš Střeleček, 'Contractualisation of Civil Litigation in the Czech Republic'; Maria Victoria Mosmann, 'Contractualisation of Civil Litigation in Argentina' 45-48; Giovanni Priori, 'Contractualisation of Civil Litigation in Peru' 354; Ramón García and Claudio Fuentes, 'Contractualisation of Civil Litigation in Chile', all in Nylund and Cabral (n 5).

parties' voluntary determinations and, therefore, tend to view procedural agreements as natural instruments of a normative framework that values the consent of the litigants.[28]

The difference between inquisitorial and adversarial systems can be misleading when considering procedural agreements. Sometimes, even jurisdictions with a consolidated adversarial tendency, such as Canada or England and Wales, do not adopt a very permissive view of procedural contracts.[29]

Moreover, although the distribution and balancing of powers among the subjects involved in a judicial process is disputed, today, one must consider the principle of cooperation, according to which, regardless of the conflict over substantive law issues, parties and judges can collaborate to a fair development of court proceedings.[30]

The principle of cooperation sets a new parameter for interpreting and understanding the interactions between judges and parties and between parties themselves. If both judges and parties are co-responsible for building and adapting proceedings, agreements about procedure do not seem as offensive challenges to the prerogatives of the court but rather as another means to achieve efficiency through dialogue and collaboration. Hence, even in jurisdictions where procedural agreements are not enforceable and do not bind judges, the principle of cooperation could lead to similar outcomes as procedural agreements. Courts tend to grant parties' joint applications and approve their joint requests when no public or third-party interest is impacted or harmed. Therefore, judicial case management, the principle of cooperation, and procedural contracts are all related topics in this trend of flexibilisation through consensual processes, with the parties and the court cooperating with shared responsibilities to drive court proceedings efficiently.[31]

Although one view could be more or less desirable from economic or social perspectives than the other, there is little benefit in labelling any of these competing variants as 'right' or 'wrong'. Different paths can lead to similar results, and even the features of this culturally dependent miscellany may point to functionally equivalent ways of providing more flexibilisation and adaptation of litigation proceedings.

---

28 Daphne Kapeliuk and Alon Klement, 'Changing the Litigation Game: An Ex Ante Perspective on Contractualized Procedures' (2013) 91 Texas Law Review 1475.

29 Sorabji (n 22) 193-195; Catherine Piché, 'Contractualisation of Civil Litigation in Canada' in Nylund and Cabral (n 5) 91-93.

30 Some jurisdictions explicitly provide for a principle of cooperation in civil procedure rules (e.g. Art. 6 of the Brazilian Civil Procedure Code). In Europe, such an ideal has been verbalised in the ELI/UNIDROIT Model European Rules of Civil Procedure (Rules 2 and 6).

31 Loïc Cadiet, 'Procès équitable et modes alternatifs de règlement des conflits' in Mireille Delmas-Marty, Horatia Muir Watt and Hélène Ruiz Fabri (eds), *Variations autour d'un droit commun* (Societé de Législation Comparée 2002) 98; Cadiet (n 16) 18-19.

5 Levelling Terminology: Agreement, Contract, Covenant, Protocol or Clause?

One of the most significant challenges for understanding procedural agreements is to define the term 'agreement' or 'contract' appropriately. Some jurisdictions use the term 'agreement' to refer to bi- or multilateral legal transactions with procedural effects entered into by the disputants.[32] Agreement, in this sense, means the mutual consent of the parties to a desired scope and intended negotiated effects that are enforceable by law.[33]

However, one should remember that court procedures involve the use of judiciary resources and, thus, entail public interests, so the concepts of contract developed in private law do not always fit the context of public law.[34] For instance, 'agreement' is a concept that differs from the notion of contract because, unlike most definitions of a contract in private law, in litigation, there is no need for the parties to have different or opposing underlying objectives. For procedural agreements or contracts, it is often the case that the parties have common or convergent goals. Moreover, a procedural agreement can alter the rules of the proceeding, and those effects do not always create any contractual obligation or legal relationship between the parties in a creditor-debtor fashion. Therefore, the consolidated contractual categories of private law are neither precise to represent all the interactions among subjects involved in a judicial procedure

32 A legal transaction ('*negócio jurídico*' or '*Rechtsgeschäft*') is a general term that entails unilateral acts. When speaking of bi- or multi-lateral legal transactions in procedural law, many legal scholars use of the term 'agreement'. In Germany, that is the case of the word '*Vereinbarung*', which has been used in this way at least since Josef Trutter, *Über prozessualische Rechtsgeschäfte* (R. Oldenbourg 1890) 194-195. In Italy, the equivalent word is '*accordo*' (as in Mario Bessone, 'Aspetti sostanziali e aspetti processuali dell´accordo di deroga alla competenza' (1965) Rivista Trimestrale di Diritto e Procedura Civile 1066, footnote 4) and in Portugal and Brazil, '*acordo*'. The term 'covenant' ('*convenção*', '*convenio*') is also frequently used in Latin America as a synonym for 'agreement'; see Cabral (n 18) 64 ff; José Carlos Barbosa Moreira, 'Convenções das partes sobre matéria processual' in J.C. Barbosa Moreira. *Temas de Direito Processual*, 3ª Série (Saraiva 1984) 89.

33 Goldschmidt uses an old taxonomy that distinguishes procedural acts according to their aptitude to produce the desired effects. According to this taxonomy, stimulative acts (*Erwirkungshandlungen*) are those in which the will of the agent does not produce the expected effects on its own power; they need the intermediation of others (e.g. the judge) to grant what was intended. Examples are allegations, motions, applications and requests. Determinant acts (*Bewirkungshandlungen*) are *causative* because they discharge the intended effects on their own without the intermediation of others. Judicial decisions are acts of this kind. James Goldschmidt, *Der Prozess als Rechtslage: eine Kritik des prozessualen Denkens* (Julius Springer 1925) 364 ff. In many legal systems, procedural agreements are determinant acts performed by the parties. See also Francesco Carnelutti, *Sistema del diritto processuale civile*, vol II (Cedam 1938) 19; Arwed Blomeyer, *Zivilprozessrecht. Erkenntnisverfahren* (2nd edn, Duncker & Humblot 1985) 162-165; Rosenberg, Schwab and Gottwald (n 20) 374.

34 Cadiet (n 16) 1.

nor are sufficient to embrace the different shades of consensually defined procedural effects.[35]

Nevertheless, the words 'pact', 'clause' and 'protocol' are also used in many jurisdictions to depict the agreement about the procedure, but these might not be optimal terms when dealing with procedural law. Although 'pact' could be a synonym for 'agreement', in some jurisdictions, it is often used to refer to specific types of procedural contracts, such as choice of court agreements (*practicum de foro propaganda*) and agreements not to sue (*pactum non petendo*). It reflects an expression frequently used in international law as equivalent to a 'convention' or 'treaty'. Furthermore, 'protocol' is a terminology often employed in international and administrative law. In some jurisdictions, it refers to agreements entered into by courts and other stakeholders (bar associations, expert unions) to regulate activities related to judicial administration or court management.[36] The term 'clause' (from Latin *clausus* or *claudere*) is indicated in Roman law as a section or chapter of a statute,[37] and, in contemporary private contractual law, it means a portion or fragment of a legal transaction or precept inserted into a contract. A legal transaction can surely be drafted in a single clause, but a contract often reflects a compound of joint clauses mingling to conform to the agreement. Hence, we should avoid expressions with the word 'clause' to refer to procedural agreements.[38]

Moreover, there is also some divergence between the concepts of contract and agreement in terms of enforceability. Not every agreement is enforceable as a contract, and, in many jurisdictions, sometimes even if parties agree to a certain effect, their consent is not enough to make it effective. This brings us to the question of whether a procedural agreement could even qualify as a contract when the court has the power to disregard it. Indeed, the label 'contract' seems misleading if the court has almost unlimited discretion to veto a whole contract or a single clause. However, if judges must apply tests to control the outcome of the negotiation, 'to protect weaker parties, ensure the proportionate use of court resources, enforce important public policies, and so forth, it would be appropriate to designate it as a contract'.[39]

Thus, in the context of procedural law, the concept of 'agreement' may be the most adequate, not only because it is broader than the term 'contract', therefore avoiding an over-excessive conceptual limitation, but also because it better fits into several peripherical phenomena related not only to contractual interplay but also to other forms

35 Despite variation in the concept of contract, some types of procedural agreements, such as those on the costs of the proceeding, could be depicted as true contracts that are valid, binding and enforceable agreements in most legal systems.

36 Activities of administrative nature; cf. Cabral (n 18) 141-151.

37 C. Grassetti, 'Clausola' in Francesco Calasso (ed), *Enciclopedia del diritto*, vol VII (Giuffré 1960) 184 ff.

38 The expression 'discrepancy clauses' (*clauses de différend*) is used in France; cf. Cadiet (n 16) 3.

39 Nylund and Cabral (n 5) 8-10.

of cooperative and consensual ways to induce (and produce) procedural effects that do not represent an actual agreement with binding force and contract-like enforceability.

The present study employs a taxonomy not to be read as a reference to a specific set of criteria. To overcome the variations and the imprecision in terminology, the labels 'contract', 'covenant' or 'agreement' should not be decisive.[40] Instead, the increase in consensual methods for dispute resolution should be the focal point. Hence, most chapters in this book will adopt a broad definition of procedural agreements, concerned not only with parties' determinations with contractual enforceability but also with an aim to explore the boundaries and contingencies of the phenomenon of consensualisation of civil litigation.

6 PROCEDURAL AGREEMENTS VERSUS SUBSTANTIVE LAW CLAUSES

There has been a lot of debate over the ideal criteria to identify when a certain agreement would be of a procedural nature. Legal systems sometimes employ diverse parameters to classify procedural agreements and differentiate them from legal transactions in substantive law, such as where the contract has been entered into, the persons involved, the subject matter of the agreement, the applicable norms or the intended effects.

For some legal scholars, an agreement would have a procedural nature whenever its subject matter would refer to the application of procedural legal rules.[41] But this reflects a qualification of the applicable norms and not of the content of the contractual clauses.[42]

Others argue that procedural agreements would qualify as such if performed within a pending judicial procedure; thus, any obligations that the parties extrajudicially agree to would belong to the realm of substantive law,[43] even if their subject matter relates to procedural rules or if the parties intend to determine procedural effects. This conclusion would imply that agreements entered into before litigation (e.g. those inserted in contracts, such as compromissory clauses) would not be of a procedural nature,[44] although they would represent a waiver with clear procedural effects. However, since procedural agreements are frequently entered into before a conflict arises outside of state courts,[45] the idea that any procedural contract must be performed inside a judicial

40 Sandrine Chassagnard-Pinet and David Hiez, Le système juridique français à l'ère de la contractualisation (Dalloz 2008) 47.

41 Josef Kohler, 'Über processrechtliche Verträge und Creationen' in Josef Kohler, *Gesammelte Beiträge zum Civilprozess* (Carl Heymanns 1894) 255-256.

42 Wagner (n 13) 32-33, 46-47.

43 Baumgärtel (n 20) 262-280; Schiedermair (n 20) 95 ff, 175 ff, differentiating direct and indirect effects.

44 Salvatore Satta, *Contributo alla dottrina dell'arbitrato* (Vita e Pensiero 1931) 48; cf. Muller (n 3) 343-344.

45 Wolfram Henckel, *Prozessrecht und materielles Recht* (Otto Schwartz 1970) 36; Francesco Carnelutti, *Lezioni di Diritto Processuale Civile*, vol IV (Cedam 1930) 405-406.

process has been rejected in legal scholarship[46] for its inconsistency with established practices such as choice of court clauses and agreements on the burden of proof.

Using another parameter, some legal scholars argue that procedural contracts are those performed by the persons involved in a procedural legal relationship.[47] This criterion is also insufficient because procedural agreements can be entered into prior to the commencement of litigation, even before any conflict arises. At that point, one can neither estimate nor identify who the procedural stakeholders in litigation would be since the judicial procedure not only does not exist yet but could never come into existence. As Josef Kohler has correctly observed, it is not about who enters into a legal transaction that determines its nature; it is up to the effects of an agreement to define whether it should qualify as substantive or procedural.[48]

In light of this, the most frequently used parameter to identify whether an agreement could qualify as a procedural contract has been the generation of procedural effects.[49] Relevant here is the aptitude of the agreement to produce legal effects in a court procedure,[50] or, in other words, its referability to an actual or potential lawsuit.[51]

Moreover, assuming that procedural agreements produce procedural effects, legal scholarship has developed two main variants to analyse whether those effects would qualify the agreement as a procedural contract.

In some jurisdictions, the nature of the legal consequences determines the nature of the contract or agreement. Whenever a contract or agreement has any actual or potential effects on court proceedings or regulates issues of a procedural nature between current or potential parties to litigation, it shall be considered a procedural contract.[52] If agreements simultaneously have substantive and procedural effects, one should verify in which ambit the effects of the agreement are to be implemented to identify what nature those legal transactions should possess and, consequently, which rules should apply.[53]

---

46 Goldschmidt (n 33) 312, n. 1616.

47 Cândido Dinamarco, *Instituições de Direito Processual Civil*, vol II (6th edn, Malheiros 2009) 484-485.

48 Kohler (n 41) 255-256.

49 Schiedermair (n 20) 32 ff, 95 ff; Baumgärtel (n 20) 185-186; Goldschmidt (n 33) 312, note 1616, 456-458; Henckel (n 45) 34 ff; Schlosser (n 18) 49; Othmar Jauernig and Burkhard Hess, *Zivilprozessrecht* (30th edn, C.H. Beck 2011) 126.

50 Emilio Betti, *Diritto processuale civile italiano* (Il Foro Italiano 1936) 277 ff.

51 Pedro Henrique Nogueira and Fredie Didier Jr., *Teoria dos fatos jurídicos processuais* (2nd edn, Juspodivm 2012) 30-37.

52 Cf. Cabral (n 18) 60-61; Nogueira and Didier (n 51) 30-37.

53 This approach is seen in sectors of specialised legal literature for a long time – Paul Oertmann, 'Der vorgängige Rechtsmittelverzicht' (1915) 45 Zeitschrift für deutschen Zivilprozeß 403-415; Karl-Heinz Schwab, 'Probleme der Prozeßhandlungslehre' in Hanns Prütting (ed), *Festschrift für Gottfried Baumgärtel zum 70. Geburtstag* (Carl Heymanns 1990) 503-512; Wagner (n 13) 29-30; Baumgärtel (n. 20) 185 ff; Schiedermair (n 20) 33 ff.

A more restrictive approach considers an agreement to have a procedural nature only if the consent of the parties interferes directly with the regulation of the proceedings.[54] The underlying rationale is that agreements can have tangible impacts on court proceedings and still be considered to belong to the domain of substantive law.[55] This intertwined relation occurs because some legal norms regulating important features of court proceedings are deemed hybrid and often considered to belong to substantive law (such as rules governing the burden of proof).[56] Therefore, the legal consequences of their application will be a parallel or mixed combination of substantive and procedural effects. For instance, a contract defining the place of performance has a substantive nature, although with an ancillary effect of altering jurisdiction and venue; an agreement regulating the sale of goods will likely be qualified as a contract of substantive law, with direct effects of transferring the property and ownership, but would also have indirect effects of changing standing to sue. In many legal systems, parties may also determine the applicable law via choice of law agreements.[57] They often can define the legal interpretation or qualification of facts, e.g. stating that a certain legal relationship is to be interpreted as a sale of goods, and those determinations are binding to the courts.[58] All these clauses impact court proceedings and can have decisive procedural effects, such as on the chamber or specialised court to which the case would be assigned. However, these stipulations appear to be clauses with predominant substantive effects, and, in many jurisdictions, they could not qualify as procedural agreements, for their procedural effects would only be indirect.

Nevertheless, a comparative analysis of these issues shows an intense variation regarding the parameters to identify contracts and agreements of a procedural nature, differentiating them from legal transactions of a substantive law nature. Whereas some procedural contracts can have direct implications on the procedure, other types of agreements have more limited effects on the powers of the court or only indirect effects through substantive law clauses.

54 Goldschmidt (n 33) 457 ff; Schiedermair (n 20) 32 ff, 43-44, 166-168; Baumgärtel (n 20) 185; Schlosser (n. 18) 49. 'Direct interference' does not mean that the effects must be the main purpose or goal of the agreement. Rosenberg, Schwab and Gottwald (n 20) 374; Jauernig and Hess (n 49) 126.

55 Schiedermair (n 20) 12 ff and 95 ff; Schlosser (n 18) 102; Wagner (n 13) 37-38, 47, 226-227.

56 Nylund, Strandberg and Tjelmeland (n 22) 341-343; Shen (n 26) 382-383.

57 Hershkoff and Resnik (n 26) 454-455.

58 ELI/UNIDROIT Model European Rules of Civil Procedure, Rule 26 (3), comments 5-7 to Rule 26.

7 Advantages and Caveats of Contractualisation of Civil Litigation

Regardless of the cultural differences in the extent of parties' autonomy in each jurisdiction, procedural agreements present many advantages to a civil justice system. Most importantly, they enable the tailoring of ordinary proceedings to the legal needs of the parties, which speaks in favour of efficiency from the perspective of the litigants, not only of the court.

However, by reducing formalities (for example, restricting evidence), procedural agreements also project agility (shorter duration) and tend to enhance not only flexibilisation and adaptation but also predictability for the litigants, favouring risk management by conferring a greater degree of foreseeability as to the time and costs involved in litigation.[59]

Moreover, procedural agreements may change how disputants approach litigation strategies. Firstly, procedural issues arise when drafting contracts; thus, litigation begins before the conflict is brought to court by designing (possible) future court proceedings already during contract drafting. Secondly, since contractual negotiations may involve anticipations of projected court procedures for potential future litigation, procedural agreements rearticulate the relationship between substantive law and procedural law. If procedural rules are modifiable, the possibility of changing default norms and formalities of court proceedings acquires value, and parties can exchange substantive rights for procedural norms and obtain a trade-off between rules of substantive law and procedural law.[60] For example, parties can negotiate discounts in the price of goods, reductions of fines, longer deadlines to comply or any other substantive law issue in exchange for a waiver of appeals (designing a procedure in a single instance, much faster) or a waiver of asset's protection in enforcement proceedings (thereby facilitating the selling of the debtor's property in case of breach of contract). The possibilities of such trade-offs are immense.

Yet, as with any other feature of a legal system, procedural agreements do not always project a pretty sight. There are also disadvantages and regulatory risks of allowing the parties to adapt court proceedings.

Indeed, a contractually defined procedure can collide with fundamental principles of civil procedure and unduly restrict constitutional guarantees to an extreme point in which the agreement presents obstacles or even a total extinction of the core protection

59 Jamie Dodge, 'The Limits of Procedural Private Ordering' (2011) 97 Virginia Law Review 731, 739; Robert J. Rhee, 'A Price Theory of Legal Bargaining: An Inquiry into the Selection of Settlement and Litigation under Uncertainty' (2006) 56 Emory Law Journal 631-632; Loïc Cadiet, 'L'économie des conventions relatives à la solution des litiges' in Bruno Deffains (dir), *L'analyse économique du droit dans les pays de droit civil* (Cujas 2002) 316.

60 Cabral (n 18) 375.

of access to justice and due process standards. Another possible downside of parties' disposition is the negotiation involving vulnerable litigants (consumers, elderly people, employees, incompetent individuals) and the lack of control over clauses included in boilerplate contracts (general terms and conditions used by professional repeat players).

Therefore, every legal system must structure means to control the excessive interference of party autonomy, safeguard procedural minimum guarantees, reduce or eliminate inequality between the parties, and build oversight mechanisms to prevent the enforcement of clauses to the detriment of weaker parties. It is paramount that the parties fully understand the implications of the agreement and make informed decisions regarding the terms of the contract. This applies to all types of contracts, including procedural contracts. Nevertheless, since procedural agreements operate in a mixed environment in which public and private interests intertwine, the presence of the judge might enable the exercise of a more intense control of clauses disfavourable to vulnerable disputants.

The key is to find parameters that could easily be applied to that goal. Standards consolidated in private law may be applicable to invalidate or disallow procedural agreements. However, because procedural contracts belong to the realm of civil procedure law, the tenets of contract law do not fully apply to them. Even if most of the contractual legal theory might be applicable, it is not clear yet which rules govern their prerequisites and formal requirements, possible nullities, means and locus of enforcement, etc.

8 Structure of this Book

As the practice of procedural agreements grows, several aspects of parties' autonomy regarding court procedures still induce interesting discussions on a theoretical level.[61] The chapters in this book relate procedural agreements to current civil litigation trends and selected aspects of contemporary civil procedure.

Florian Eichel and Rorick Tovar Galván explore choice of court agreements (CCAs), procedural contracts by which parties agree upon jurisdiction and venue. They discuss forum selection clauses, investigating the role of contract law in determining the enforceability of CCAs and considering the underlying interests behind the negotiation of such agreements. It highlights the dual nature of these types of agreements (both procedural and substantive) and their close relationship with choice of law clauses. The authors further discuss the issue of consensus and interpretation of CCAs, as well as the various approaches to the limits and tests that must be implemented to ensure flexibility but with predictability and certainty about their enforceable effects.

61 For further discussions, Nylund and Cabral (n 5) 31 ff.

Magne Strandberg discusses evidentiary agreements. Since evidence law has always been placed amid substantive law, legal needs and procedural regulative effects, it was natural that agreements of the parties about evidence would be very important for predicting the costs and outcomes of litigation. However, evidentiary agreements are also very controversial not only because proof is decisive for the result of the dispute but also due to their crucial impacts over the powers of the judge to admit and evaluate evidence, activities that were historically deemed to be related to core aspects of civil justice and, therefore, respectful to public interests. Especially when entered into before the dispute has arisen, evidentiary agreements tend to be challenged or disregarded by one of the parties after the conflict has been brought to court, which shows the importance of understanding their limits and possibilities. He argues that there is a close relationship between certain aspects of evidence and substantive law provisions (for example, the burden of proof and standards of proof), and this proximity suggests that party autonomy over evidentiary default rules might be similar to freedom of contract.

Henrik Bellander deals with the topic of procedural agreements about the costs of litigation. He investigates how parties' contractual stipulations can impact the disputants' behaviour and their incentives to litigate or settle, how agreements on the distribution of costs between the litigants may affect the parties' control of litigation risks, and to which limits these clauses should be restricted in light of relevant third-party or public interests. The author investigates different factors to be considered, inter alia the type of interests involved, the burdens the agreement might have on the parties, and its impacts on the court. He suggests some parameters to test the validity of such agreements in a broader concept that entails norms of both procedural and substantive nature.

Vigita Vėbraitė investigates some possibilities of procedural agreements regarding appeals. Departing from what is considered in many jurisdictions as the right to appeal, even inserted in some constitutions as a fundamental guarantee of court procedures, she provides comparative insights on the extent to which parties' appeal waivers are to be permissible.

Anna Nylund discusses the subject of agreements related to alternative dispute resolution. She investigates intersections between ADR and court proceedings from three perspectives: (i) the enforceability of ADR agreements instead of litigation or arbitration, (ii) whether agreements obtained in ADR processes should be considered enforceable and (iii) whether they should have res judicata or estoppel effects, barring the parties from initiating or re-litigating a dispute or claim that has been settled in ADR.

Alain Ancery and Bart Krans remind us that in litigation, some issues require ex officio application of imperative statutory rules deriving from EU law, especially in conflicts involving consumers and other weaker litigants. They discuss cases and circumstances under which courts are required to take a more active approach, inter alia, by applying default rules on their own motion and rejecting some effects of procedural agreements. The authors provide an overview of EU consumer protection legislation and case law, its impact on national civil procedure, and some frequently used examples of procedural contracts.

Wolfgang Hau studies the emergence of International Commercial Courts (ICCs), a hybrid structure between state judiciary and international arbitration with a strong emphasis on party autonomy and flexible procedural design. In many countries, a market of specialised state courts offering some previously available services only in arbitration (such as proceedings being conducted in a foreign language) has emerged. Hau investigates why countries worldwide establish ICCs, either as specialised court divisions or standalone courts. He discusses their advantages and downsides, arguing for their potential for saving time and reducing expenditure while implementing successful principles and practices of arbitration within court proceedings. He searches for a balance between flexibilisation, adaptation and the rule of law, considering the impact of ICCs on the justice system, and he questions whether the public resources that go into creating an effective ICC would be better invested in general civil justice infrastructure.

Alan Uzelac questions the traditional view of the legal rules of civil procedure as mandatory, by which a procedure defined by parties' agreements would be disallowed. On the contrary, he observes that case management powers enable courts to determine the flexibilisation of proceedings, which shows that not every default rule of procedure is supposed to be imperative. However, the author raises concerns on whether the parties should be allowed to impose the form and pace of the procedure, and, instead of bilateral contractualisation, the author argues in favour of multilateral cooperation with a focus on joint and shared obligations of the judge, the parties and all other participants in the proceedings to secure a fair, efficient, inexpensive and proportionate procedure.

Shusuke Kakiuchi shows how the increasing complexity of the social and economic aspects of contemporary conflicts, as well as their entanglement with court structures with overloaded dockets, creates the need to adapt civil litigation procedures so that the judicial relief is suitable to respond to the ever-changing needs of the parties. He argues that within the boundaries of public interests, it should be possible for the parties to deviate from statutory norms. He analyses the challenges that procedural contracts need to overcome to provide an effective adaptation tool to achieve fair adjudication of disputes with more predictability, less time and lower costs.

In the concluding chapter, Anna Nylund revisits key topics related to procedural agreements in light of the discussions in the book. These topics are the boundaries between procedural contracts, substantive law and the flexibilisation of court proceedings; the cultural, systemic and regulatory contexts such agreements operate in; the limits of procedural agreements; and how courts should deal with procedural contracts.

9 Conclusions and Topics for Future Research

Procedural agreements change parties' strategies and interactions. They may profoundly impact some aspects of the civil justice landscape. However, there are still many issues in need of further clarification. Such topics are the existing and inherent limits to party autonomy in litigation, how judges' oversight and control over the agreed procedural rules should be performed, the means to enforce binding contractual determinations, and the mechanisms for the parties to react to a breach of procedural contracts.

Jurisdiction Clauses and Procedural Contracts

Florian Eichel and Rorick Tovar Galván

1 Introduction and Terminology

Choice of court agreements (CCAs) are contracts concluded between two or more parties under which they agree to submit their disputes to at least one designated court.[1] They may be concluded in regard to a legal dispute or potential disputes arising out of a legal relationship between the parties. In practice, most terms and conditions of a contract usually contain such a 'jurisdiction clause'. As CCAs are frequently agreed upon when the parties enter into or modify a contractual relationship, i.e. long before a legal dispute arises, the law on CCAs is closely interwoven with the general contract law. The present chapter focuses mainly on this interrelation of the law on CCAs with the general contract law. It aims at identifying the legal aspects in which procedural law interacts with contract law in order to find out to what extent the procedural law on CCAs is influenced by contract law or even has to rely on it. Particular attention will be paid to the phenomenon of a 'fairness control' of CCAs and the extent to which this control may have its roots in contract law.

As regards the legal framework of the research, we assume that there is a global understanding of the function and key attributes of a CCA, although the limits and conditions of validity may differ from one legal system to another. This chapter is, therefore, not particularly framed in a European or 'Brussels-/Lugano-perspective'. It likewise refers to case law or legislation of either civil law or common law jurisdictions sharing this global understanding. As regards terminology, we refer to 'outbound' CCAs when they aim to redirect litigation to a court other than the one where the suit was filed and to 'inbound' CCAs when they extend or confirm the jurisdiction of a court where the proceeding is brought.[2] CCAs are 'exclusive' if the contractual parties agree that disputes can only be decided by the chosen court(s). Conversely, 'nonexclusive'

---

1 Trevor C. Hartley, Civil Jurisdiction and Judgments in Europe – The Brussels I Regulation, the Lugano Convention, and the Hague Choice of Court Convention (OUP 2017), para. 13.03; James O'Hara, 'Strategies for Avoiding a Jurisdiction Clause in International Litigation' (2020) 94 Australian Law Journal 267.

2 John Coyle and Katherine C. Richardson, 'Enforcing Inbound Forum Selection Clauses in State Court' (2021) 53 Arizona State Law Journal 73. The terms 'inbound' and 'outbound' broadly correspond with the terms 'prorogation' and 'derogation' – see Kevin M. Clermont, 'Governing Law on Forum-Selection Agreements' (2015) 66 Hastings Law Journal 645; Peter Hay, 'Forum Selection Clauses – Procedural Tools

CCAs do not prevent the parties from litigating in another court than the chosen one but facilitate establishing jurisdiction in the chosen forum.[3]

First, this chapter examines the meaning of the dual nature of CCAs (Section 2.1), their close similarity with the choice of law clauses (Section 2.2) and their independence from the main contract (Section 2.3). Next, it highlights some interfaces with contract law, such as the issue of consensus (Section 3.1) and interpretation (Section 3.2). The last part deals with the role of contract law in setting limits on CCAs (Section 4.1), the various interests behind them (Section 4.2), and the existing approaches for the implementation of such limits. In this regard, some insights into law and economics are used to determine the pros and cons of clear-cut and discretionary rules (Section 4.3).

2 Jurisdiction Clauses as Contracts of a Dual Nature

2.1 *Fundaments of CCAs and the Role of Contract Law*

Although CCAs are contracts, their enforceability cannot be solely justified with the 'freedom of contract', the fundamental principle of private law.[4] The rule that parties are free to create contractual obligations does not automatically mean that they are free to create a jurisdiction. In the case of real estate issues, for example, individuals are widely free to stipulate the terms of their contracts, but they are often not allowed to choose the competent court.[5] In consequence, the fundament of the freedom to determine jurisdiction is seen as a matter of public law.[6] However, since CCAs are contracts, their enforceability depends not only on procedural law but also on contract law. This is why they are defined as contracts of a dual nature – agreements combining procedural and substantive law elements.[7] In the case of CCAs, this twofold nature does not mean that, in addition to procedural provisions, the contract law applies as such.[8] Moreover, due

---

or Contractual Obligations? Conceptualization and Remedies in American and German Law' (2021) 35 Emory International Law Review 7.

3 Tiong Min Yeo, 'The Contractual Basis of the Enforcement of Exclusive and Non-Exclusive Choice of Court Agreements' (2005) 17 Singapore Academy of Law Journal 307.

4 It is only one pillar among others, O'Hara (n 1) 271.

5 See, e.g. Art. 24.1 Regulation (EU) No. 1215/2012 of 12 December 2012 on jurisdiction and the recognition and enforcement of judgements in civil and commercial matters (recast) [2012] OJ L 351/289 (Brussels Ibis Regulation); Art. 22, para. 1, Convention on jurisdiction and the recognition and enforcement of judgments in civil and commercial matters [2009] OJ L 147/5 (2007 Lugano Convention).

6 Adrian Briggs, 'Choice of Forum and Submission to Jurisdiction' in Jürgen Basedow, Giesela Rühl, Franco Ferrari and Pedro De Miguel Asensio (eds), *Encyclopedia of Private International Law*, vol I (Edward Elgar 2017) 304.

7 Hay (n 2) 7.

8 This might be the approach for court settlements; cf. in German law Leo Rosenberg, Karl Heinz Schwab and Peter Gottwald, *Zivilprozessrecht* (18th edn, CH Beck 2018) Sec. 131, para. 36.

to the procedural effects of CCAs, contract law has to be applied in a way that takes into account the procedural interests behind CCAs. What that means will be shown throughout this chapter.

2.2 *Close Relationship with Choice of Law Clauses*

CCAs share many similarities with choice of law agreements. Firstly, the doctrine of separability is equally applicable to choice of law agreements; like CCAs, they are regarded to be a contract which is separate from the main contract.[9] Secondly, both types of agreements are the 'backbone' of a contract. They do not refer to a specific stipulation but affect the contract as a whole.[10] Thirdly, both agreements are intertwined in various regards, for example, when jurisdiction follows the maxim *qui elegit iudicem, elegit ius*.[11] Considering their functional interdependence, in practice, they are drafted in consideration of each other.[12] Last but not least, both types of agreements are contracts of a dual nature.[13] As such, they face similar challenges in contract law, like their incorporation in a contract by way of standard terms, the question of to which extent they are subject to contractual fairness control, or conflict-of-laws issues.[14] This is why lawmakers and courts should examine whether these contract law issues can be treated coherently for both agreements.

2.3 *CCAs as 'Independent' Contracts: The Doctrine of Separability*

However, CCAs stand 'on their own feet'. If they are inserted in a contract, challenges to the validity and existence of the main contract do not necessarily call into question the enforceability of the CCA.[15] Their contractual enforceability has to be examined

9 Daniel Girsberger, Thomas Kadner Graziano and Jan Neels, 'General Comparative Report' in Daniel Girsberger, Thomas Kadner Graziano and Jan Neels (eds), *Choice of Law in International Commercial Contracts – Global Perspectives on the Hague Principles* (OUP 2021), para. 1.342.

10 Wolfgang Hau, 'Gerichtsstandsklauseln' in Walter Lindacher and Thomas Pfeiffer (eds), *AGB-Recht: Kommentar* (7th edn, C.H. Beck 2020), para. G158.

11 Girsberger, Kadner Graziano and Neels (n 9), para. 1.263 ff; Dieter Martiny, 'Rom I-VO Art. 3 Freie Rechtswahl' in Jan von Hein (ed), *Münchener Kommentar zum Bürgerlichen Gesetzbuch: BGB*, vol 13 (8th edn, C.H. Beck 2021), para. 49. For the influence of a choice of law clause on the CCAs, see Ulrich Magnus 'Article 25' in Ulrich Magnus and Peter Mankowski (eds), *European Commentaries on Private International Law – Commentary Brussels Ibis Regulation*, vol 1 (Otto Schmidt 2023), para. 82a.

12 Tanya Monestier, 'When Forum Selection Clauses Meet Choice of Law Clauses' (2019) 69 American University Law Review 327; O'Hara (n 1) 267. See also I.7. of the Hague Principles on Choice of Law in International Commercial Contracts.

13 A choice of law provision has its effects on the level of conflict of laws but is created as a contract.

14 Martiny (n 11), para. 102 ff.

15 See also Peter Mankowski, 'Art 25 Brüssel Ia-VO' in Thomas Rauscher (ed), *Europäisches Zivilprozess- und Kollisionsrecht EuZPR/EuIPR*, vol 1 (5th edn, Otto Schmidt 2021), para. 109.

separately. This doctrine of separability[16] is supposed to be a global concept.[17] How separate a CCA is depends on how strictly or liberally the courts apply the doctrine. This is exemplified by fraud defences in cases where a person tricks another person into signing an agreement which contains a CCA.[18] If the fraudulent statements only concerned the main contract, would this be enough to invalidate the CCA? Or would it be necessary to prove that the fraud specifically referred to the choice of court clause? Similar issues arise when analysing the effects of a CCA on a successor in title: is an assignee bound by a CCA even if the assignment contract does not mention the existence of the CCA in the main contract?[19] The more rigidly the doctrine of separability is applied in these cases, the harder it is to question the validity of the CCA. In fraud cases, this would be detrimental to a party that has evidently been betrayed. This shows that it cannot be ignored that the validity of the main contract and the CCA can be interrelated and influenced by each other, although the CCA, in theory, is a separate contract. In these situations, contract law cannot be applied without taking into account the procedural significance and consequences of a CCA.

3 The Interfaces between CCAs and Contract Law

3.1 *Consent and Form of CCAs*

As for any other contract, the validity of a CCA raises general questions of contract law, like formation and consensus, incorporation of standard terms, capacity, misrepresentation, duress and so on. For international CCAs, the basic question is, which contract law applies? Often, no explicit conflict rule determines the applicable contract law for CCAs.[20] This is why the question is subject to profound academic discussion.[21] Instead of going into a deeper analysis of these issues, we want to highlight the relationship between

16 Also referred to as 'the doctrine of severability', see Briggs (n 6) 308.

17 See Art. 3 lit d of the 2005 Hague Choice of Court Convention; Art. 25, para. 5 Brussels Ibis Regulation.

18 With references to case law, see John Coyle, William Dodge and Aaron Simowitz, 'Choice of Law in the American Courts in 2021: Thirty-Fifth Annual Survey' Social Science Research Network (31 January 2022) 22 and fn. 76, https://ssrn.com/abstract=4022722 (accessed 3 January 2024).

19 Cf. ECJ Case C-519/19 *Ryanair DAC v. DelayFix* [2020] ECLI:EU:C:2020:933, para. 35; Magnus (n 11), paras. 161-162.

20 Art. 5 (1) Convention of 30 June 2005 on Choice of Court Agreements (2005 Hague Choice of Court Convention) and Art. 25, para. 1 (1) Brussels Ibis Regulation contain only *renvoi* provisions referring to the conflict-of-law rules of the chosen state; see Trevor Hartley and Masato Dogauchi, *Explanatory Report on the Hague Convention on Choice of Court Agreements* (Permanent Bureau of the Conference 2013), para. 125, and Recital No. 20 Brussels Ibis Regulation); the EU conflict rules on contracts exclude CCAs from their scope of application (Art. 1, para. 2 lit e Rome I Regulation).

21 See among many others Barbara Lindenmayr, *Vereinbarung über die internationale Zuständigkeit und das darauf anwendbare Recht* (Duncker & Humblot 2002); Clermont (n 2) 661, 673.

the requirement of consensus and formal requirements for CCAs. Due to the backbone character of a CCA, it is crucial for a court to examine whether the CCA was subject to a consensus of the parties. This can be particularly difficult if the contract consists of several documents or the CCA is contained in standard forms. The importance of establishing the consensus is underlined by statutory provisions or case law which require the drafter of a CCA to make it more visible to the other party either in terms of its position in standard forms[22] or through typographical requirements (bold print, capital letters, type size provisions or the like).[23] Moreover, it is quite common that statutes provide that CCAs have to be 'in writing' to be enforceable.[24]

As regards the interpretation of these form requirements and their influence on enforceability, one can distinguish between two prevailing concepts. On the one hand, there is a 'procedural approach'. According to this approach, the agreement of the parties does not need to be (entirely) in writing as long as there is written evidence of a consensus between the parties regarding the CCA. This is the concept underlying Article 3 of the 2005 Hague Choice of Court Convention.[25] The form is not understood as an element of the consensus but as a separate element aiming at facilitating the evidence. Consequently, it does not affect the validity of the CCA if the parties merely refer orally to standard terms containing a CCA and are permanently displayed on the website of the party that provided the standard terms.[26] On the other hand, there is a 'substantive approach', which regards the consensus and the formal requirements as two sides of one coin. According to this approach, the form is seen to be the 'vehicle' of consensus.[27] The fact that the formal requirements are fulfilled makes it almost

22 See Swiss Federal Court BGE 128 I 273 E. 2.3; BGE 91 I 11, 14 E. 3. Whether these decisions are still applicable is in dispute among scholars, see Patricia Dietschy-Martenet, 'Article 17' in Isabelle Chabloz, Patricia Dietschy-Martenet and Michel Heinzmann (eds), *Petit commentaire CPC Code de procédure civile* (Helbing Lichtenhahn 2020), para. 19; contra Ulrich Haas and Michael Schlumpf, 'Article 17' in Paul Oberhammer, Tanja Domej and Ulrich Haas (eds), *Kurzkommentar ZPO Schweizerische Zivilprozessordnung* (3rd edn, Helbing Lichtenhahn 2021), para. 19 ff.

23 Helen Hershkoff and Judith Resnik, 'Contractualisation of Civil Litigation in the United States: Procedure, Contract, Public Authority, Autonomy, Aggregate Litigation, and Power' in Anna Nylund and Antonio Cabral (eds), *Contractualisation of Civil Litigation* (Intersentia 2023) 419, 447 ff; John Coyle and Katherine Robinson, 'Enforcing Outbound Forum Selection Clauses in State Court' (2021) 96 Indiana Law Journal 1138 ff.

24 See Art. 3 lit. c of the 2005 Hague Choice of Court Convention, Art. 25, para. 1 (3) Brussels Ibis Regulation, and Art. 63 Sec. 1 Brazilian Code of Civil Procedure (Lei No 13.105 of 16 March 2015).

25 Convention of 30 June 2005 on Choice of Court Agreements. See Andreas Bucher, 'La Convention de La Haye sur les accords d'élection de for' (2006) 16 Revue Suisse de Droit International et Européen 37; Florian Eichel, *AGB-Gerichtsstandsklauseln im deutsch-amerikanischen Handelsverkehr: zugleich ein Beitrag zum Einfluss des Haager Übereinkommens über Gerichtsstandsvereinbarungen vom 30.6. 2005* (Jenaer Wissenschaftliche Verlagsgesellschaft 2007) 255-257.

26 Hartley (n 1), para. 13.132; cf. Hartley and Dogauchi (n 20), paras. 113-114.

27 Ingo Saenger, 'Internationale Gerichtsstandsvereinbarungen nach EuGVÜ und LugÜ' (1997) 110 Zeitschrift für Zivilprozess 484; Thomas Rauscher, 'Gerichtsstandsbeeinflussende AGB im Geltungsbereich des EuGVÜ' (1991) 104 Zeitschrift für Zivilprozess 278.

impossible to deny that there has been a consensus regarding the CCA.[28] Where the formal requirements follow the substantive approach, their interpretation is rather rigid. Noncompliance makes the CCA unenforceable. According to the European Court of Justice (ECJ) settled case law, the approach followed by the Brussels Regulations is substantive.[29] Likewise, the above-mentioned typographical requirements have this approach as they aim at ensuring consensus by bringing the clause to the other party's attention.[30]

In conclusion, the concept of consensus, which is a core principle of contract law, is overlaid with form requirements, which usually come from procedural law and respond to the particular backbone character of a CCA. How strongly these procedural requirements influence or push back the applicable contract law depends on whether they follow a mere 'procedural' or a 'substantive' approach.[31]

3.2 *Interpretation*

3.2.1 Regime of Interpretation

Disputes on the relevance of a CCA are often caused by the wording of the clause giving rise to different interpretations. In the EU Member States, for example, there is some uncertainty on whether a broadly drafted CCA applies to tort or antitrust claims.[32] In the US, it is often in dispute if a CCA is exclusive or nonexclusive,[33] as nonexclusive CCAs are of higher importance there than, for example, in Europe.[34] As mentioned above, there is a lack of explicit conflict rules determining the contract law which is applicable to international CCAs. This also affects the interpretation because interpretation happens against the background of a certain legal system. We suggest that there should be two

28 Mankowski (n 15), para. 217.

29 'The purpose of the formal requirements ... is to ensure that the consensus between the parties is in fact established' – see Case 24/76 *Estasis Salotti v. Rüwa* [1976] ECLI:EU:C:1976:177, para. 7. See also ECJ Case 25/76 *Galeries Segoura SPRL v. Société Rahim Bonakdarian* [1976] ECLI:EU:C:1976:178; Hartley (n 1), para. 13.58.

30 Ulrich Haas and Johanna Hug, 'Gerichtsstandsklauseln in Allgemeinen Geschäftsbedingungen' (2021) 54 Schweizerische Zeitschrift für Zivilprozess- und Zwangsvollstreckungsrecht 474; in general, Yonathan Arbel and Andrew Toler, 'All-caps' (2020) 17 Journal of Empirical Legal Studies 867.

31 As Art. 25 Brussels Ibis Regulation follows the substantive approach, its form requirements prevail over the rules of the applicable contract law on the inclusion of standard terms – see Peter Gottwald, 'Art 25 Brüssel Ia-VO' in Wolfgang Krüger and Thomas Rauscher (eds), *Münchener Kommentar zur Zivilprozessordnung mit Gerichtsverfassungsgesetz und Nebengesetzen*, vol 3 (6th edn, C.H. Beck 2022), para. 79; Art. 3 lit. c of the 2005 Hague Choice of Court Convention does not have such an effect, see Eichel (n 25) 258-259.

32 Florian Eichel, 'Gerichtsstandsvereinbarungen und europarechtliche Auslegungsregeln im Kontext des Delikts- und Kartellrechts' (2021) 41 Praxis des Internationalen Privat- und Verfahrensrechtsx 143 ff.

33 Maral Kilejian and Christianne Edlund, 'Enforceability of Choice of Forum and Choice of Law Provisions' (2012) 32 Franchise Law Journal 81.

34 Eichel (n 25) 209.

regimes governing the interpretation of a CCA, depending on whether procedural or substantive aspects are concerned. Procedural questions like whether a CCA is exclusive or not should be subject to the *lex fori* of the designated court because it affects the jurisdiction of the said court. By contrast, the interpretation of the scope of the CCA regarding any claims arising out of the legal relationship between the parties should be subject to the law governing the main contract.[35] The argument is that the wording of a CCA that is integrated into the main contract will most commonly follow the wording of the main contract and the law applicable to it.[36] Here, the specific context with the main contract influences how a CCA is interpreted.

3.2.2 Relation to a Particular Legal Relationship ('Definiteness')

Frequently, provisions on CCAs provide that they are only enforceable if they refer to a 'particular legal relationship' (hereinafter called 'concept of definiteness'[37]). The underlying concept is widely recognised.[38] It results from the very nature of the CCA as a contract. The concept urges a court to examine if – according to the parties' expectations – the CCA had really been concluded to cover the type of claim which is in dispute. If the parties intended to apply the CCA to their future relationship or on a specific contract, it is not permissible to apply the CCA to prior disputes or other contracts because this would be contrary to the will of the parties. The scope of the CCA must be foreseeable for both parties at the time of signing in order to avoid a party being taken by surprise.[39]

However, the CCA must only refer to a determinable claim that may give rise to a dispute and not a particular lawsuit.[40] The ECJ missed that point when it required the 'foreseeability of the dispute'.[41] If that were true, a CCA would never be applicable to lawsuits based on fraud, which, as such, are not foreseeable. Arguing with the foreseeability of the lawsuit is only justified in certain cases. Disputes arising out of a

---

35 O'Hara (n 1) 275; Swiss Federal Court, 4A_559/2022 of 3 August 2023, E. 5.1.2; opting for the *lex fori*: Chukwuma Okoli, 'The Contractual Function of a Choice of Court Agreement in Nigerian Jurisprudence' (2020) conflictoflaws.net, https://conflictoflaws.net/2020/the-contractual-function-of-a-choice-of-court-agreement-in-nigerian-jurisprudence/ (accessed 3 January 2024).

36 Eichel (n 32) 146.

37 In German 'Bestimmtheitserfordernis'. Astrid Stadler and Christian Krüger, 'Art. 25' in Hans-Joachim Musielak and Wolfgang Voit (eds), *Zivilprozessordnung* (20th edn, Verlag Franz Vahlen 2023), para. 6.

38 Art. 25 Brussels Ibis; Art. 3(a) of the 2005 Hague Choice of Court Convention; Art. 63 Sec. 1 Brazilian Code of Civil Procedure (n 24).

39 Cf. Case C-214/89 *Powell Duffryn plc v. Wolfgang Petereit* [1992] ECLI:EU:C:1992:115, para. 31; Georg Kodek, 'Gerichtsstandsvereinbarungen im Kartellrecht' in Dietmar Czernich and Reinhold Geimer (eds), *Streitbeilegungsklauseln im Internationalen Vertragsrecht* (Helbing Lichtenhahn 2018), para. 17.

40 Christoph Thole 'Artikel 25' in Friedrich Stein and Martin Jonas (eds), *Kommentar zur Zivilprozessordnung* (23rd edn, Mohr Siebeck 2022), para. 121; Polina Westerhoven and Kristina Sirakova, 'Erfassen allgemein formulierte Gerichtsstandsvereinbarungen Schadensersatzklagen wegen Missbrauchs marktbeherrschender Stellung?' (2019) 6 Praxis des Internationalen Privat- und Verfahrensrechts 494 ff.

41 Case C-352/13 *Cartel Damage Claims (CDC) Hydrogen Peroxide SA v. Evonik Degussa GmbH and Others* [2015] ECLI:EU:C:2015:335, para. 70.

tort, which has been committed prior to the conclusion of a CCA, may not be covered by the CCA if the damaged parties did not know the tort and if there are reasons to assume that they would not have agreed to the CCA if they had known the tort at the time of conclusion.[42] Hence, the foreseeability of the specific claim does not play a role unless the dispute has arisen out of circumstances prior to the conclusion of the CCA.

4 LIMITING CHOICE OF COURT AGREEMENTS

It is commonly emphasised that the parties are free to determine jurisdiction by agreement in civil and commercial matters.[43] However, there are more limits than it may seem at first sight. Very often, provisions on CCAs do not explicitly mention all of the limits: Some international instruments that unify the validity requirements of CCAs even leave it to another lawmaker to set up limits. In Europe, for example, the Brussels Ibis Regulation[44] establishes the requirements for the enforcement of international CCAs but relies on the national contract law of the EU Member States for the substantive validity of a CCA.[45] Likewise, the 2005 Hague Choice of Court Convention covers mainly the formal validity of jurisdictional clauses, whereas the question of whether the CCA is null and void is subject to the law of the state of the chosen court (including the choice of law rules).[46] In the United States, there are various limits that depend on the type of the main contract and are imposed by state statutory laws.[47]

The following section will show which role contract law plays among the limits to the enforceability of a CCA. As contract law is often the basis for an 'individual fairness test' of CCAs, the following section also explores the interests behind the limits of enforceability because they could generate the criteria which are weighed up in such an individual fairness test. The last section examines under which circumstances there is a need for such an individual fairness test.

42 Eichel (n 32) 148 ff.

43 See O'Hara (n 1) 267, who criticises the common perspective as a biased pro-enforcement view.

44 See n 5.

45 See Art. 25, para. 1 Brussels Ibis Regulation.

46 See Art. 5, para. 1, 6 lit a, 9 lit a of the 2005 Hague Choice of Court Convention; Hartley and Dogauchi (n 20), para. 125.

47 See in detail Coyle and Richardson (n 2) 1113; Hay (n 2) 16.

4.1 *Variety of Limits and the Role of Contract Law*

4.1.1 *Variety of Limits*

Common exceptions to the enforceability of CCAs are provided by exclusive jurisdictions that are typically not at the disposal of the parties.[48] Other provisions restrict CCAs by defining a limited circle of courts which may be the subject of a CCA.[49] Some limits only address outbound CCAs,[50] while others set limits to inbound CCAs by requiring the parties or the lawsuit to have certain connections to the forum.[51] There are limits which only address certain effects of a CCA: either they state that a CCA cannot affect the subject matter jurisdiction[52] or they eliminate the binding effect by providing that a court which examines its jurisdiction shall consider the CCA, but only as a factor among others.[53] Other limits refer to the characteristics of one or both parties, e.g. provisions voiding CCAs signed on behalf of children under age 18[54] or by consumers.[55] Some limits are set up by provisions which ban or impose further requirements on CCAs once they are contained in a certain type of contract-like consumer,[56] franchise,[57] insurance,[58] labour,[59] construction,[60] student debt[61] or even 'seed contracts'.[62] The enforceability of a

48 E.g. in real estate, certain corporate or patent litigation, Luis de Lima Pinheiro, 'Article 24' in Ulrich Magnus and Peter Mankowski (n 11), para. 3.

49 Art. 4 Council Regulation (EC) No. 4/2009 of 18 December 2008 on jurisdiction, applicable law, recognition and enforcement of decisions and cooperation in matters relating to maintenance obligations (2009) OJ L 7/138.

50 CAL CIV PROC CODE § 116.225 (Code of Civil Procedure of the US state California); Art. 5, para. 2 Swiss Federal Act on Private International Law (SR 291; hereafter PILA).

51 Art. 5, para. 3 PILA (n 50); see Andrea Bonomi, 'Accords d'élection de for: une révision de l'article 5 LDIP à l'occasion de l'adhésion de la Suisse à la Convention de La Haye de 2005?' (2023) Swiss Review of International and European Law (SRIEL) 597, 607 ff.

52 Cf. Dominik Vock and Christoph Nater, 'Article 4' in Karl Spühler, Luca Tenchio and Dominik Infanger (eds), *Basler Kommentar Schweizerische Zivilprozessordnung* (3rd edn, Helbing Lichtenhahn 2017), para. 5.

53 Stewart Organization, *Inc v. Ricoh Corp*, 487 US 22 (1988); Hay (n 2) 12-14; David Pearson, 'Transfer of Venue under 28 U.S.C. 1404(a): All Things to All People, or Cracking under the Weight of the Forum Selection Clause Comment' (2002) 75 Temple Law Review 929; O'Hara (n 1) 279.

54 Art. 4(3) Council Regulation (EC) No. 4/2009 of 18 December 2008 on jurisdiction, applicable law, recognition and enforcement of decisions and cooperation in matters relating to maintenance obligations [2009] OJ L 7/138.

55 Art. 114(2) Swiss PILA (n 50).

56 Art. 19 Brussels Ibis Regulation; CAL CIV PROC CODE § 116.225 (Code of Civil Procedure of the US state California); IND CODE ANN § 24-4.5-1-201(6)(c) (Code of the US state Indiana).

57 CAL BUS & PROF CODE § 20040.5 (Business and Professions Code of the US state California); LA STAT ANN § 32:1261(A)(1)(a)(v) (Revised Statutes of the US state Louisiana).

58 Art. 15 Brussels Ibis Regulation; VA CODE ANN § 38.2-312 (Code of the US state Virginia).

59 Art. 23 Brussels Ibis Regulation; CAL LAB CODE § 925(a)(1) (Labor Code of the US state California); LA STAT ANN § 22:868(A)(2) (Revised Statutes of the US state Louisiana).

60 CAL. CIV. PROC. CODE § 410.42(a) (Code of Civil Procedure of the US state California); LA STAT ANN § 9:2779(B)(1) (Revised Statutes of the US state Louisiana); IND CODE ANN § 32-28-3-17(2) (Code of the US state Indiana).

61 Hershkoff and Resnik (n 23) 446.

62 IN Code § 15-15-6-9 (Code of the US state Indiana).

CCA may also depend on whether it has been concluded before or after the dispute or the claim has arisen.[63] In the latter case, a CCA in business-to-consumer contracts raises fewer concerns because the protected party can better assess the consequences of the clause when the dispute has already arisen.[64] Last but not least, a CCA may be subject to public policy control.[65]

4.1.2 *The Role of Contract Law*

Apart from all these limits that specifically address CCAs, there are restrictions to the enforceability of a CCA that immediately arise from contract law. Among these are not only limits which reflect core contractual concerns like incapacity or missing authority to conclude a CCA. Moreover, there are instruments of contract law which take into account the procedural impact of a CCA. One example is the contractual concept of *clausula rebus sic stantibus*, whereby a CCA can be void when exceptional circumstances which have been decisive for the selection of a court or jurisdiction have changed so that the CCA cannot reasonably be performed as it has been intended at the time of conclusion.[66]

Another example of instruments of contract law considering procedural aspects is discretionary tests, which allow the examination of the enforceability of a CCA in light of all the circumstances of the case. In the form of 'individual fairness tests' like the doctrine of unconscionability, contract law can be either the basis for these discretionary tests,[67] an integral part of such tests[68] or at least a source of ideas to define an 'abusive' CCA.[69]

4.2 *Interests Underpinning the Limits*

The above-mentioned limits serve various interests, which may be classified as either procedural, substantive or public.

---

63 Art. 19(2) 1 Brussels Ibis Regulation; LA STAT ANN § 23:921(A)(2) (Revised Statutes of the US state Louisiana).

64 Peter Mankowski 'Introduction to Articles 17-19' in Ulrich Magnus and Peter Mankowski (n 11), para. 12.

65 Art. 6 lit c of the 2005 Hague Choice of Court Convention; Federal Court of Australia *Epic Games, Inc v. Apple Inc [2021] FCAFC 122*, para. 86 f; O'Hara (n 1) 280.

66 Art. 6 lit d of the 2005 Hague Choice of Court Convention; Ved Nanda and Ralph Lake, *The Law of Transnational Business Transactions* (Clark Boardman Callaghan 2020) Sec. 3:16.

67 Such as under the Brussels Ibis Regulation, see Section 4.3.1 of this chapter.

68 Canada: Supreme Court of Canada *Douez v. Facebook Inc*, 2017 SCC 33, para. 28; US: Hay (n 2) 12, 15 ff. Likewise, in Australia: according to O'Hara (n 1) 276 f, but not yet decided.

69 Art. 5, para. 2 Swiss PILA (n 50) is intended to refer to the standard term problematic (Botschaft zum Bundesgesetz über das internationale Privatrecht of 10th November 1982, BBl 1983 I 263, para. 213.5). Similarly, Art. 63, Sec. 3 and 4 of the Brazilian Code of Civil Procedure (n 24), knows a procedural rule on good faith (Art. 5) and might, therefore, not depend on contract law.

4.2.1 *Procedural Interests*

We classify interests as procedural when they aim at facilitating the pending proceeding for the sake of either the parties or the courts. Limits which ensure that the chosen court has close connections to the lawsuit, to the matter in dispute, the applicable law or to the means of proof ('appropriate forum')[70] are procedural when they intend to increase the efficiency of the proceeding. This lies in the public interest of a good administration of justice but as well in the interest of the parties getting a cheaper and faster 'day in court'. Provisions that ban outbound CCAs to avoid that no court is competent (*negativer Justizkonflikt*) or to safeguard that a party will not be deprived of fundamental procedural rights by the foreign court serve procedural interests likewise. The French Supreme Court, in setting aside an asymmetric CCA, referred to the lack of predictability.[71] Predictability and certainty are also acknowledged procedural interests in the law of international jurisdiction.[72]

A common pattern in justifying the setting aside of CCAs relates to a distinction in procedural doctrine between a so-called one-shotter and a repeat player.[73] The 'one-shotter' stands for the economically weaker and legally less experienced party who is (at most) occasionally involved in litigation. By contrast, the 'repeat player' is frequently engaged in similar litigation and has (due to higher resources and the professional background) more effective access to justice. The imbalance resulting from these different starting points may get so high that the weaker party would *de facto* be deprived of its 'day in court' if litigation did not take place in their home country, all the more in international litigation. Although this view has its roots in the US, it is not only US courts[74] that refer to this imbalance when setting aside a CCA. The ECJ also takes it into account when assessing the validity of a CCA: if a CCA would oblige a

70 O'Hara (n 1) 278 ff. See for Art. 4 Regulation (EC) No. 4/2009 Marianne Andrae, 'Art 4 EG-UntVO' in Thomas Rauscher (ed), *Europäisches Zivilprozess- und Kollisionsrecht EuZPR/EuIPR*, vol. 4 (4th edn, Otto Schmidt 2016), para. 3 (in German 'sachnahes Forum'). For Art. 24 Brussels Ibis Regulation, see Peter Mankowski, 'Art 24 Brüssel Ia-VO' in Thomas Rauscher (ed), *Europäisches Zivilprozess- und Kollisionsrecht EuZPR/EuIPR*, vol. 1 (5th edn, Ottoschmidt 2021), para. 3.

71 Cour de cassation, civile, Chambre civile 1, 7 February 2018, 16-24.497, ECLI:FR:CCASS:2018:C100165 (available at https://www.legifrance.gouv.fr/juri/id/JURITEXT000036635588 (accessed 3 January 2024); see also Cour de cassation, civile, Chambre civile 1, 3 October 2018, 17-21.309 ECLI:FR:CCASS:2018:C100910 (available at https://www.legifrance.gouv.fr/juri/id/JURITEXT000037495393 (accessed 3 January 2024); furthermore, see François Mailhé, 'France: A Game of Asymmetries, Optional and Asymmetrical Choice of Court Agreements Under French Case Law' in Mary Keyes (ed), *Optional Choice of Court Agreements in Private International Law* (Springer 2020) 208.

72 O'Hara (n 1) 270 ff.

73 Also for the following Marc Galanter, 'Why the Haves Come Out Ahead: Speculations on the Limits of Legal Change' (1974) 9 Law & Society Review 97 f; Dörner Heinrich, '"One-shotter" gegen "repeat player" – Zum Verständnis der Art. 13 Abs. 2 und 11 Abs. 1 lit. b EuGVVO (EuGH, S. 196)' (2018) 38 *Praxis des Internationalen Privat- und Verfahrensrechts* 158.

74 *Kubis & Perszyk Associates, Inc v. Sun Microsystems, Inc*, 146 N.J. 176 (N.J. 1996) 680 A.2d 618, para. 193 ff; Nanda and Lake (n 66) Sec. 3:9.

consumer to litigate 'a long way from his domicile', the ECJ reasons that the CCA would cause the consumer 'to forgo any legal remedy' when the lawsuit only concerns 'limited amounts of money'.[75] If a 'one-shotter' is involved, this reasoning leaves room to consider the value of the claim in relation to the hypothetical costs of litigating abroad. By providing consumers an option to litigate at home, the Brussels Ibis Regulation also follows this reasoning but leaves it to the consumers to determine whether it is worth litigating abroad.[76] This is why the equivalent restrictions of CCAs (Art. 19 Brussels Ibis) merely aim at ensuring that the consumers' freedom to choose the forum cannot be circumvented by recourse to a CCA.[77]

4.2.2 *Substantive Interests*

If the enforcement of an outbound CCA is denied because mandatory provisions of the substantive law of the forum would not apply in the designated court,[78] the interests served by such a denial are substantive in nature as they aim at enforcing substantive law. The same is true for provisions of contract law which protect a party against undue influence or fraud. However, it is less clear for provisions directed against unfair CCAs in standard terms. If they try to counterbalance a weaker negotiation position of the party or an information deficit, they might be referred to as substantive when it does not matter if the unfair term is substantive or procedural in nature. If, however, the CCA is measured by a notion of 'procedural justice', it might be that the above-mentioned procedural interests are also taken into account. In such a case, an instrument of substantive contract law (e.g. 'unconscionability', or in German law, '*Inhaltskontrolle*') is also used to protect procedural interests.[79]

4.2.3 *Public Interests*

We refer to interests as public when they reach beyond the specific proceedings. Provisions that prevent the courts of a state from being chosen as a 'neutral forum' aim at protecting the limited judicial resources against excessive workload or the taxpayer's money.[80] When the burden of jury duty or the difficulties linked to the application of foreign law are taken into consideration, these are also public interests.[81] The rationale

75 Case C-243/08 *Pannon GSM Zrt. v. Erzsébet Sustikné Győrfi* [2009] ECLI:EU:C:2009:350, para. 41; Case C-137/08 *VB Pénzügyi Lízing Zrt. v. Ferenc Schneider* [2010] ECLI:EU:C:2010:659, para. 54.

76 Case C-464/01 *Gruber v. Bay Wa AG* [2005] ECLI:EU:C:2005:32, para. 34; Mankowski (n 64), para. 3.

77 Paul Jenard, *Report on the Convention on Jurisdiction and the Enforcement of Judgments in Civil and Commercial Matters Signed at Brussels*, 27 September 1968 [1979] OJ C59/1 33; Carl Friedrich Nordmeier, 'Art. 15 Brüssel Ia-VO' in Wieczorek and Schütze (eds), *Zivilprozessordnung und Nebengesetze Großkommentar*, vol 14 (5th edn, De Gruyter 2022), para. 2.

78 Federal Court of Australia *Epic Games, Inc v. Apple Inc [2021] FCAFC 122*, para. 86 f; O'Hara (n 1) 280.

79 Cf. Case C-243/08 *Pannon GSM*, para. 40 f; Case C-137/08 *VB Pénzügyi Lízing*, para. 53 f.

80 See Art. 5, para. 3 Swiss PILA (n 50) and Botschaft (n 69), para. 213.6.

81 Hannah Buxbaum, 'Forum Selection in International Contract Litigation: The Role of Judicial Discretion' (2004) 12 Willamette Journal of International Law and Dispute Resolution 190.

behind excluding CCAs in lawsuits on immovable property lies in strong public interests due to the *erga-omnes* effect of the decision[82] or is justified by a perception of territorial sovereignty.[83] Some provisions forbidding CCAs in certain kinds of contracts are said to be of a protectionist nature, attributable to the political influence of local industry.[84]

4.2.4 *Different Interests on the Domestic and the International Levels*

Restrictions of CCAs often differ according to whether international or domestic CCAs are concerned, whereby the former respond to a higher level of protection at the international level. In Switzerland, for example, domestic CCAs are subject to lower control than international CCAs.[85] Regarding outbound CCAs, this takes into account that only international CCAs could deprive a party of the protection by provisions, which are part of the Swiss *ordre public*.[86] However, there are also examples of provisions on CCAs that are not automatically more liberal on the domestic level than on the international level. In German law, consumers are facing fewer restrictions on the international level (Section 38, para. 2, ZPO) than on the domestic level (Section 38, para. 1, ZPO).[87] In the US, in Federal courts outbound CCAs may be better enforceable on the international level than on the domestic level as in domestic cases the provision of Title 28 of USC, Section 1404(a), may be applicable.[88]

4.2.5 *Interim Conclusion*

It has been shown that a variety of restrictions to the enforceability of CCAs serve a bunch of different interests. The list of interests as identified above may be far from being

82 Case C-433/19 *Ellmes Property Services Limited v. SP* [2020] ECLI:EU:C:2020:482, Opinion of AG Szpunar, para. 62.

83 Peter Mankowski, 'Art 24 Brüssel Ia-VO' in Thomas Rauscher (n 15), para. 44; for another view, see Dennis Solomon, 'Der Immobiliargerichtsstand im Europäischen Zuständigkeitsrecht' in Herbert Kronke and Karsten Thorn (eds), *Grenzen überwinden – Prinzipien bewahren Festschrift für Bernd von Hoffmann* (Gieseking 2012) 728 ff.

84 Coyle and Robinson (n 23) 1109; Cara Reichard, 'Keeping Litigation at Home: The Role of States in Preventing Unjust Choice of Forum' (2020) 129 Yale Law Journal 906; Frederic Lyon and Douglas Ackerman, 'Controlling Disputes by Controlling the Forum: Forum Selection Clauses in Construction Contracts' (2002) 22 Construction Contracts 16.

85 Cf. Art. 17 Swiss Civil Procedure Code vis-à-vis Art. 5, paras. 2 and 3 Swiss PILA (n 50).

86 Andreas Bucher 'Article 5' in Andreas Bucher (ed), *Loi sur le droit international privé – Convention de Lugano* (Helbing Lichtenhahn 2011), para. 29; critically Pascal Grolimund and Eva Bachofner, 'Article 5' in Pascal Grolimund, Leander Loacker and Anton Schnyder (eds), *Basler Kommentar Internationales Privatrecht* (4th edn, Helbing Lichtenhahn 2020), para. 58; however, highlighting the little importance of this provision in practice Bonomi (n 51) 612.

87 German Code of Civil Procedure (ZPO) Sec. 38, paras. 1 and 2 subject to 29c, cf. Christian Heinrich, '§ 38' in Hans-Joachim Musielak and Wolfgang Voit (eds), *Zivilprozessordnung: ZPO mit Gerichtsverfassungsgesetz* (20th edn, Verlag Franz Vahlen 2023), para. 15; Haimo Schack, *Internationales Zivilverfahrensrecht mit internationalem Insolvenz- und Schiedsverfahrensrecht* (7th edn, C.H. Beck 2017), para. 502. The German Code of Civil Procedure in English is available at https://www.gesetze-im-internet.de/englisch_zpo/index.html (accessed 3 January 2024).

88 Nanda and Lake (n 66) Sec. 3:12; Eichel (n 25) 153 ff.

complete. However, this list will be important for determining criteria for a discretionary fairness test which are derived from contract law (e.g. the concept of unconscionability; see Section 4.1.2 of the present chapter). Whether and when there is need for such a discretionary test will be explored in the following sections.

4.3 *Implementation of the Limits by a Discretionary or Nondiscretionary Approach*

Regarding the implementation of the limits, one can distinguish between a discretionary approach and a nondiscretionary approach. A nondiscretionary approach defines the requirements for setting aside a CCA more precisely so that the court has no other option than to disregard the CCA when it holds that these requirements are fulfilled. A discretionary approach allows the judge to weigh various factors to determine whether the CCA will be enforced. It allows courts to take into account a broader understanding of 'fairness', considering various interests.

4.3.1 Status Quo

In the law of jurisdiction, the discretionary approach can mainly be found in common law countries, whereas civil law countries, for instance, the European Brussels Ibis regime, are known to rely on clear-cut rules in order to strengthen predictability for the parties. Turning to CCAs, this difference between the Common Law and the Brussels Ibis system is much less distinctive. In the US, there are many detailed statutory restrictions on CCAs for specific contracts.[89] Clear-cut rules are employed to address imbalances within a particular business sector in a general way so that lawyers can assess to what extent CCAs will be enforced. Apart from such provisions, there is a discretionary approach in the US, which is not solely based on procedural grounds but also on contract law.[90] In the interest of party autonomy, it is based on the assumption that a CCA is presumptively valid.[91]

Such a coexistence of both approaches can likewise be observed in the Brussels Ibis regime. Clear-cut limits for outbound CCAs are mainly defined by exclusive jurisdiction clauses (Art. 24, Brussels Ibis Regulation). In addition to these limits, the Brussels Ibis regime allows a discretionary approach, which the ECJ has constantly developed.[92] This

89 See Section 4.1.1 of this chapter.

90 Hay (n 2) 12, 15 ff.

91 *Bremen v. Zapata Off-Shore Co.*, 407 U.S. 1, 10 (1972) ('such clauses are *prima facie* valid'); O'Hara (n 1) 283; Magnus (n 11), para. 79a.

92 Case C-519/19 *Ryanair DAC v. DelayFix*, paras. 57-61; C-240/98 to C-244/98 *Océano Grupo Editorial SA v. Roció Murciano Quintero* [2000] ECLI:EU:C:2000:346, para. 24; C-243/08 *Pannon GSM*, para. 40; C-137/08 *VB Pénzügyi Lízing*, para. 53. Confirming the applicability of international CCAs, but critical towards fairness tests Thole (n 40) 37.

approach comes from the contract law on standard terms which is strongly influenced by European law.[93] Its idea is that a CCA as a contractual stipulation is also subject to the fairness test according to Article 3 of the EU Directive on Unfair Terms if the CCA has not been individually negotiated. A CCA is held unenforceable if it – contrary to good faith – causes a significant imbalance in the parties' rights and the obligations arising under the contract. That can be assumed for a CCA, which confers exclusive jurisdiction to the courts of the seller or supplier to the detriment of a consumer if it hinders the consumer's right to take legal action. However, assessing the unfairness of a CCA in this regard requires to consider the nature of the services of the main contract and all the circumstances surrounding the conclusion of the contract.[94]

What can be derived from these observations is that regardless of the basic jurisdictional approach, there is apparently a need for both the discretionary approach and the nondiscretionary approach in each jurisdiction. Clear-cut rules in favour of persons needing protection do not apparently exclude the need for a discretionary approach. In the following lines, this phenomenon shall be explained by a recourse to law and economics, which shows that both the nondiscretionary clear-cut rules, on the one hand, and a standard-oriented discretionary approach, on the other hand, have their advantages and disadvantages depending on the context.

4.3.2 *Advantages and Disadvantages of the Approaches*

Speaking from a more general legal perspective, the imposition of limits on CCAs can be done by means of rules or standards. The term rule refers to legal provisions whose application leaves no room for discretion due to the precision of their wording.[95] They distinguish permissible from non-permissible conduct in a clear-cut way. The following provision on CCAs is an example of a *rule*: 'no insurance contract shall contain any condition, stipulation or agreement depriving the domestic courts of jurisdiction in actions against the insurer.'[96] By contrast, standards are flexible legal provisions whose concretisation requires a more elaborated hermeneutic process to apply them to the individual case, as they leave a considerable margin of discretion to the judge.[97] A standard is a provision according to which a CCA has no effect if it results in abusively

93 Council Directive 93/13/EEC of 5 April 1993 on unfair terms in consumer contracts [1993] OJ L95/29; Stadler and Krüger (n 37), para. 2c.

94 Case C-519/19 *Ryanair DAC v. DelayFix*, paras. 57-61; M. Thon, 'AGB-Kontrolle und Drittwirkung von Gerichtsstandsvereinbarungen im Anwendungsbereich der EuGVVO – Rolle rückwärts in puncto Rechtssicherheit?' (2022) 3 Praxis des Internationalen Privat- und Verfahrensrechts 236 ff.

95 Isaac Ehrlich and Richard Posner, 'An Economic Analysis of Legal Rulemaking' (1974) 3 Journal of Legal Studies 258-259; Hans-Bernd Schaefer, 'Legal Rules and Standards' in Charles Rowley and Friedrich Schneider (eds), *Encyclopedia of Public Choice* (Kluwer 2004) 347; Gisela Rühl, *Statut und Effizienz. Ökonomische Grundlagen des Internationalen Privatrechts* (Mohr Siebeck 2011) 311; Lous Kaplow, 'Rules Versus Standards: An Economic Analysis' (1992) 42 Duke Law Journal 559-560.

96 Shortened version of VA CODE ANN § 38.2-312 (Code of the US state Virginia).

97 Schaefer (n 95) 347; Ehrlich and Posner (n 95) 258.

depriving a party of the protection granted to it by national law. Both approaches have advantages and disadvantages depending on the legal system's characteristics or the provision's subject matter.

The use of precise rules has, among others, two advantages. First, the enforcement and compliance costs for the courts or parties are lower. Due to the precision of their wording, the hermeneutic process to determine their meaning and scope is not overly complicated.[98] If rules are used to establish limits on CCAs, less time will be needed to reach a decision.[99] Second, rules promote legal certainty, which allows individuals to align their contracts with the law and to foresee the outcome of a dispute.[100] However, there are also drawbacks to using rules. The lack of discretion can prevent courts from considering the case's particular circumstances.[101] Furthermore, there is a risk of over- or under-regulation.[102] Rigid rules may ignore the passing of time; their wording might cover cases that need not always be treated in the same way due to cultural, social or economic changes. An example of a risk of overregulation would be a rule that invalidates outbound CCAs in franchise contracts in order to ensure the application of the law of the forum that protects the franchisee.[103] Such a rule would keep invalidating CCAs even when the franchise laws abroad guarantee higher protection.

The use of standards allows courts to easily adapt the law to current needs and developments: standards permit the courts not only to take into consideration all the circumstances of a case but also to reach a decision where the existence (or nonexistence) of rules no longer respond to the interests at stake. In the example given, standards instead of rules would allow the courts to take into account that the franchisee receives better protection when the CCA is enforced. Discretion brings thus a higher dynamism and flexibility into the legal system. However, the enforcement and compliance costs for courts and the parties are relatively high since standards require a more elaborate process of interpretation to determine their content and scope.[104] Courts will have to invest more time and resources in adjudicating.[105] The parties will have more difficulties in predicting how the courts would apply a provision,[106] namely, to foresee whether a CCA will finally be enforced. Furthermore, the lack of precision can lead to more mistakes being made when applying them.[107] In countries where the judiciary is

98 Schaefer (n 95) 347 f.

99 Cf. Ehrlich and Posner (n 95) 265-266.

100 Rühl (n 95) 313; Ehrlich and Posner (n 95) 262, 265.

101 Schaefer (n 95) 347.

102 Rühl (n 95) 314; Ehrlich and Posner (n 95) 268.

103 Cf. Daniel A. Crane, 'Tesla, Dealer Franchise Laws, and the Politics of Crony Capitalism' (2016) 101 Iowa Law Review 577; Douglas C. Beryr, David M. Byers and Daniel J. Oates, 'State Regulation of Franchising: The Washington Experience Revisited' (2009) 32 Seattle University Law Review 816-817.

104 Schaefer (n 95) 348.

105 Ehrlich and Posner (n 95) 265-266.

106 Rühl (n 95) 313.

107 Ibid., 314.

poorly paid, poorly equipped, less qualified, slow, or prone to corruption, standards might be less suited to provide equal and uniform application of the law. However, in countries where the influence of interest groups on the legislature is strong, the use of standards can counterbalance the power of these groups because the court system as a whole cannot be influenced by interest groups in the same way.[108] And as regards the uncertainty, it can become smaller over time. Once case law made by precedents of higher courts has been established, the use of standards can provide as much legal certainty as rules.[109]

Whether rules or standards are the better instrument also depends on the subject matter of regulation. For phenomena that have been handled by the courts over years or decades, rules will be preferable to standards because lawmakers have valuable data to define the scope of a provision precisely.[110] Likewise, these data might enable the lawmaker to better foresee and consider further developments so that there should be no need for subsequent reforms in the medium term that reduce the adaptation costs. Furthermore, a high frequency of similar cases coming to courts makes rules preferable to standards.[111] Based on these thoughts, it could be concluded that with today's experience, it might be easier to draft a provision protecting procedurally 'weaker parties' (i.e. 'one-shotters' like consumers, employees, franchisees and the like) against unfair CCAs in the form of a 'rule'. The reason is that litigation of weaker parties is far more established than at the time when consumer or franchisee legislation began to appear. In addition, the internet economy, as well as globalisation, which both created new challenges to the protection of weaker parties, have produced a valuable number of cases so that the interests at stake can be better evaluated. In any case, today, it is much clearer what a weaker party is and what situations create a need for protection than 30 years ago. However, standards are preferable to rules if rather new or more heterogeneous areas of law are affected, which arises in only a small number of cases or, as far as areas of law are concerned, where economic and social conditions are in frequent change.[112] This is why it seems that every legal system is at least in need of a 'back-up provision' to fill the gaps that remain outside the scope of special rules on CCAs. For this conclusion, the above-mentioned jurisprudence of the ECJ might be sort of proof because the Brussels Ibis Regulation has established provisions protecting consumers, insurance clients and employees, but apparently there are still enough number of cases where discretionary fairness is needed.

---

108 Schaefer (n 95) 349.
109 Ibid.
110 Schaefer (n 95) 348; Rühl (n 95) 315 ff; 319.
111 Schaefer (n 95) 348.
112 Ibid.

4.3.3 Conclusions

Contract law can be the instrument to examine the enforceability of a CCA on an individual and discretionary basis. Such a discretionary 'fairness test' comes into play where the nondiscretionary 'rules' of procedural law reach their limits and in situations where a discretionary, 'standards-based' test has its strengths according to what has been laid down above. The criteria which have to be weighed up in such a fairness test could be equivalent to the procedural and substantive interests which (exemplarily) have been described above. Consequently, due to this dual nature of a CCA, it is not unusual that contract law can be an instrument to enforce procedural interests, whereas the public interests should not play a role in such a fairness test as contract law only balances the interests of the parties. For the sake of certainty, public interests should be enforced by 'rules'. In the interest of party autonomy, a discretionary fairness test should allow the consideration of all the circumstances of the case, and it should be based on the assumption that a CCA is presumptively valid.

Evidentiary Contracts in Civil Proceedings

Magne Strandberg

1 Introduction

At a very general level, an important relationship seems to exist between contracts, facts and evidence. Avoiding or reducing factual difficulties is one of the main functions of writing a contract. Well-defined contractual clauses specify the matters that must be proven in a later dispute and leave out issues that are hard to prove. For instance, clauses on strict liability leave out tricky issues concerning who knew what, and limitation of liability to direct loss leaves out tricky issues of causation. In practice, parties to a contract may still disagree on factual issues relevant to their dispute, but the contract may affect evidential issues, and evidentiary clauses may become relevant also for cases which, from a substantial point of view, do not belong to contract law. By allowing evidentiary clauses, parties may have found a regulation that works better for their dispute. For instance, a well-defined disclosure clause may provide parties access to more evidence within a simplified framework, which would save time and money compared to regular disclosure proceedings. However, contracts on matters of evidence may also become highly troublesome. While most aspects of evidence are normally regulated by a set of public rules, which would usually be regarded as relatively balanced, freedom of contract may allow stronger parties to use their bargaining power to establish evidentiary rules unfavourable to a weaker party. Evidentiary contracts may also turn problematic if courts are left with a less robust evidential situation or if the costs are enhanced.[1]

Evidentiary contracts could have been approached from a purely theoretical or normative point of view. Such an approach could highlight basic and foundational aspects and could stress the pure arguments in favour of freedom of contract on evidential issues compared to arguments in favour of leaving these matters to general lawmakers within parliament, ministries, or Supreme Courts. However, purely theoretical answers are hard to justify for these matters. Whether evidential contracts should be allowed and under what circumstances, depends on the legal framework which they operate within. Whether evidential contracts are destructive or constructive may vary from one legal tradition to another; the need for such contracts depends on

1 See Anna Nylund and Antonio Cabral, 'General Report: Contractualisation of Civil Litigation' in Anna Nylund and Antonio Cabral (eds), *Contractualisation of Civil Litigation* (Intersentia 2023) 29-30.

existing national law, and in some countries, the lawmaker may assume that parties will adjust proceedings by entering a contract, while other lawmakers may take a completely opposite starting point. Therefore, I will bring in examples from Germany, England and Wales, the United States, and the Scandinavian countries to find a variety of experiences from countries that represent different procedural traditions. While I will include examples from these jurisdictions, my article is not genuinely comparative. A full-blown comparative analysis of these matters would have to include both evidence law, contract law and a number of legal mechanisms which may serve as functional equivalents to regulations in contract.[2] The format of a book chapter does not allow for such a broad and comprehensive analysis.

Within these jurisdictions, one finds general discussions on whether and on what criteria parties may enter into contracts on procedural issues. In Scandinavia, and especially in Sweden, most scholars argue that contracts on procedural issues are invalid unless explicitly allowed for in the procedural code.[3] In Germany, some scholars argue in favour of a general right to enter into procedural contracts, while others argue in favour of regarding procedural law as not generally negotiable.[4] In US law, while a rather massive theoretical discussion is found concerning procedural contracts,[5] the most practically important issues concerning evidentiary contracts are regulated in Federal Rules of Civil Procedure (FRCP).[6] Even though the possibilities for regulating procedural issues in contracts seem to vary quite significantly between these countries, the very debates on the contractualisation of procedural issues suggest that the freedom to agree on procedural issues is not as wide, general and straightforward as the right to enter into contracts on those substantive issues which a regular civil dispute concerns. Whenever a lawsuit before a state court concerns a private law issue, parties are generally free to agree on substantive matters, but they are not necessarily

2 Several articles on the methodological requirements for comparative civil procedure law are found in Loïc Cadiet, Hess Burkhard and Marta Requejo Isidro (eds), *Approaches to Procedural Law. The Pluralism of Methods* (Nomos 2017).

3 Lotta Maunsbach, *Avtal om rätten till domstolsprövning. Processuella överenskommelsers giltighet i svensk rätt* (1st edn, Norstedts Juridik 2015) 100-104; Peter Westberg, *Civilrättsskipning* (2nd edn, Norstedts Juridik 2013) 283-284; Peter Westberg, *Konflikt och Kontrakt* (Jure 2020) 107-110. The situation in Norway is slightly more unclear and perhaps somewhat in transition, see Anna Nylund, Magne Strandberg and Marit Tjelmeland, 'Contractualisation of Civil Litigation in Norway: Flexibility and Cooperation in a Rule-Based Tradition' in Anna Nylund and Antonio Cabral (eds), *Contractualisation of Civil Litigation* (Intersentia 2023) 333-348.

4 Felix Maultzsch and Stefan Klingbeil, 'Contractualisation of Civil Litigation in Germany: A Development Towards More Party Autonomy' in Anna Nylund and Antonio Cabral (eds), *Contractualisation of Civil Litigation* (Intersentia 2023) 235-236; Gerhard Wagner, *Prozeßverträge. Privatautonomie im Verfahrensrecht* (Mohr Siebeck 1998).

5 Helen Hershkoff and Judith Resnik, 'Contractualisation of Civil Litigation in the United States: Procedure, Contract, Public Authority, Autonomy, Aggregate Litigation, and Power' in Anna Nylund and Antonio Cabral (eds), *Contractualisation of Civil Litigation* (Intersentia 2023) 419-506.

6 Federal Rules of Civil Procedure rule 29, see Section 2.4 below.

free to agree on procedural matters. Matters of evidence, however, are closely linked to substantive law, and the freedom of contract concerning substantive issues may apply to matters of evidence. Whenever such freedom of contract concerning evidence derives from substantive law, the freedom is independent of procedural matters, such as whether the dispute is dealt with by a state court, an arbitration court or a complaints board.

In principle, the subject of contractualisation of evidence is as wide, rich and complex as evidence law itself. Therefore, I must leave out some issues, and in the present chapter I will discuss contracts concerning access to evidence (Section 2), burden of proof (Section 3) and standard of evidence (Section 4). I will not deal with contracts concerning admissibility, taking or presentation of evidence. Those issues are too complex and detailed to be adequately dealt with in the rather short format of this article. Taking and presenting evidence would involve not only situations where parties agree vis-à-vis the court on, for instance, the admissibility of certain issues but also whether a party may waive his right to keep information secret and whether such a waiver may be taken by a binding contract. Involved are also matters concerning public interest, proportionality and increases of state costs as a by-product of the parties' agreement.

2 CONTRACTS CONCERNING ACCESS TO EVIDENCE

2.1 *Comparative Overview*

Even though all party-driven systems of civil procedure law meet difficulties when a party lacks access to important evidence, the solutions differ quite fundamentally from one tradition to another.[7] Except for a few types of substantive rights on which international conventions prescribe wide-ranging disclosure of evidence, the problem of access to evidence is left to national law.[8]

---

7 See Peter L. Murray and Rolf Stürner, *German Civil Justice* (Carolina Academic Press 2004) 239-244 and 589-610; Remme Verkerk, *Fact-Finding in Civil Litigation. A Comparative Perspective* (Intersentia 2010); Aleš Galiç, 'Disclosure of Documents in Civil Procedure: The Privilege against Self-Incrimination or a Quest for Procedural Fairness and Substantive Justice' in C.H. van Rhee and Alan Uzelac (eds), *Evidence in Contemporary Civil Procedure* (Intersentia 2015) 33-55.

8 On a global level: Agreement on Trade-Related Aspects of Intellectual Property Rights, Annex 1C of the Agreement Establishing the World Trade Organisation in Marrakesh Declaration of 15 April 1994. On a European level: European Parliament and Council Directive 2004/48/EC of 29 April 2004 on the enforcement of intellectual property rights [2004] OJ L195/16, and European Parliament and Council Directive 2014/104/EU of 26 November 24 on certain rules governing actions for damages under national law for infringements of the competition law [2014] OJ L349/1.

In common law, the tradition has been to open up, put all the cards on the table, and to provide all parties with a right to access evidence in the possession of the opposite party or any third party. Illustrating the long history of this tradition is a leading case which was decided as early as in 1882, when the English Court of Appeal set up a very broad obligation to disclose evidence and did so by insisting on a broad criterion of potential relevance.[9] In the United States, the tradition of open and broad discovery of evidence was further elaborated when the FRCP was established in 1938.[10] The requirement of relevance was further relaxed, and innovative discovery devices were introduced. Later, US rules of discovery have been somewhat narrowed and modified,[11] but the essence of the rules is still in line with the very open and broad rules decided in 1938. Discovery is still the most characteristic element of American civil procedure law; most cases are decided during discovery and do not go to trial.[12] The US approach to access to evidence is so open and broad compared to other countries that even American scholars describe US discovery as exceptional and extreme.[13] In England and Wales, the tradition is fundamentally similar to that of the US, but the rules on discovery have never been as far-reaching as their US counterpart. The softer English tradition became even more so after the Woolf reform in the late 1990s. In order to emphasise the differences from US discovery, the English rules got the name 'disclosure', and the rights to access evidence were modified.[14] Interestingly, in both the Woolf reform and in later English reforms of civil procedure law, the very broad right to discover evidence has been regarded as a key problem for the effectivity of legal proceedings.[15]

In Germany, both the historical and the current state of the law are the complete opposite of the Anglo-American tradition. A general duty to give access to evidence

9 *Compagnie Financiere et Commerciale du Pacifique v. Peruvian Guano Co* (1882) 11 Q.B.D. 55.

10 Richard Marcus, 'Looking Backward to 1938' (2014) 162 University of Pennsylvania Law Review 1691, 1693-1695; Stephen N. Subrin, 'Fishing Expeditions Allowed: The Historical Background of the 1938 Federal Discovery Rules' (1998) 39 Boston College Law Review 691-745; John H. Langbein, 'The Demise of Trial in American Civil Procedure: How It Happened, Is It Convergent with European Civil Procedure?' in C.H. van Rhee and Alan Uzelac (eds), *Truth and Efficiency in Civil Litigation. Fundamental Aspects of Fact-finding and Evidence-taking in a Comparative Context* (Intersentia 2012) 119, 132-133.

11 Richard L. Marcus, 'Discovery Containment Redux' (1998) 39 Boston College Law Review 747-784.

12 Margaret Woo, 'The Disappearing Trial: Retrenchment of Litigation in North America' in C.H. van Rhee and Alan Uzelac (eds), *Transformation of Civil Justice. Unity and Diversity* (Springer 2018) 145-157.

13 Stephen N. Subrin, 'Discovery in Global Perspective: Are We Nuts?' (2002) 52 DePaul Law Review 299-318; Richard L. Marcus, 'Putting American Procedural Exceptionalism into a Globalized Context' (2005) 53 The American Journal of Comparative Law 709-740; Richard L. Marcus, 'Extremism in the Pursuit of Truth is our Virtue: The American Infatuation with Broad Discovery' in A. Uzelac and C.H. van Rhee, *Truth and Efficiency in Civil Litigation* (n 10) 165-188.

14 CPR ch 31. Further reading: Neil Andrews, *Andrews on Civil Proceedings* (Intersentia 2019) 245-272.

15 On reforms of disclosure rules after the entering into force of CPR: Rupert Jackson, 'Review of Civil Litigation Costs' (2010) TSO 364-374. A Disclosure Working Group has been established since 2016, and a recent product of its work is the Disclosure Pilot Scheme, see https://www.judiciary.uk/announcements/update-on-the-operation-of-the-disclosure-pilot-scheme-disclosure-pilot-july-2021/ (accessed 18 September 2022).

('*Aufklärungspflicht*') has been suggested in the literature,[16] but the suggested doctrine is far more modified than its common law counterparts and has been accepted neither by the Federal Supreme Court (*Bundesgerichtshof*)[17] nor by a majority of scholars.[18] Instead, German courts and the prevailing academic tradition regard access to evidence as a problem of substantive law.[19] However, a general right to access information is not found in German law. While a legal basis for access to certain types of evidence is found in German substantive law for specific kinds of cases and, under exceptional circumstances, in the general doctrine of *Treu und Glauben*,[20] such rules merely provide parties with a rather limited right to access evidence.[21] From a procedural standpoint, a reform for establishing wider rights to access evidence was suggested in the 1990s, but the suggestion did not pass. Instead, a 2003 reform rephrased Sections 142-144 of the German CCP, which even after the reform grants judges limited power to order access to evidence after request from a party, and only when the requested evidence is well specified.

Middle-way solutions are found in Scandinavian rules on *edisjonsplikt*, which provide a right to access evidence in the possession of the opposite party or a third party after request and, if necessary, by court order. Characteristic of these solutions is that parties have a right to access evidence, but it is conditional and with no right to access all possibly relevant and non-privileged evidence.[22] Rules on *edisjonsplikt* have existed at least since the first part of the 1900s. The rules have been extended by both

16 Rolf Stürner, *Die Aufklärungspflicht der Parteien des Zivilprozesses* (JCB Mohr 1976); Rolf Stürner, 'Parteipflichten bei der Sachverhaltsaufklärung im Zivilprozeß. Zugleich ein Beitrag zur Lehre von der Beweisvereitelung' (1985) 98 Zeitschrift für Zivilprozeß 237-256.

17 E.g. BGH NJW 1990, 3151; BGH NJW 2007, 155, 156.

18 Peter Gottwald, 'Urteilsanmerkung' (1979) 92 Zeitschrift für Zivilprozeß 364 ff.; Peter Ahrens, 'Zur Aufklärungspflicht der nicht beweisbelasteten Partei im Zivilprozeß' (1983) 96 Zeitschrift für Zivilprozeß 1-24; Hanns Prütting, *Gegenwartsprobleme der Beweislast* (C.H. Beck 1983) 33-34 and 137 ff.; Gerhard Lüke, 'Der Informationsanspruch im Zivilrecht' (1986) 25 Juristische Schulung 2-7; Johann Braun, *Lehrbuch des Zivilprozeßrecht* (Mohr Siebeck 2014) 103-106; Hans-Jürgen Ahrens, *Der Beweis im Zivilprozess* (Otto Schmidt 2015) 113-114; Gottfried Baumgärtel, Hans-Willi Laumen and Hanns Prütting, *Handbuch der Bewislast. Grundlagen* (3rd edn, Carl Heymanns 2016) 560; Reinhard Greger, *Zöller Zivilprozessordnung* (34th edn, Otto Schmidt 2022) 853; Christian Gomille, *Informationsproblem und Wahrheitspflicht* (Mohr Siebeck 2016) 142 ff.; Wolfgang Lüke, *Zivilprozessrecht I* (11th edn, C.H. Beck 2020) 20.

19 E.g. BGH NJW 1990, 3151; BGH NJW 2007, 155, 156; Baumgärtel et al. (n 18) 308, 561; Ahrens (n 18) 1087.

20 See Section 2.2 below.

21 Further reading: Stephan Saß, *Die Beschaffung von Informationen und Beweisen* (Gardez 2002); Daniel Waterstraat, 'Informationspflichten der nicht risikobelasteten Partei im Zivilprozess' (2005) 118 Zeitschrift für Zivilprozeß 459 ff.; Baumgärtel et al. (n 18) 296-308.

22 The Scandinavian rules are very similar to ELI/UNIDROIT Model Rules Part VII Section 2, see Fernando Gascón Inchausti and Michael Stürner, 'Access to Information and Evidence in the ELI/UNIDROIT European Rules on Civil Procedure: Some Fundamental Aspects' (2019) 24 *Uniform Law Review* 14-41; Michael Stürner, 'The ELI/UNIDROIT European Rules of Civil Procedure: Access to Information and Evidence' in Fernando Gascon Inchausti and Burkhard Hess (eds), *The Future of the European Law of Civil Procedure* (Intersentia 2020) 205-222.

legal reforms and adjustments initiated by the Supreme Courts from the late 1980s onwards. While the conditions for a right to access evidence may vary in detail from one Scandinavian country to another, in general, these criteria must be met before a request for access to evidence is successful: First, the request must specify in reasonable detail the requested evidence, but the requirement is rather relaxed and is normally fulfilled whenever the cluster of evidence is reasonably specified according what one may expect under the circumstances.[23] For instance, a cluster of evidence would be sufficiently specified if a party asked for all documents contained in a company's accounting, including attachments for the period 2015 to 2020. Such a request would also be sufficiently specified if a party asked for all correspondence between the opposite party and a specific third party within a specified number of months or perhaps years. Second, the requested evidence must be relevant,[24] but even this requirement is rather relaxed inter alia because it may be hard to decide on the relevance of a piece of evidence before it is disclosed. Third, the request must be proportionate, which means that the costs for giving access must be reasonable given the value of the dispute.[25] Fourth, the evidence must be admissible, which covers all issues of privilege in the United States and England, in addition to issues like trade secrets.[26]

2.2 *Contracts as Legal Basis for Access to Evidence*

Apparently, all these general systems of denying or accepting access to evidence face genuine practical difficulties which may be of concern to parties or prospective parties to a lawsuit. Since at least some of these potential problems should be foreseeable, an interesting issue is whether parties to a contract could bindingly deal with these flaws of access to evidence law. In general, the nature of the right to access evidence suggests that it is a matter which should be subject to freedom of contract. In contrast to some other aspects of evidence law, such as admittance of evidence, parties may provide each other with access to evidence without even involving the court, and they may do so before commencement, at a preparatory stage or during a main hearing stage. In its pure form, access to evidence is a matter inter partes.

Especially in countries lacking general procedural rights on access to evidence, contracts may serve as an important legal basis for access to evidence. Such an agreement could take the form of a separate access to information contract or an access to information clause within a contract. Such a clause may run independently of

23 Norwegian CCP Section 26-6, Swedish Supreme Court practice, e.g. NJA 1959 p. 230.
24 Norwegian CCP Section 21-5, Swedish CCP Chapter 38 Section 2 first subsection and Swedish Supreme Court ruling NJA 1988 p. 652 and NJA 2002 p. 41.
25 Norwegian CCP Section 26-5 (3), Swedish Supreme Court practice, see NJA 1998 p. 829.
26 Norwegian CCP Section 21-5, Swedish CCP Chapter 38 Section 2 second subsection.

any underlying dispute or disagreement, but it may also explicitly relate to solving of disputes between the parties. Such a clause may, for instance, read:

> Whenever a dispute arises because of matters related to this contract, all parties to the contract shall provide all other parties to the contract with all relevant evidence.

In general, such contracts are binding and valid. In many jurisdictions, such clauses will be regarded as dealing with a substantive issue that the parties are free to agree on – it is just simply any person's right to share information or objects containing information in his possession. In Germany, CCP Section 422 regulates certain procedural questions for enforcing access to evidence based on substantive law and thereby presupposes the existence and validity of such rights.[27] The most important kinds of such rights are access to evidence based on a property right (*dingliches Recht*) and on a contractual right (*obligatorisches Recht*).[28] Such a contractual right may be based on statutory provisions, general principles such as the doctrine of *Treu und Glauben* ('good faith obligation') or the contract itself.

Probably influenced by German law, Scandinavian codes of procedural law traditionally entail explicit provisions which presuppose the validity of duties to disclose evidence based on substantive law.[29] Such a substantial duty to disclose evidence (*materiell edisjonsplikt*) is regarded as a parallel to the procedural duty to disclose evidence (*prosessuell edisjonsplikt*).[30] As in Germany, such a substantial right to get access to evidence may be based on a property right or a contractual right, including rights based on statutory provisions, general principles of contract law or the contract itself.[31] Since these rights are based on substantive law, the provisions found in procedural codes are mere reminders of the rights and imply that such a substantial duty prevails even though the document or property may be evidence in an ongoing lawsuit. Under the Norwegian civil procedure reform of 2005, that effect was regarded as self-evident, and the previous provision on substantive rights to access evidence was removed from the procedural code.[32]

---

27 German CCP 422: 'The opponent is under obligation to produce the record or document if, pursuant to the stipulations of civil law, the party tendering evidence may demand the surrender or production of the record or document.'

28 Ahrens (n 18) 670, rn. 36.

29 Swedish CCP Chapter 38 Section 3; the Norwegian Code of 1915 (tvistemålsloven) Section 250 second subsection.

30 Per Olof Ekelöf, Henrik Edelstam and Lars Heuman, *Rättegång IV* (7th edn, Norstedt Juridik 2009) 273-275; Peter Westberg, *Anskaffning av bevisning i dispositiva tvistemål* (Norstedts Juridik 2010) 181-205.

31 Ekelöf et al. (n 30) 274-275; Westberg (n 30) 198-200.

32 NOU 2001: 32 *Rett på sak* 977.

Since a contract on access to evidence is regarded as substantive in nature, the validity of such a contract depends on substantive law and probably, first and foremost, on requirements found in general contract law or specialised contract law for the specific objects or information. Probably, questions concerning the validity of such a contract will be of interest at least in three circumstances.

First, if a clause is highly imbalanced, for instance, if one party is obliged to give access to all evidence in his possession, while the opposite party is not obliged to give access to any sort of information. Imbalanced contracts are a well-known problem, and in most jurisdictions, contract law will provide at least some rules or mechanisms for handling such situations. Nevertheless, the implications of an evidentiary contract for the underlying proceeding may give reason to provide special rules for these contracts, and in extreme cases a state court could, at least in principle, be entitled to apply ECHR Article 6 in order to prevent massive differences in the parties' opportunities to prove their case.

Second, the validity of an access to evidence contract may become questionable if the contract implies a waiver of an evidential privilege or a reason for keeping information inadmissible. Although such contracts come with numerous nuances, as a starting point, one should acknowledge the legal categorisation of the issues. As these contracts are substantive in nature, an evidential privilege or a rule on inadmissibility applicable for litigation does not (directly) affect the validity of a substantial contract concerning the right to information. For instance, if two parties to a contract under Norwegian law agree to disclose evidence containing trade secrets, such a contractual clause is valid regardless of the rule on the inadmissibility of such information in Norwegian CCP Section 22-10. If a party in accordance with such a contract has gained access to trade secrets, that evidence is admissible since the contract would be regarded as a waiver of the right to hold trade secrets inadmissible. However, the reason for keeping information privileged or inadmissible may become relevant under contract law and may justify a boundary for the freedom of contract. If a clause contained in an insurance policy implies that all private parties are obliged to disclose all sensitive information concerning their private life or their physical or mental health, it may cause trouble, for instance, under ECHR Article 8, GDPR, and in most jurisdictions also under national law.

Third, if disclosing information in accordance with a contract would infringe on the right of a third party (i.e. a person or legal entity who is not a party to the contract), the contract is not binding for the third party. Such a contract clause may still become valid between the parties to the contract; for instance, one of the parties could be liable for damages, but it will not have any practical effect for the third party.

2.3 *Non-Disclosure Agreements: Contracts as a Legal Basis for Setting Aside Procedural Rules on Access to Evidence?*

In jurisdictions containing procedural rules giving parties a right to access evidence in the possession of the opposite party or a third party, a potentially important question is whether parties to a contract can agree that information shall be kept non-disclosed. A contract clause may instruct the setting aside of procedural rules on access to evidence, for instance, that no party shall request access to evidence based on Scandinavian rules on *edisjonsplikt* or English rules on disclosure, or it may exclude the application of such rules for certain types of information or information arising from a specific source. If parties enter into such a contract and act according to it, rules on access to evidence will not apply unless the court has a duty or power to order access to evidence on its own motion. In Scandinavian law and common law countries, the court cannot order such access, which means that such an agreement between the parties will have effect. In Germany, on the other hand, the court may order access to evidence ex officio based on CCP Sections 142-144 and, according to the prevailing view, that competence cannot be limited by a contract between the parties.[33]

What if a party requires access to evidence under civil procedural rules even though he has agreed not to do so in a contract? In US law, such a problem has occurred concerning so-called 'non-disclosure agreements' (NDA), which limits the extension of discovery, for instance, for certain pieces of evidence or for information on, for instance, a specified event or relationship.[34] Scholars seem to disagree on whether such contract clauses are rare or frequent,[35] but NDAs seem to be frequently used in employment contracts and in some other branches.[36] However, an NDA is not necessarily a barrier towards discovery. In general, parties may waive their right to discovery, but such a waiver is not necessarily given (full) effect and may very well have a rational and justifiable reason for avoiding the potentially extreme effects of US discovery. Very few exceptions apply to the general rules on discovery;[37] the basic idea of discovery is that all relevant and non-privileged evidence shall be disclosed, and a piece of evidence is not directly regarded as privileged on the basis of an NDA clause.[38]

In Scandinavian law, it is uncertain whether parties to a contract may waive their right to access evidence in the possession of the opposite party or any third party. Scholars starting from a principle of non-validity of procedural contracts will probably

33 Maultzsch and Klingbeil (n 4) 246-248 with further references.

34 Hershkoff and Resnik (n 5) 493-496.

35 Ibid., Section 3.6.

36 Jeffrey Steven Gordon, 'Silence for Sale' (2020) 71 Alabama Law Review 1109 ff., 1123.

37 Richard Marcus et al., *Civil Procedure. A Modern Approach* (7th edn, West Academic Publishing 2018) 396-431.

38 Hershkoff and Resnik (n 5) Section 3.6 with references to court practice.

conclude that the provisions on *edisjonsplikt* do not explicitly open for contractual arrangements, and therefore such a contract will stay invalid. Furthermore, parties are not allowed to agree on any evidential privileges or extend the rules on inadmissibility,[39] which may also suggest that parties are not allowed to set aside the rules for *edisjonsplikt* since it is quite similar to inadmissibility. However, a doctrine on waiver could be developed and partly accepted by the courts, for instance, if parties waive the right to request access to evidence based on rules on *edisjonsplikt* and replace these rules with other criteria for access to evidence.

2.4 Contracts or Agreements within the Application of Procedural Rules on Access to Evidence

Since most sets of rules concerning access to evidence tend to result in complicated, expensive, time-consuming, and not always foreseeable ways of practical applications or effectuation in concrete cases, parties may very well have a reasonable need for clarifying matters in a contract either at a very early stage or when a case is pending. May the parties in a contract regulate aspects such as how evidence is to be disclosed, when disclosure shall take place, or which expert to involve in securing or filtering the evidence? May they agree on additional discovery devices or non-application of certain requirements within the set of rules or perhaps set up another requirement than the one set up in the law?

US law is based on an assumption that a majority of discovery proceedings should be, and actually will be, conducted by agreement between parties and counsels. Attorneys are obliged to attempt to solve issues of discovery in good faith and in accordance with an agreed discovery plan which is also submitted to court.[40] FRCP Rule 29 allows parties to agree on – to stipulate – elements other than those found in FRCP, unless the court orders otherwise:

> Unless the court orders otherwise, the parties may stipulate that:
> (a) a deposition may be taken before any person, at any time or place, on any notice, and in the manner specified—in which event it may be used in the same way as any other deposition; and
> (b) other procedures governing or limiting discovery be modified—but a stipulation extending the time for any form of discovery must have court approval if it would interfere with the time set for completing discovery, for hearing a motion, or for trial.

39 Norwegian CCP Section 21-5.

40 FRCP Rule 26(f). Jay E. Grenig, 'Stipulations Regarding Discovery Procedure' (1998) 21 American Journal of Trial Advocacy 547-564.

Normally, parties do not need the court's approval of a stipulation, but any stipulation which varies the procedures set up in FRCP could be superseded by a court order.[41] The court's approval is necessary, however, if a stipulation extends timelines compared to what has been set up in a court-imposed schedule.[42]

In Norwegian law, parties cannot, in contract, set up requirements for access to evidence which deviate from a provision on *edisjonsplikt* in the code Chapter 26, which does not entail any provision similar to FRCP Rule 29. But parties may agree on matters not prescribed in the code, for instance, methods or details for how, when and where to effectuate access to evidence, and the code does not entail detailed provisions on enforcement of access to evidence orders. A case decided by the Supreme Court in 2020[43] suggests that parties are both allowed and encouraged to agree on practical matters concerning how access to evidence shall be enforced. Although the Supreme Court did not explicitly leave matters of access to evidence to contracts to the parties, the nature of access to evidence rules was emphasised, in particular their feature of working inter-partes based on a principle of cooperation. The role of the court seems to be of a 'secondary' nature, where court orders are granted when parties are not able to agree.[44]

3 Contracts Concerning the Burden of Proof

In Germany, common law countries and Scandinavia, the burden of proof is a matter of law and, in general, is allocated to the party who has the advantage of having a substantive rule applied or to the party who alleges certain facts.[45] If a contract defines the conditions for a legal effect and for certain defences, allocations of the burden are a by-product of those definitions. However, parties may also directly regulate the burden of proof in a contract, for instance, by prescribing that a specific party has the burden of proof for a defined matter and thereby allocate the burden of proof differently from what the general rules would imply. In contrast to most other procedural contracts, contractual clauses on the burden of proof are normally taken at a very early stage and normally when a contract on the substantive issue is entered.

41 Grenig (n 40) 561.

42 Ibid., 562.

43 Norwegian Supreme Court, 21 December 2021, HR-2020-2469-A.

44 Magne Strandberg, 'Bevistilgang og rollefordeling' in Torbjörn Andersson, Eric Bylander and Henrik Bellander (eds), *Processrättsliga studier tillägnade Bengt Lindell* (Iustus 2021) 277-295.

45 On German law Maultzsch and Klingbeil (n 4) 245-256. On English law: Adrian Keane and Paul McKeown, *The Modern Law of Evidence* (OUP 2016) 106. The allocation of the burden of proof varies somewhat in Swedish and Danish law, see Magne Strandberg, 'Standards of Evidence in Scandinavia' in Luboš Tichý (ed), *Standard of Proof in Europe* (Mohr Siebeck 2019) 135-159, 144-145, 155-156.

Although it is somewhat uncertain whether such explicit contractual clauses on the burden of proof are frequent, all jurisdictions allow them.[46] In all jurisdictions, the connection between the burden of proof and substantive law is the justification of that freedom of contract,[47] which is especially important in jurisdictions starting from a principle of non-validity of procedural contracts. While some argue that the burden of proof *is* substantive law, others argue that the burden of proof derives from, or is determined by, substantive law.[48] Regardless of whether the relationship between the burden of proof and substantive law is described ontologically or derivatively, contractual freedoms concerning the burden of proof follow the freedom to enter into contracts on the substantive issue. If the parties may enter into contracts on the substantive issue, they may also agree on allocation of the burden of proof. Arguably, limits of the freedom of contract concerning the substantive issue apply similarly to the burden of proof clauses. If, for instance, a substantive contract is valid only in writing, a burden of proof clause for such a substantive issue must probably also be in writing.

In Europe, special boundaries for the freedom to enter into contracts apply in consumer law. May a company and a consumer agree on a contractual clause on the burden of proof which is unfavourable for the consumer compared to the general rules? In Germany, the Civil Code Section 309 number 12 makes ineffective any standard business term that allocates the burden of proof to a consumer for a fact within the sphere of responsibility of the professional party. Furthermore, the following is pursuant to the Civil Code Section 312k:[49]

> (1) No agreements deviating from the provisions of this subtitle may be made, unless otherwise provided, that are to the disadvantage of the consumer or the customer. Unless otherwise provided, the provisions of this subtitle apply even if they are circumvented by other constructions.

Norwegian law does not contain a general provision on the effect of burden of proof clauses in consumer contracts. In Norway, consumer law is regulated in a rather fragmented manner by separate Acts for the sale of goods, insurance, financial contracts, etc. Typically, one of the first sections of such an Act declares the invariability of terms or conditions which are unfavourable to the consumer, for instance, Consumer Purchases Act,[50] Section 3, first subsection:

---

46 Maultzsch and Klingbeil (n 4) 245-246, Nylund et al. (n 3), 341-343, John Sorabji, 'Contractualisation of Civil Litigation in England and Wales: Party Autonomy, Contracts and Procedure' in Anna Nylund and Antonio Cabral (eds), *Contractualisation of Civil Litigation* (Intersentia 2023) 202-203.

47 Maultzsch and Klingbeil (n 4) 245-246, Nylund et al. (n 3) 342, Sorabji (n 46) 202.

48 See also ELI/UNIDROIT Rule 25 (1) third sentence.

49 The translation is found here: German Civil Code BGB (gesetze-im-internet.de (accessed 4 March 2024).

50 Act relating to consumer purchases (Act 2002 no 34) Section 3 first subsection. An unofficial English translation is found here: https://lovdata.no/dokument/NLE/lov/2002-06-21-34 (accessed 4 March 2024).

> Terms and conditions less favourable to the consumer than those flowing from the provisions of this Act may not be agreed or enforced.

If a Norwegian consumer protection act entails a provision on the burden of proof,[51] a contract clause setting up a rule that is unfavourable for the consumer is not binding. However, most acts concerning consumer law only entail substantive rules and do not explicitly regulate the burden of proof. Therefore, it has been argued that such provisions do not exclude clauses regulating the burden of proof in a way that sets a consumer in a less favourable position than general principles of evidence law.[52] According to that opinion, such clauses may become invalid merely on the basis of general contract law principles, which would mean that at least some contractual regulations of the burden of proof are invalid but far from all such regulations. In my view, the burden of proof could be regarded as a side effect or an implication of the substantive provisions. An allocation of the burden of proof seems to be implied by the statutory provisions and thereby not permissible when it poses a disadvantage to the consumer. The practical effect of a consumer law regulation may be seriously diminished if parties are allowed to regulate this freely in a contract. Such a burden of proof clause may also become invalid because of EU law.[53]

Whether a contractual clause on the burden of proof is valid, first and foremost, depends on general contract law and specific contract law whenever applicable to the specific contract. However, one may argue that some additional requirements for the validity of such a clause must apply, such as matters of effectivity of other elements of the contracts. If a standard of evidence is impossible to fulfil, it may be regarded as a waiver of the right to any sort of effective remedy. In the end, matters of a fair trial in ECHR Article 6 could perhaps be an issue.

4 Contracts Concerning the Standard of Evidence

The standard of evidence for civil cases varies considerably from one legal family to another. While common law countries apply a low more-probable-than-not standard,[54] Germanic countries apply a significantly higher standard requiring that the judge must

51 Examples are found in the Act on Insurance Contracts (Act 1989 no 69) Section 21-1 and in the Financial Agreements Act (Act 2020 no 146) Sections 3-5 to 3-7.

52 Arnulf Tverberg, *Forbrukerkjøpsloven med kommentarer* (Gyldendal 2008) 140.

53 See Alain Ancery and Bart Krans, this volume.

54 John Sorabji, 'The English Approach to the Standard of Proof in Civil Proceedings' in Luboš Tichý (ed), *Standard of Proof in Europe* (Mohr Siebeck 2019) 249-269; David Kaye in Broun (ed), *McCormick on Evidence* (7th edn, West Academic Publishing 2014) 715-724.

be convinced of the truth of the statement in question.[55] In Scandinavia, the standard varies from one country to another. While Norwegian law applies the more-probable-than-not standard as a main rule, the Swedish normal standard is similar to the Germanic standard, although the number of exceptions is quite high.[56] At least in international contracts involving parties from different legal traditions, these massive differences suggest that parties have a need to clarify the standard of evidence in the contract.

However, surprising differences occur also in the freedom of contract concerning the standard of evidence. In Scandinavia, the standard of evidence is regarded as a matter of substantive law, or at least an element very closely related to substantive law.[57] Therefore, even in countries with a restrictive approach to procedural contracts, parties are free to enter into a contract that sets up a standard of evidence deviating from the general principles. The close relationship between the standard of evidence and substantive law is apparent on several levels: the standard of evidence is a part of the final judgment and directly affects the decision taken on the merits, and the standard of evidence directly affects the risk of a substantive error between the parties.

German law, on the other hand, does not accept contracts on the standard of evidence.[58] The abstract and general character of the standard of evidence implies that it is not amenable to an agreement between the parties because any change to the standard of evidence would represent an interference with the established legal structure.[59] The standard of evidence is regarded as based on German CCP Section 286 and thereby closely linked to the principle of free evaluation of evidence, which cannot be enshrined by agreements between the parties.[60] Moreover, the standard of evidence is regarded as a matter of procedural law, also in situations where the standard is defined in a Code or Act concerning substantive matters.[61] In line with these reasons for considering the standard of evidence as non-permissible, most scholars regard the standard of evidence as *lex fori*.[62]

These fundamental differences concerning the freedom to regulate the standard of evidence in a contract are explained by a paradigmatic difference between Scandinavian and German legal methodology. Although plausible arguments may be put forward in favour of both the Scandinavian and the German systematisation of the standard of evidence, the systematisation itself is typically far more important within German

55 Baumgärtel et al. (n 18) 94; Ahrens (n 18) 349-353; Leo Rosenberg, Karl Heinz Schwab and Peter Gottwald, *Zivilprozessrecht* (18th edn, C. H. Beck 2018) 685-686.

56 Strandberg (n 45) 143, 149, 156.

57 Maunsbach (n 3) 349, Westberg, *Konflikt och kontrakt* (n 3) 565-569.

58 E.g. Baumgärtel et al. (n 18) 93.

59 Ibid.

60 Reinhard Greger, *Zöller Zivilprosessordnung* (34th edn, Otto Schmidt Verlag 2022) 859, rn. 8.

61 Wolfgang Hau, 'Dogmatik im Dienst von Gerechtigkeit, Rechssicherheit und Rechtsentwicklung' in Moritz Brinkmann et al (edn), *Festschrift für Hanns Prütting* (Carl Heymanns Verlag 2018) 325-355, 333.

62 Hau (n 61) 334 and Baumgärtel et al. (n 18) 92.

legal thinking. While Scandinavian legal methodology would emphasise arguments from systematisation, in general, arguments based on the (societal) consequences of legal regulation are far more important. Although the actual consequences of a legal regulation may be impossible or highly challenging to foresee, in practical legal reasoning, avoiding consequential paradoxes would regularly be of high importance. From a Scandinavian point of view, the German acceptance of contracts concerning the burden of proof would be regarded as incoherent with the non-allowance of contracts concerning the standard of proof. While German contractors are not allowed to reduce the high standard of evidence, they are allowed to direct that high standard of evidence against the opposite party.

However, this Scandinavian argument is based on a particular approach concerning the relationship between the burden of proof and the standard of evidence. In the Scandinavian doctrine of evidence, the burden of proof and the standard of evidence are together regarded as containing one single decision rule or one single threshold for sufficient proof. That element of Scandinavian evidential theory was developed in the 1940s[63] and elaborated and published internationally by Ekelöf and others in the 1960s.[64] Even though these Scandinavian theories are well known in Germany,[65] German theory of evidence is simply based on a different general view concerning the relationships between the burden of proof, the standard of evidence and the evaluation of evidence. Those differences in systematisation may be due to a number of reasons, but, apparently, the key role of the non-liquet concept within the German burden of proof theories implies or suggests a specific systematisation. The function of the burden of proof is to handle *non-liquet* situations,[66] and such a situation appears whenever sufficient evidence has not been adduced in favour of any factual assertion by any party. Implied, then, is that the judge must apply both the standard of evidence and the principle of free evaluation of evidence before the burden of proof may become applicable and decisive. In Scandinavia, on the other hand, the pairing of the standard of evidence and the burden of proof into one operative criterion implies a disappearance of the entire non-liquet problem, and the very concept of non-liquet has more or less been abolished from Scandinavian theories of evidence.

63 Sjur Brækhus, 'Et par bemærkninger til bevislæren' (1940) 5 Stud Jur 5-11; Torstein Eckhoff, *Tvilsrisikoen (Bevisbyrden)* (Tanum 1943) 9-21; Per Olof Bolding, *Bevisbördan och den juridiska tekniken* (Appelbergs Boktryckeri 1951) 132-147.

64 Per Olof Ekelöf, 'Beweiswürdigung, Beweislast und Beweis des ersten Anscheins' (1962) 75 Zeitschrift für Zivilprozeß 289-301; Per Olof Bolding, 'Aspects of the Burden of Proof' (1960) Scandinavian Studies in Law 9-27.

65 E.g. Richard Motsch, *Vom rechstgenügenden Beweis* (Duncker & Humblot 1983) 37-55; Prütting (n 18) 71-73; Mark Schweizer, *Beweiswürdigung und Bewismaß* (Mohr Siebeck 2015) 155-167.

66 Hans-Joachim Musielak, *Die Grundlagen der Beweislast im Zivilprozess* (de Greuter 1975) 19-21, Prütting (n 18) 14-17, Baumgärtel et al. (n 18) 170.

Apparently, the German discussions on the Scandinavian theories have put too much emphasis on the more-probable-than-not standard. The Scandinavian systematisation is a general systematisation of any standard of evidence and any allocation of the burden of proof; it does not presuppose a particular standard of evidence. Ekelöf never accepted the more-probable-than-not-standard, which he criticised over many decades, and Swedish law has never developed such a standard as a main rule for civil cases – it is an exception that merely applies to certain matters.[67] My personal view is that the-more-probable-than-not-standard is not well justified,[68] but I would still argue in favour of the Scandinavian systematisation of the standard of evidence and the burden of proof. Anyway, the impact on the freedom of contract highlights the potential importance of rather theoretical and deep-level systematisation of evidence law.

67 Strandberg (n 45) 146-147.

68 Magne Strandberg, 'The More-Probable-Than-Not-Standard: A Critical Approach' in Luboš Tichý (ed), *Standard of Proof in Europe* (Mohr Siebeck 2019) 65-92.

Procedural Agreements and Litigation Costs

Henrik Bellander

1 Introduction and Outline

Litigation costs have long been subject to the interest of legislators and academics, not least in comparative procedural literature. Often, attention has been drawn to how legal costs are increasing and how high attorneys' fees, the risk of bearing costs and the financial differences between the parties can hinder the impact of substantive law.[1] Solutions to this problem have shifted from an instrumental view on the design of statutory cost rules in themselves, like consistently implemented main rules and predictable criteria,[2] towards helping the parties to finance the costs of the proceedings – through a reduction of the fees for courts, state legal aid or private legal expenses insurances[3] – and, further, to questions on how to avoid or limit costs (as well as avoiding or limiting litigation or trials) through the use of conciliation or mediation – leading to settlement agreements between the parties.[4] The discussion has also been about the fact that high attorney costs can be avoided or limited in various ways within the framework of the relationship between client and counsel through different kinds of risk agreements or through the use of different kinds of commercial financing solutions from third parties.[5]

---

1 See Marcel Storme, 'Tomorrow's Civil Trial' in Vyutas Nekrosius et al. (eds), *The Recent Tendencies of Development in Civil Procedure Law – Between East and West* (Justitia 2007) 20; Mario Cappelletti and Bryant Garth, 'Access to Justice: The Worldwide Movement to Make Rights Effective: A General Report' in Mauro Cappelletti and Bryan Garth (eds), *Access to Justice Vol I: A World Survey* (Giuffrè Editore/Sijthoff/Noordhoff 1978) 10.

2 An early example would be the Austrian Zivilprozessordnung of 1898, with a concise 'looser pays' main rule in § 41.1 combined with few and well-defined exceptions in § 44 and § 45. The law was originally based on Franz Klein's ideas on a 'social civil procedure' and influenced by Rudolf Pollak's theories on costs. A recent example is the UK; see Harry Woolf, Access to Justice: Final Report (HM Stationary Office 1995) and Rupert Jackson, *Review of Civil Litigation Costs: Final Report* (The Stationary Office 2010).

3 See about legal aid in the first wave of the Access to Justice movement Michel Zander in Mauro Cappelletti (ed), *Access to Justice and the Welfare State* (Sijthoff/Brulylant/Klett-Cotta/Le Monnier 1981) 27-48 and for more recent examples Christopher Hodges, Stefan Vogenauer and Magdalena Tulibacka (eds), *The Costs and Funding of Civil Litigation: A Comparative Perspective* (C.H. Beck 2010) 96-100.

4 Mauro Cappelletti et al., *Towards Equal Justice: A Comparative Study of Legal Aid in Modern Societies (Text and materials)* (Giuffré Editore/Dobbs Ferry/Oceana Publications 1975).

5 In the UK, for example, the legislature has identified risk agreements and third-party funding as alternatives to public funding, starting with the comprehensive reform of 1999 (the Civil Procedure Rules). See Woolf (n 2), especially Chapter 7, Jackson (n 2), and UK Legal Aid, Sentencing and Punishment of Offenders Bill 2010-2011.

In this landscape of legal relations, regulations and agreements, the focus has also shifted to questions about states' interests to let parties modify, regulate or control the cost effects, fully or to some extent, by their procedural dispositions or by agreements. Proposals for alternative rules are often discussed. These proposals often seek greater flexibility, allowing costs to be managed and rules to be adapted for the best possible effects in relation to the circumstances of the individual cases. The discussion on the design of cost rules often also raises parameters of interest to the parties in individual cases, such as mechanisms to encourage or discourage litigation or achieve more predictable risks. Against this background, the parties may also have an interest in entering into various agreements intended to modify or supplement the cost rules.

This chapter outlines various legal approaches to such procedural contracts on litigation costs. Section 2 is an inventory of both specific and more abstract issues relevant to agreement on litigation costs in a wider sense. Section 3 contains an attempt to summarise and draw conclusions on more methodological aspects of dealing with procedural agreements on costs. The aim of the chapter is to problematise agreements on costs at a general level, irrespective of what national regulations are intended. Comparative examples are provided mainly in the footnotes, primarily from a Nordic and European perspective.

2 An Inventory of Relevant Topics and Problems

2.1 Cost Agreements in Relation to Statutory Cost Rules

A natural starting point for an examination of agreements on litigation costs is the procedural rules on costs which such agreements are meant to modify in some way. In a strict sense, cost rules could be described as rules directed against the court regulating the assessment of reimbursable litigation costs and the distribution of these costs in the relationship between the parties (claimant and defendant).[6] This regulates the extent of and the circumstances under which there is a liability for reimbursement.[7]

Even if common traits might be detected, such rules are subject to endless variations between and within legal orders. When it comes to cost-shifting, one common narrative or categorisation is the distinction between those legal orders where shifting of costs between the parties is the main rule (often described as the English rule)[8] and those

6 Hodges et al. (n 3), 12-20.

7 The term 'costs' is often used to denote only recoverable expenses, while other 'expenses' may also be non-recoverable.

8 Here we find most European countries, see Hodges et al. (n 3), 12-20.

where no shifting is the starting point (the American rule).[9] However, they both usually come with a variety of exceptions, e.g. depending on the subject matter of the case (e.g. consumer or employment law),[10] the value in dispute (small claim tracks),[11] the procedural conduct of the parties or the courts' discretion. For certain situations, one-way shifting rules may also exist to enhance the protection of weaker parties.[12]

The same kind of variety is also apparent when it comes to rules on cost assessment, regulating what kind of expenses – like fees for witnesses, experts, courts[13] and lawyers – are recoverable and to what extent. Here we find solutions with different kinds of tariffs[14] or more general rules on reasonability.[15] The separation of rules on cost assessment from rules on cost-shifting is also deceptive. A rule on shifting combined with a rule on assessment limiting the recoverable costs could have much the same effect as a rule on no shifting.[16]

Furthermore, the more formal or procedural rules on how cost issues are handled in litigation are often overlooked. For example, the effects and impact of substantive cost rules may be affected by imposing certain documentation or evidentiary requirements for certain cost items. Similarly, there may be major differences between countries regarding at what stages during the process cost issues are addressed, affecting parties' abilities to predict and control costs.[17]

Considering all such differences, a study of details in specific cost agreements would not be fruitful. Even if the focus here is the parties' own regulation of the costs in their agreement (designed as a modification of statutory rules and their effects), and these differences as such might be of second-grade importance, every attempt to formulate

9 See the US Federal Rules on Civil Procedure, Rule 54(d).

10 See, e.g. as an exception from the American rule, the US Fair Housing Act, Section 813 (c), stipulates that the prevailing party in a civil action regarding discriminatory housing practice may, at court's discretion, be allowed a reasonable attorney's fees and costs.

11 See, e.g. the English Civil Procedure Rules, rule 27.14.

12 E.g. 'Qualified one-way costs shifting' according to the English Civil Procedure Rules, rules 44.13-44.17.

13 Another set of rules may govern the parties' responsibility towards the court or state for fees connected to the litigation. Filing a claim in court in some countries is combined with considerable court fees, sometimes calculated as a percentage based on the amount in dispute and/or as instalments due to be paid at different stages of the procedure. In other countries, court fees are flat and more symbolic. See Hodges et al. (n 3) 75.

14 See the German Zivilprozessordnung, Section 91 and the Attorney Remuneration Act.

15 See, e.g. the Swedish Code on Judicial Procedure (1942:740) Chapter 18 Section 8.

16 See the Swedish rule on small claims, the Swedish Code on Judicial Procedure (1942:740) Chapter 18 Section 8a and the US Supreme Court ruling in *Alyeska Pipeline Service Company v. The Wilderness Society* (421 US 241, 1977).

17 In England, a cost capping order may be issued at an early stage of the procedure, and cost issues could be dealt with in a meeting subsequent to the ruling in the case, see Civil Procedure Rules, part 3, practice direction 3F and rule 47, while in Sweden the assessment of costs is left to the final stage of the hearing and dealt with in connection with the ruling in substance, see the Swedish Code on Judicial Procedure (1942:740) Chapter 18 Section 14.

general conclusions on how such provisions may be formulated, their possible effects or legal problems they may involve would be unsuccessful.

However, the differences on a statutory level between countries could teach us something about considerations that must be made when regulating the same issues in a contract.

First, a provision on cost, by law or agreement, may not be seen as isolated but must always be considered in relation to other provisions related to them. The effects of a rule on shifting certain costs under certain conditions may be altered by a rule on how to calculate these costs, just as a provision on how to calculate certain costs could be altered by a provision on the evidence or claims being put forth in the proceedings, etc. What is gained by one rule may be taken back by another, and the effects of altering one rule may be limited if others are altered too.

Second, when limiting the scope to rules regulating the shifting of costs between the parties, these provisions do not directly regulate how costs arise for each party or how they may be finally regulated, for example, in a broader legal context – like rules on legal representation by lawyers – and a wider circle of subjects – not least the lawyers representing the parties. So even if a study of agreements between the parties leads us to limit the relevant considerations to agreements on cost assessment and cost-shifting between the parties of the dispute, the effects of and boundaries of such agreements must be regarded in this more complex context.

Third, due to the variety of possible combinations of rules to modify in a contract, it is more fruitful to focus on the intended effects than to go into details on the means to reach them, like specific provisions. If we limit ourselves to cost assessment and cost-shifting between the parties to the dispute, a variety of effects of contracts could be relevant.

One aim could be to limit the cost liability by regulating what shall or not shall constitute a reimbursable cost, by linking the size of recoverable costs to the subject matter of the dispute or by agreeing on general foundations for how the costs are to be shifted, e.g. that each party shall bear its own cost.

Another aim could be to make the allocation of costs depending on how the court assesses certain claims or issues, substantial or procedural. This could include financial incentives or sanctions for the procedure to be carried out in a certain way.

Parties could also have incentives to make procedural provisions on how the cost liability should be tried, e.g. that cost issues are to be decided by the court more freely or based on equality rather than strict application of rules, that cost issues should be dealt with separately in a subsequent procedure, instead of within the main trial or on the evidence or invocations required for different costs.

2.2 Cost Issues between Parties in the Context of Representation and Legal Aid

Often separated from but closely connected to the cost rules touched on in the previous section is the regulation of legal representation. Rules demanding or allowing parties to be represented in court set the framework for how much of the costs arise. We can find legal orders that require parties to be represented in court, legal orders where a certain profession, normally members of the bar, has a monopoly on such representation, or legal orders with both of these solutions.[18] In other countries, parties are free to choose to be represented or not, to choose representatives with lower demands on their qualifications or both of these. Again, exceptions and details in such regulation also provide for a set of in-between positions, e.g. where representation and/or specific qualification for representatives is prescribed for proceedings in higher instances only or depending on the size of the claims in dispute.

Rules or professional standards for lawyers also include provisions on the details of and limitations for how lawyers' fees are calculated, invoiced and due for payment. Here, another demarcation may be systems where contingency or success fees, calculated in relation to the values in dispute, are allowed and those systems where such fees are prohibited and, where allowed, if they are common or rare.[19]

Further along the line, we find that cost-related procedural agreements could also be seen in relation to parties' funding of litigation, also introducing further actors and legal regulations to take into consideration. Here, we find traditional forms of financing like publicly funded legal aid. In a legal environment with increased complexity, increasing costs for legal representation, experts and evidence and less public financing, a strategy both for the parties and the state is to find private solutions. Legal aid insurance, governed by insurance contracts, has long been an important factor for dispute funding, fragmenting and distributing the risk and costs on an insurance collective. In recent decades, along with an increased interest in distributing the risk also on lawyers with risk agreements, third-party funding solutions have been

18 Different approaches in the Nordic countries may illustrate this. In Denmark and Sweden, a special professional title ('*advokat*') is linked to membership in the respective countries' bar associations, and by law these associations have a protected status and the main responsibility to supervise the conduct of their members. In Norway, the Norwegian Bar Association has voluntary membership, while the Supervisory Council for the Legal Community and a Disciplinary Board are responsible for supervising all lawyers. In Norway and Denmark, lawyers have a monopoly on representing parties in courts, and in Norway, representation of a lawyer is required for procedure in higher courts. Sweden, on the other hand, has neither a requirement on representation nor a monopoly for members of the bar.

19 For a comparative overview, see Michael Faure, Fokke Fernhout and Niels Philipsen, 'No Cure, No Pay and Contingency Fees' in Mark Tuil and Louis Visscher (eds), *New Trends in Financing Civil Litigation in Europe* (Edward Elgar 2010) 33, 41.

more common.[20] Such financing also comes at a cost and must be dealt with in the contractual relationships between the party and the financier, not seldom linked to the action taken in and the outcome of the trial. Here, too, the extent of legal regulation is shifting between countries; while state legal aid is normally strictly regulated in statutes, private solutions are less regulated.

These relationships, between one of the parties and their lawyer and/or financier, are not the primary interest when dealing with cost agreements between the parties.[21] However, these factors may explain a party's strategy to control the risk by reaching an agreement with the other party of the dispute, and they are of interest in a number of ways.

First, even if the degree of legal regulation varies, this is an area that is, to a large extent, already governed by agreements and contracts rather than by legislation. Contracts between one of the parties and its lawyer or funder indirectly set the frames for the party's expenses that are later subject to rules on cost-shifting and cost assessment. Such contracts govern how and when costs arise for a party (e.g. their size and when they are due), and they may also regulate what costs a winning or losing party finally bears (e.g. if the funder also contributes by paying the counterparty's costs in case of defeat). Hence, they enable parties to modify the effects of statutory cost rules and to control the economic outcome of litigation.

Second, the dispute between the parties, seen as an asset or a risk, is marred by many unpredictable variables that must be managed efficiently. The future size and distribution of cost is one variable that parties often want to control or be able to predict. A strategy for a party to manage these unpredictable risks is to involve third parties. Ways to reallocate the risk could be a legal counsel with a success fee or commission agreement, insurance solutions or third-party funders.[22] Therefore, these agreements could be considered as an alternative to agreements modifying cost rules in a stricter sense. The same logic and rationality may lie behind an agreement with a financier and the counterparty.

Third, a contract on costs between the parties could also be used or seen as a complement to agreements between a party and a lawyer, regulating the liability for

20 See, e.g. Christopher Hodges, John Peysner and Angus Nurse, *Litigation Funding: Status and Issues* (Oxford Center for Socio-Legal Studies 2012), Simon Latham and Augusta Venture (eds), *The Third Party Litigation Funding Review* (6th edn, The Law Reviews 2022), and Jérôme Saulnier, Klaus Müllerwith and Ivona Koronthalyova, 'European Added Value Unit', *Responsible Private Funding of Litigation* (European Parliamentary Research Service 2021).

21 Some countries with cost shifting may include provisions on the responsibility between the losing party and the winning party's lawyer. I understand the Brazilian system with 'defeat-based honorary fees' as an obligation for the defeated party to pay the winning party's attorney directly, while most procedural orders separate these obligations.

22 See Tuil and Visscher (n 19), Latham and Venture (n 20); Saulnier et al. (n 20). This risk could also be managed by transferring the disputed rights – involving new parties in the dispute that have not been a party in the original substantial relationship.

costs between the parties in relation to the provisions of a contract with a third party (insurer, attorney, financing company, organisation, etc.), e.g. to give a suitable effect on the whole.

Fourth, the parties' relationship with third parties is normally not subject to the court's decision on cost-shifting or cost assessment. Instead, the contractual rights and obligations in these relations are finally established outside the main trial. They may also be subject to subsequent or separate disputes, tried in court, between one of the original parties and a third party (e.g. an attorney claiming further compensation from its client or a winning party claiming compensation from the losing party's funder, etc.).

To sum up, the effects of agreements on costs should be seen from a broader perspective where other possible means to control, modify and redistribute cost risks are taken into consideration. Both the incurrence of costs and the final distribution of the liability for costs may be a result of contracts and litigation not between the parties to the dispute but between one of the parties and a third party. The possible contractual redistribution of liability of costs to subjects other than the parties to the dispute and the possible outcome of subsequent litigation regarding this liability in relation to a third party should be taken into account.

2.3 *Costs and Litigation Contracts in General*

Another natural starting point for an examination of agreements on costs could be to relate these to the context of different possible forms of litigation contracts in a broader sense.[23] Such agreement could range from, inter alia, dispute resolution agreements or clauses with cost provisions entered by the parties in connection with entering into a substantive contractual relationship, situations where parties formally or informally reach consensus on cost issues before the court,[24] settlement agreements fully or partly ending the dispute or even agreements made subsequent to the trial, e.g. in connection to enforcement stages, in order to modify the outcome. Finding the typical or ideal form for an agreement on litigation costs among these is probably impossible. Cost issues could be relevant to include in all these kinds of procedural contracts.

Within arbitration, we normally find full freedom for the parties to agree also on cost issues. Even if this chapter focuses on cost issues in courts rather than arbitration agreements or institutional rules for arbitration, such alternatives for parties and legislators could still be relevant when discussing party autonomy and other interests.

---

23 From a Swedish perspective, procedural contracts have recently been subject to two extensive studies, see Lotta Maunsbach, *Avtal om rätten till domstolsprövning* (Norstedts 2015) and Peter Westberg, *Konflikt och kontrakt* (Jure 2020).

24 On agreements to consent to procedural action, see Westberg (n 23) 146.

The line between pure arbitration and strict court procedure is seldom definitive, and parties may often, by contract, create other private procedures that can replace the court process in part or in whole and provide alternatives to other forms of procedural dispositions.[25]

As mentioned previously, the risk of liability for litigation costs is an important factor for parties to control and an incentive to reach agreements. As with funding described previously, another strategy for the state and the parties to solve problems associated with costly court procedures and improve access to courts is the tendency towards increased use of alternative dispute resolution (ADR), mediation and incentives to settle.[26] An efficient way to sanction an agreement prescribing obligations to engage in mediation procedure could be to let it have an effect on the liability for costs in a subsequent trial if no settlement is reached.[27] A settlement agreement in itself also normally not only ends the dispute in substance but also regulates the liability for costs incurred. A result of mediation or settlement negotiations could also be that the parties agree only to settle some aspects or parts of their dispute, leaving only the remaining parts for the court to decide on. Also, in such situations, clauses regulating the costs, with effect in the ongoing trial, would be a natural element. There might even be situations where a settlement is reached in cost issues only, leaving the substantial dispute to be tried by the court, or the opposite situation where a settlement may be reached in substance but not on the costs.

Even if not by 'contract' in the strict sense, consensus between the parties could also be manifested in the form of conclusive action or by parties' refraining from action within the procedure.[28] Cost decisions are traditionally subject to parties' dispositions insofar as liability requires that it is initiated on parties' incentive by a claim. Parties could sometimes also indirectly agree on the application of a set of cost rules by choosing a small-claims track or by shaping the substantial claim in one way or another.

Another strategy to improve access to court has also been to make procedural rules more flexible, allowing for party dispositions.[29] This may also open the way for

25 Like pre-trial referee, rent-a-judge, '*Schiedsgutachten*', expertise-arbitrage, etc. See further Julian DM Lew, Loukas A Mistelis and Stefan Kroll, *Comparative International Commercial Arbitration* (Kluwer 2003) 1-31-1-54.

26 See Maurits Barendrecht, 'Legal Aid, Accessible Courts or Legal Information? Three Access to Justice Strategies Compared' (2011) 11 Global Jurist 1.

27 Such considerations may also be prescribed in statutory cost rules, e.g. the Norwegian Dispute Act (Lov 17. juni 2005 nr 90) Chapter 20, Section 20-2 (3) b or the English Civil Procedure Rules, rule 44.3 (a).

28 Nylund and Cabral point to increasing 'flexibilisation, cooperation, and fragmentation' of dispute resolution; Anna Nylund and Antonio Cabral, 'General Report: Contractualisation of Civil Litigation' in Anna Nylund and Antonio Cabral (eds), *Contractualisation of Civil Litigation* (Intersentia 2023) 19-21.

29 In Sweden, a trend from fixed rules on procedure, via flexibility for courts, to allowing more and more dispositions by the parties may be seen. See further Anna Wallerman, 'Towards an EU Law Doctrine on the Exercise of Discretion in National Courts? The Member States' Self-imposed Limits on National Procedural Autonomy' (2016) 53 Common Market Law Review 339; Westberg (n 23) 15.

situations where consensus is reached between the parties in detail on the application of cost rules. By seeking greater flexibility in the national process, one of the purposes can also be to provide a more attractive alternative to arbitration.[30]

Hence, very different types of consensus or agreements may have to be taken into consideration when discussing procedural agreements on costs. From a theoretical standpoint, the agreements that fall in between the classical arbitration agreement and the mediation, negotiation or settlement agreement, ending the whole dispute, are the most interesting. From an economic viewpoint, the possibility and strategy to settle a dispute and allocate the risk with a third party could be seen as interconnected. The willingness and incentives to settle with the other party are an alternative to finding a better economic result involving third parties. Hence, also settlements in only a part of a dispute, with the regulation of cost issues between the parties, should be seen as an alternative or a complement to handling this in a relationship with a third party.

2.4 *The Relation between Private and Public Law and between Contract and Procedural Law*

The contractual side of agreements on cost also needs to be seen in relation to the legal framework of contract law and procedural law at large. Just as with other litigation contracts, cost-related contracts occur in the borderland between contract law and procedural law and between private law and public law. Contractual law sets one standard for the parties' ability to and ways to conclude an agreement, how they should be interpreted and what effects a breach of the agreement may have. The procedural context sets another standard for parties' legal acts and their effects, where acting under the responsibility for costs is one important factor in itself. There is also an unclear border between what is to be regarded as or regulated by the parties as a substantial claim and what should be handled as a litigation cost. This normally boils down to questions about whether an agreement is valid at all between the parties, to what extent and how it could be adjusted or set aside and whether it is also binding for the court so that it may affect the court's application of procedural rules.

Agreements on litigation costs could also be framed in relation to conceptions of mandatory and non-mandatory law and party autonomy. Here, some countries more generously and explicitly allow parties to agree on modifications of their procedural regulation,[31] while others explicitly indicate that certain paragraphs or chapters may be

---

30 Per Henrik Lindblom, 'Allmän domstol som alternativt tvistlösningsorgan' in Per Henrik Lindblom (ed), *Studier i processrätt* (Norstedts 1993) 109.

31 The most evident example is Art. 190 in the 2015 Brazilian Civil Procedure Code.

subject to contract.[32] At the other end of the scale, some countries generally prohibit or have a more restrictive approach to litigation contracts.[33]

A normal demarcation of the area where litigation agreements could be allowed, if at all, is whether only parties' interests or also public interests are at stake.[34] As noted previously, cost issues are more or less subject to party dispositions, whereas claims need to be put forth, and the outcome may depend on evidence of costs claimed from the parties, etc. Hence, cost rules may be regarded as a regulation of a purely private law claim between the parties only, as a tort-based compensation.[35]

However, different cost rules and different cost regimes, also within the same legal order, are subject to changing views in this respect. The liability for costs may also be regarded as an expression of a legal relationship not only between the parties but also to sanction the parties' duties to the state or the court.[36] From a legal realist's or an instrumentalist's perspective, they may be treated as a means to control parties' behaviour at large or within the procedure.[37] From a socioeconomic or law-and-economics perspective, one would say that there is a public interest at stake in every litigation: the efficient and substantial correct application of private law legislation.[38] Also, where cost-shifting between parties requires that claims for costs are put forth by the parties, once claimed, the distribution and assessment of these costs are often used as leverage to sanction the adherence to other procedural rules.

---

32 E.g. the Norwegian Dispute Act (Lov 17. juni 2005 nr 90) Chapter 20, Section 20-1 (2) states that compensation for legal costs pursuant to the chapter can be claimed when provided by law or agreed between the parties.

33 Some scholars would place Sweden in this section, arguing that procedural agreements are void in principle unless expressly permitted by law, see Maunsbach (n 23) 33. As this position is founded mainly on an opinion expressed by the Council of Legislation 80 years ago rather than something expressed in the legal text, as the Supreme Court since then has expressed that some forms of procedural agreements have effect, as the legislature since then has given more leeway to parties' dispositions, and as the *de facto* effects of procedural agreements can often be accomplished through the parties' procedural actions, I have argued for a somewhat more permissive view; see Henrik Bellander, *Rättegångskostnader* (Iustus 2017) 347.

34 See Nylund and Cabral (n 28). Again, Art. 190 of the 2015 Brazilian Civil Procedure could serve as an example.

35 This view could be traced back to the dominant view up to the late-19th century in German legal theory, represented by Weber. See Adolph Dieterich Weber, *Über die Processkosten, deren Vergütung und Compensation* (2 edn, Schwerin 1790).

36 This view could be traced back to the German legal concept of *Prozessrechtsverhältnis* as developed by Oscar Bülow, see Heinrich Degenkolb, 'Die Lehre vom Prozetzrechtsverhältnis. (Ein Gedenkblatt)' (1908) 103 Archiv für die civilistische Praxis 385.

37 This has been the main viewpoint in Sweden since the mid-20th century; see Bellander (n 33) 51. A recent example of extending this view to third-party funding issues is the European Parliament resolution of 13 September 2022 with recommendations to the Commission on Responsible private funding of litigation (2020/2130(INL)).

38 What would be described as a 'cost of error', see Richard Posner, 'An Economic Approach to Legal Procedure and Judicial Administration' (1973) 2 Journal of Legal Studies 399. For an economic analysis regarding possible regulation of funding of litigation from an EU perspective, see Saulnier et al. (n 20).

The right to or freedom from cost reimbursement also has important EU and ECHR law aspects – as it concerns parties' rights to and states' duty to ensure efficient legal remedies and a fair trial.[39] Here, concepts of horizontal or vertical effects also come into play. Further, such norms may not always affect the application of procedural rules within a trial but may lead to a redistribution of the costs in a subsequent trial. Within EU law, it would also be easy to find examples where substantial claims are subject to party autonomy, but when put forth in a court, the public interest in these matters limits the freedom of parties and the court.[40]

At least from a European perspective, national cost regimes have a mixture of rules originating from and balancing all of these approaches. In many regimes, the 'English rule' was consistently implemented during the 19th or early 20th century, and arguments about giving the winning party full protection by full recoverability of costs were limited solely by an assessment of their reasonableness.[41] In the second half of the 20th century, these rules have often been supplemented by different limitations and restrictions that apply to the costs with the introduction of different fast-track or small-claims track proceedings, where considerations like encouraging litigation and foreseeability of the cost risks have been the rationale.[42]

Further, the lines between mandatory, non-mandatory and unregulated areas of procedure are often blurred and dependent on the substantive law context. The distinction between, on the one hand, mandatory and non-mandatory private law rules and, on the other hand, claims or facts dispositive within a procedure and non-mandatory procedural rules is fraudulent and partly illusory. Private law claims with public law elements, e.g. with connections to consumer law or competition law, also call for procedural treatment where party autonomy plays a less prominent role.[43] This could affect not only the application of parties' contracts in substance but also their procedural contracts.

Apart from contractual effects outside of the trial, there are also statutory norms regarding costs that have no effect on the application of cost rules but need to be enforced

39 See, e.g. *Stankiewicz v. Poland*, App no 46917/99 (ECHR 6 April 2006) and case C-205/15 *Toma and Biroul Executorului Judecătoresc Horațiu-Vasile Cruduleci* [2016] ECLI:EU:C:2016:499.

40 See, e.g. case C-352/13 *Cartel Damage Claims Hydrogen Peroxide SA (CDC) v. Akzo Nobel NV* [2015] ECLI: EU:C:2015:335 and more recently case C-30/19 *Diskrimineringsombudsmannen v. Braathens Regional Aviation AB* [2021] EU:C:2021:269. See further Bart Krans and Anna Nylund (eds), *Procedural Autonomy Across Europe* (Intersentia 2020).

41 Still noticeable in, e.g. the Norwegian Dispute Act (Lov 17 juni 2005 nr 90) Chapter 20, Section 20-5 (1), the Swedish Code on Judicial Procedure (1942:740) Chapter 18, para. 8 and the English Civil Procedure Rules, part 44, rule 44.3.

42 See, e.g. the Norwegian Dispute Act (Lov 17 juni 2005 nr 90) Chapter 20, Section 20-5 (2) and Section 10-5, the Swedish Code on Judicial Procedure (1942:740) Chapter 18, para. 8a and the English Civil Procedure Rules, part 45, rule 45.38.

43 See, e.g. Case C-352/13 *Cartel Damage Claims Hydrogen Peroxide SA (CDC) v. Akzo Nobel NV* [2015] ECLI:EU:C:2015:335.

by the parties in subsequent proceedings (e.g. claims based on EU law regarding the right to effective remedies or the right to a fair trial). Hence, the view should not be limited to the effects within the trial.

Adding to the list of possible considerations, different substantive law contexts could have different effects on cost agreements both within and outside the procedure.[44] For example, some cost agreement issues may be investigated ex officio by the court (e.g. if limiting – or providing – a party's right to efficient remedies for substantial EU law-based rights), others may call for more active case management by the court (e.g. in order to bring an inferior party's attention to their implications), and yet others may not affect the court within the proceedings aimed at but instead may be brought up in subsequent proceedings (e.g. claims for costs covered by the agreement based on its contractual law effects, but that have been unrecoverable according to non-dispositive cost rules).

3 Conclusions

3.1 *Sprawling Considerations, Grey Areas and Sliding Scales*

To sum up, agreements on litigation costs could be varied infinitely, referring to a multitude of procedural statutes involving many different parties, concluded at different stages of a dispute (also before and after a trial), dealing with a number of sprawling and connected issues and calling for numerous and sometimes conflicting considerations.[45]

These agreements raise questions within many 'grey areas' of law: between dispute and consensus, between public and private interests, between subject matter and procedure, between contract law and procedural law, between international and national law, between mandatory law and party autonomy, etc. Further, the questions they raise seldom have black-or-white or yes-or-no answers but are rather to be found on sets of sliding scales. Instead of agreements being either binding or not binding or either subject to full party autonomy or ex officio application of non-mandatory rules, agreements may be binding in some aspects but not in others, and they may have different effects inside and outside the trial.

A more formalistic proceduralist way to deal with this could be to try to separate these questions, e.g. only focusing on agreements to modify courts' application of procedural rules and without regard to private law effects, with the aim of defining and clarifying the borders between private law and procedural law, the nature of certain

44 See Alain Ancery and Bart Krans in this volume.

45 See Sections 2.1 to 2.4 above.

cost rules, identification of public interests, etc. This approach could be suitable from the perspective of a national court when the question is whether the parties' contract or specific national cost rules should be applied in the ruling on costs. But depending on what perspective one may have and the question at hand, one might have to make other considerations. I therefore argue for a somewhat different approach.

3.2 *Considerations: Tentative Examples*

The area of acceptable contracts shifts according to circumstances in the case or the type of issue that is regulated. This calls for a range of tests to assess whether the court, within the limits of national legislation, should strike down (or uphold) a contract on costs. Drawing from the foregoing inventory, at least the following questions are relevant:[46]

1. What kind of agreement is in question?
   a. A settlement agreement ending the dispute as a whole or in part, with implications for costs.
   b. An agreement on or by refraining from or taking procedural action (claiming cost liability etc.).
   c. Substantial provisions in an agreement overlap the scope of cost rules.
   d. An agreement explicitly addressing the court's application of statutory cost rules.

2. What possible effects may the agreement have on the costs?
   a. The agreement limits or controls the cost risk for the parties (shifting and/or cost assessment, etc.).
   b. The agreement connects the cost risk to certain factors, like the outcome of specific decisions, in order to sanction specific procedural behaviour from the parties.
   c. The agreement limits or sets frames for the courts' cost decision, e.g. with reference to equity, tariffs, the sum at dispute, etc.
   d. The agreement regulates the procedure in itself regarding the decision on costs, e.g. with requirements on evidence or when and how the decision should be made.

46 These categories overlap and may not be separable. Procedural provisions demanding specific evidence for some costs to be recoverable may practically limit the responsibility etc.

3. What interests and/or which parties are affected by the agreement?
   a. The agreement only concerns parties and their interests, i.e. the plaintiff and the defendant).
   b. The agreement also affects third parties and their interests, e.g. lawyers, insurers, etc.
   c. The agreement affects courts', state or other public interests, e.g. the workload for the court or how the trial should be conducted.
   d. The agreement has international law and/or human rights implications, e.g. limiting or ensuring the right to a fair trial for one of the parties.

4. What possible effect may the agreement be given on the relationship between the parties?
   a. The agreement should have no binding effect at all (nullity).
   b. The agreement may be subject to adjustment due to fairness etc.
   c. The agreement may have an effect within the application of the substantial agreement as part of the ruling over the substantial claim.
   d. The agreement has effect as a private law responsibility (e.g. where non-fulfilment is sanctioned by liability for damages).

5. What possible effect may the agreement be given in relation to the court?
   a. The agreement should have no effect at all on the court.
   b. The agreement may have an effect on the substantial outcome of the dispute.
   c. The agreement may have an effect depending on the parties' procedural dispositions (claims put forth, size of claims, consent, etc.).
   d. The agreement may have an effect on the court's application of cost rules.

These questions overlap and may not be separable. Procedural provisions demanding specific evidence for some costs to be recoverable may practically limit the responsibility etc. However, they could serve as a tentative list of relevant factors to consider when regulating cost issues in a procedural agreement or for the court when taking a position on their effect.

For a court faced with an agreement with the provision on costs, the main question is whether the agreement has an effect on their application of statutory cost rules or not (questions no 5a and 5c). The most central consideration in this perspective is probably whether the contractual disposition concerns a legal norm (procedural or substantial) that can be considered non-mandatory and subject to party autonomy. If a disposition of the application of the norm has adverse effects on interests outside the relationship between the parties (e.g. the court's or third parties' interests), it could be an argument for limiting the legal effects of the agreement (question 3b and 3c). It should also be assessed whether the agreed disposition with regard to factors like the time when the agreement was concluded, the parties' equality in arms, whether certain applications of the provisions affect a party's fundamental right to judicial review under the European Convention on Human Rights (ECHR), etc. This could affect the validity of the agreement but may also lead to other 'softer' effects on how an agreement on costs should be treated – affecting not only the validity but also being subject to adjustment. An important note here is that statutory rules on costs could be insufficient in some jurisdictions and in some substantive law and party-related contexts. Consequently, cost agreements between the parties could be needed in order to achieve adequate protection for either party.[47]

From the perspective of parties considering concluding procedural agreements on cost issues, further considerations have to be made. Also, from a legal comparatist perspective, all possible variations in cost rules and different national ways to treat them also call for a more holistic and pragmatic approach to facilitate comparisons and understanding.

A less formalistic and more effect-oriented view on litigation agreements shows us that the same effects as with an agreement directly affecting the court's application of statutory cost rules may often be achieved by alternative means by the parties – acting within areas left to party disposition and autonomy. As long as the parties are able to achieve corresponding results through other dispositions, e.g. in a settlement agreement, in the substantive provisions of an agreement or by their action in the procedure,[48] this suggests that the disposition in a procedural agreement cannot be generally dismissed per se. Such an evaluation of the agreement should also take into consideration to what extent the parties' liability for costs may be tried again, redistributed or even reversed in subsequent proceedings.

Unlike many other kinds of procedural agreements, the application of cost rules and agreements on cost rules has direct economic effects on the parties. They indirectly affect the parties' procedural choices and behaviours, the handling of the subject matter in the case, or the possibility of the parties being successful in proving their case. If cost-related economic sanctions are awarded directly in the proceeding or only indirectly through a civil law claim in a parallel or subsequent proceeding, the effect on the parties' economic outcome and the indirect effect on the parties' behaviour may be equivalent. Once a dispute arises, such agreements may also lead to additional uncertainty and costly 'procedures within the procedure' regarding the validity and effect of such agreements, which also has to be taken into consideration.

---

47 E.g. individuals and companies with successful claims against the state in Swedish administrative courts are, as a main rule, not entitled to reimbursement for costs according to national procedural law (The Administrative Court Procedure Act, 1971:29) but may claim such compensation separately as damages based on Swedish constitutional law, the EU Charter of Fundamental Rights, Art. 47, and ECHR, Art. 6.1. Also see ECtHR judgment in case *Černius and Rinkevičius v. Lithuania* (App no 73579/17 and 14620/18).

48 E.g. by the parties' claims for cost reimbursement or invocation of facts with regard to the costs.

If the conclusion is that parties may achieve the requested effect (question 2) by a contractually binding private law obligation, by the substantial provisions in their agreement or by taking action or refraining from taking action within the procedure, the question remains whether they should be given effect only within the framework of the substantive review of the case, e.g. affecting the size of the substantial claim in dispute, or, if contractually binding, leading to subsequent claims. One could also argue that such possibilities show that the pursued dispositions in themselves fall within the scope of the permissible and that this could 'spill over' onto the question of the procedural validity of such agreements and their procedural effects on the application of certain cost rules.

Agreements Concerning Appeals: The Right to Waive the Appeal

Vigita Vėbraitė

1 Introduction

The concept of agreement in civil procedure is known in many different countries on different continents, and it is usually understood as an agreement to settle a civil dispute or, for instance, choice of court or arbitration agreements. A broader concept of procedural agreements, for instance, agreements regarding case management or litigation costs, has only recently been discussed in more detail in different countries. For example, in some South American countries, such as Brazil, agreements in civil proceedings play a much more significant role than in most Eastern European countries. It can be agreed that many jurisdictions are moving towards a progressive loosening of procedural formalities in litigation, allowing the parties to determine by contract, in a manner that binds the judge, the shape and form of proceedings before state courts.[1]

The ELI/UNIDROIT Model European Rules of Civil Procedure have been a strong incentive to start new discussions regarding the contractualisation of civil proceedings in Europe.[2] The Brazilian rules were officially published in 2020 and introduced new ideas for many jurisdictions on how civil proceedings can become more flexible. This chapter analyses possibilities to waive the right to appeal and will not discuss different ways in which the proceedings in appellate courts could be shaped using procedural agreements.

Agreements on waiver of the right to appeal are also quite a new phenomenon in many jurisdictions, and not all jurisdictions allow such agreements, while some allow them only in a limited manner. Quite commonly, codes of civil procedure simply do not regulate this question, and courts have to decide how far party autonomy can be allowed in the appeal procedure.

This chapter analyses different positions on the waiver of the right to appeal. It explores how constitutional law influences such waivers and whether views on constitutional limits on such agreements could change in the near future in jurisdictions that do not currently accept such agreements. It explores whether agreements concerning appeals

1 Antonio Cabral, 'Designing Procedure by Contract: Litigation Agreements in Contemporary Civil Procedure' (2019) 9 International Journal of Procedural Law 380.

2 ELI/UNIDROIT Model European Rules of Civil Procedure <www.undroit.org/instruments/civil-procedure/eli-undroit-rules/ > (accessed 1 December 2023).

could become a broadly applied institute of civil procedure. The chapter is devoted to the first appeal and does not discuss the right to waive access to the second appeal.

2 Different Approaches to the Right to Appeal

The appeal proceedings and right to appeal are understood in different ways in separate jurisdictions. It could be agreed that contemporary legal systems share a tension between the wish to remove errors by exposing judgments to several layers of control and the wish to protect civil rights and obligations in a concrete and effective way, not theoretical and illusory.[3] It is even said that differences in the approach to appeals are considerably greater than the differences in the approach to the judicial proceedings that gave rise to the decisions that might or might not be appealed.[4]

For instance, the appeal can be heard *de novo*, which means that the appellate court decides on the facts without deferring to the first instance court's judgment. Also, appeal proceedings can be understood only as the appellate court analysing the factual and legal grounds of the appeal and verifying the absence of absolute grounds for the invalidity of the judgment of the first court. Also, in some jurisdictions, the right to appeal hinges on the appellate court permitting it when certain conditions are met.

For instance, in England, nearly all appeals require the court to give its permission in response to the appellant's speedy request to the first instance court. If the lower court refuses permission, a fresh application for permission can be made to the appeal court.[5] In countries with a common law system, it is usually said that they may be restricted because appeals are expensive and cause delays. It is regarded that a dissatisfied litigant's right should not be to appeal but to have his request to appeal considered.[6] Quite a different tradition can be found in most Eastern and Central European countries, which have had socialist systems for a long time. For example, in Croatia, the basic rule is that all decisions on the merits are subject to appeal.[7]

The right to appeal and the right to waive the right to appeal can also depend on constitutional legal tradition or regional legal rules or recommendations.

3 Alan Uzelac and C.H. Van Rhee, 'Appeals and other Means of Recourse against Judgments in the Context of the Effective Protection of Civil Rights and Obligations' in Alan Uzelac and C.H. van Rhee (eds), *Nobody's Perfect: Comparative Essays on Appeals and Other Means of Recourse against Judicial Decisions in Civil Matters* (Intersentia 2014) 3.

4 Ibid., 2.

5 Neil Andrews, *Contracts and English Dispute Resolution* (Jigakusha 2010) 285.

6 Michael Zander, *Cases and Materials on the English Legal System* (Cambridge University Press 2012) 659.

7 Alan Uzelac, 'Features and Shortcomings of Appellate Review in Civil and Administrative Cases in Croatia' in Alan Uzelac and C.H. van Rhee (eds), *Nobody's Perfect: Comparative Essays on Appeals and Other Means of Recourse against Judicial Decisions in Civil Matters* (Intersentia 2014) 239.

Recommendation No. R(95)5 of the Committee of Ministers of the Council of Europe[8] acknowledges the possibility of limiting the right of appeal. Such limitations must be introduced by law and be compatible with the fundamental principles of justice. ELI/UNIDROIT Model Rules also stress the importance of limiting the right to appeal. According to the ELI/UNIDOIT Model Rules, the parties cannot invoke new facts or evidence in appellate proceedings unless a limited exception applies.[9] The Rules adopt the approach that while there is a right to appeal, it can only be exercised with the appellate court's permission and in accordance with the provisions that limit the access to and scope of such proceedings.[10]

3 Influence of International Rules and Constitutional Law on the Possibility of Waiving the Right to Appeal

When discussing procedural rights, it is necessary to mention the European Convention on Human Rights,[11] Article 6 and Protocol 7 and the case law of the European Court of Human Rights (ECtHR). Article 6 of the Convention clearly states that everyone is entitled to a fair public hearing by an independent, impartial tribunal within a reasonable time. It is important to note that according to the case law of ECtHR Article 6 of the Convention, it does not include the absolute right to appeal.

The Court has stated in many judgments that the right of access to the courts is not absolute. This applies in particular where the conditions of admissibility of an appeal are concerned since, by its very nature, it calls for regulation by the state, which enjoys a certain margin of appreciation in this regard.[12] It could be said that ECtHR jurisprudence mostly does not contradict agreements on waiver of the right to appeal if national laws allow it. The ECtHR has, for instance, stated that

> ...the manner in which Article 6 § 1 applies to courts of appeal or of cassation depends on the special features of the proceedings concerned and account must be taken of the entirety of the proceedings conducted in the domestic legal order.[13]

8 Recommendation No. R (95)5 of the Committee of Ministers of the Council of Europe Concerning the Introduction and Improvement of the Functioning of Appeal Systems and Procedures in Civil and Commercial Cases.

9 Rolf Stürner, 'Model European Rules of Civil Procedure: An Introduction to Their Basic Conceptions' (2022) 86 Rabels Zeitschrift 455.

10 ELI/UNIDROIT Model European Rules of Civil Procedure (n 2).

11 The 1950 Convention for the Protection of Human Rights and Fundamental Freedoms.

12 E.g. *Stanev v. Bulgaria*, no. 36760/06 (ECtHR, 17 January 2012), para. 230; *Zubac v. Croatia*, no. 40160/12 (ECtHR, 5 April 2018), para. 78.

13 *Kozlica v. Croatia*, no. 29182/03, para. 32.

Until now, the ECtHR has not opined specifically on the right to waive the right to appeal in civil cases. However, a different approach applies to criminal cases. Article 2 of Protocol Number 7 of the Convention[14] states that everyone convicted of a criminal offence by a tribunal shall have the right to have his conviction or sentence reviewed by a higher tribunal.

Moreover, the Charter of Fundamental Rights of the European Union[15] also does recognise an absolute right to appeal. Article 47 of the Charter only mentions access to justice but does not enshrine the right to appeal. It is important that the European Parliament resolution[16] on common minimum standards of civil procedure also does not state that the right to appeal is absolute. Article 8 only stresses that Member States must ensure that courts or tribunals provide sufficiently detailed reasoned decisions within a reasonable time to enable parties to effectively use any right to review the decision or lodge an appeal.

Nevertheless, in some jurisdictions, the jurisprudence of the national constitutional court is much stricter, establishing a right to appeal for civil justice, not just criminal cases. For instance, in several rulings, the Constitutional Court of Lithuania has stated that the right to apply to court is absolute; the right of a person to apply to court cannot be restricted, nor may the use of the right be unreasonably burdensome. The constitutional right to appeal, as interpreted in the context of other provisions of the Constitution, also implies that procedural rules enabling citizens to lodge an appeal with at least one court of higher instance against any final act adopted by a court of general jurisdiction must be established.[17] In a more recent ruling, the Constitutional Court of Lithuania stressed that under the Constitution and the constitutional principle of the rule of law, the right to lodge an appeal at least once against any final act of a court of first instance must be possible to ensure that the higher court can correct potential mistakes. This is an inseparable part of the constitutional right to access to court and the right to due process.[18]

Similar positions can also be found in the jurisprudence of the Constitutional Court of Latvia or the Constitutional Court of Romania. These courts noted that the obligation of representation and assistance through a lawyer in the exercise of an appeal

14 Protocol No. 7 of 22 November 1984 to Convention for the Protection of Human Rights and Fundamental Freedoms.

15 Charter of Fundamental Rights of the European Union [2012] OJ C 326/391.

16 European Parliament Recommendations on Common Minimum Standards of Civil Procedure [2018]OJ C334/39.

17 Ruling of Constitutional Court of Lithuania, no 35/03-11/06 (21 September 2006), paras. 51-53; Ruling of Constitutional Court of Lithuania, no 26/07 (24 October 2007), paras 62-63.

18 Ruling of Constitutional Court of Lithuania, no. K9-N3/2019 (1 March 2019), para. 28.

amounted to a condition of admissibility to exercise a legal remedy, which limited the right to a court and judicial defence.[19]

These examples show that in some jurisdictions, constitutional law does not create conditions for parties to a dispute to waive their rights to appeal. Even if the parties agreed to waive their rights, the courts would most likely have an obligation to allow an appeal by one of the parties. While the Constitutional Courts devoted their discussions to the questions of representation in appeal proceedings, the Courts have stressed the importance of the right to appeal in a broad manner and broadly explained the right for parties to appeal.[20]

The situation is quite different in some European jurisdictions, such as Scandinavia; the right to waive the right to appeal is considered normal. For instance, Article 21 subsection 2 of the Constitution of Finland states that provisions concerning the publicity of proceedings, the right to be heard, the right to receive a reasoned decision and the right of appeal, as well as the other guarantees of a fair trial and good governance shall be laid down by an Act.[21] According to Chapter 25 Section 5 of the Code of Judicial Procedure,[22] the declaration of intent to appeal is a prerequisite for filing an appeal. This means that parties have the right to waive their right to appeal. The prospective appellant must give either oral or written notification of its intention to appeal. The notice may be limited to a part of the judgment, thus restricting the possibility to appeal to that part of the judgment.[23] Pursuant to Chapter 25 Section 2, the parties may agree to waive the right to appeal for a specific dispute or all disputes arising from specific circumstances. So far, no constitutional problems have arisen in Finland regarding appeals waivers.

In Norway, Section 95 of the Constitution on fair trial rights remains silent on the right to appeal. Pursuant to Section 29-6 of the Norwegian Dispute Act,[24] the right to appeal must be expressly waived. Before the ruling is pronounced, the right to appeal may only be waived if the waiver is mutual. Even if the right of appeal has been waived before the ruling, an appeal may be brought on the grounds of procedural errors.

It can be mentioned that, in most countries, constitutions and jurisprudence of constitutional courts allow restrictions of second appeal. For instance, Article 350 of the Code of Civil Procedure of Lithuania[25] states that a selection panel formed

19 Judgment of Constitutional Court of Latvia, no. 485/2015 (30 September 2015); Judgment of Constitutional Court of Romania, no. 2014/462 (17 September 2014).

20 Kalvis Torgans, et al., *Civilprocesa likuma komentāri*, I, II un III daļa, (Riga 2020) 335.

21 The Constitution of Finland, 11 June 1999.

22 The Code of Judicial Procedure of Finland, Legal Act no 4/1734 with amendments, https://www.finlex.fi/en/laki/kaannokset/1734/ (accessed 22 November 2023).

23 Laura Ervo, *Civil Justice in Finland* (Jigakusha 2009) 182.

24 Dispute Act of Norway of 17 June 2005, https://lovdata.no/dokument/NLE/lov/2005-06-17-90?q=the%20dispute%20actm (accessed 22 November 2023).

25 The Code of Civil Procedure of Lithuania, Legal Act no 36-1340/2022 with amendments.

of three judges decides the question of accepting a cassation appeal. Recently, the Constitutional Court of Lithuania confirmed that taking into account the specifics of the institution of cassation, the constitutional purpose of the cassation procedure, as well as the particularities of the examination of cases under the cassation procedure, the legislature may establish conditions for lodging an appeal to the Supreme Court of Lithuania. These restrictions include, inter alia, conditions, time limits and certain requirements for drawing up a cassation appeal.[26] Nevertheless, it is unclear whether a selection panel would accept a cassation appeal when the legal requirements to accept a cassation appeal are met but the parties have agreed to waive the right to a second appeal. The author believes that the public interest in ensuring uniform interpretation and application of law and forming coherent and consistent case law would prevail and the cassation appeal would be accepted.

For instance, a different approach is found in the United States. The US Supreme Court has repeatedly declined to consider the right to appeal as a due process right in civil and criminal cases.[27] Such argument forms a fertile soil for allowing appeal waivers, as some scholars and practitioners advocated for.

The different approaches to the right to appeal show variations in legal cultures and levels of the principle of party disposition in civil procedure. In some jurisdictions, agreements on procedural rules are allowed broadly, and in others, most of such agreements are regarded as belonging exclusively to the arbitration domain. Next, the rules on appeals waivers from selected jurisdictions that allow the right to appeal to be waived will be explored and compared.

4 Regulating Appeals Waivers

4.1 *Argentina and Brazil*

While appeals waivers have traditionally not been allowed in South American jurisdictions, new or recently amended codes of civil procedure allow them. For instance, the new Brazilian Code of Civil Procedure, which entered into force in 2016, allows the parties to dispose of, at their convenience, their advantageous legal situations, as well as to shape how their respective procedural legal duties will be fulfilled and how their legal

26 Ruling of Constitutional Court of Lithuania, no KT205A-N16/2021 (30 December 2021), para. 48.

27 John B. Oakely and Vikram Amar, *American Civil Procedure: A Guide to Civil Adjudication in US Courts* (Kluwer Law International 2009) 201.

burdens will be divided among them throughout the judicial process.[28] Interestingly, the aim is to allow the parties to expedite the procedure, including a waiver of future appeals so that the case will thereby be heard more quickly by a single judge trial in the first instance. Article 999 of the Code[29] states that the waiver of the right to appeal does not depend on the other party's acceptance; it can be done unilaterally.

A different situation can be found in Argentina. Even if the draft version of the new Code of Civil and Commercial Procedure has been presented and discussed by different interested groups, only generic rules enabling different agreements have yet been included.[30] Till now, no clear rules regarding waiving the right to appeal have been clearly included. Still, there is a possibility that Argentina will follow new traditions of the Brazilian Code of Civil Procedure.

4.2 *England and Wales*

It should be stressed that there is no general right to appeal a judgment or order in English civil procedure. To pursue an appeal, parties must obtain permission from either the court whose decision is to be appealed or from the appeal court.[31] An agreement not to appeal or not to seek permission to appeal would, in effect, operate as a jurisdictional ouster of the appeal court's jurisdiction.

English law generally treats jurisdictional ouster clauses as inimical to the rule of law and void on public policy grounds. Parties may not have a right to appeal but only a right to seek permission to appeal. An agreement purported to stop a party or parties from exercising that right to seek permission would be a complete ouster. As such, it is likely that such an agreement would not be upheld.[32]

---

28 Antonio Cabral and Pedro Henrique Nogueira, 'Contractualisation of Civil Litigation in Brazil: Party Autonomy and Procedural Agreements' in Anna Nylund and Antonio Cabral (eds), *Contractualisation of Civil Litigation* (Intersentia 2023) 85.

29 Code of Civil Procedure of Brazil, Act no 13.105, https://www.lawyerinbrazil.com/articles/brazilian-civil-procedure-code-in-english (accessed 22 September 2023).

30 Maria Victoria Mosmann, 'Contractualisation of Civil Litigation in Argentina: Current Status of the Legislation and Prospects of Procedural Agreements' in Anna Nylund and Antonio Cabral (eds), *Contractualisation of Civil Litigation* (Intersentia 2023) 49.

31 Adrian Zuckerman, *Civil Procedure: Principles and Practice* (3rd edn, Sweet & Maxwell 2013) 1212-1214.

32 John Sorabji, Contractualisation of Civil Litigation in England and Wales: Party Autonomy, Contracts and Procedure' in Anna Nylund and Antonio Cabral (eds), *Contractualisation of Civil Litigation* (Intersentia 2023) 208.

4.3 Germany

The attitude towards recognising procedural agreements in German law has become increasingly permissive over the years. This trend mirrors a general development under which civil litigation is no longer primarily seen as a sovereign means of dispute resolution but as a kind of service for the parties.[33] Also, waiver of the right to appeal is generally permissible under German law. According to Article 515 of the German Code of Civil Procedure, such a waiver on the right to a first appeal is not dependent on the opponent's acceptance of the waiver. The code allows a unilateral waiver of the right to appeal.[34]

The waivers of the right to appeal are only unilateral declarations of the parties. However, it is also accepted that the parties may enter a contractual obligation not to appeal a judgment.[35] There is widespread consensus that the agreed waiver of a right to appeal is relevant in a lawsuit only if the opponent raises an objection based on it. In this case, the court will dismiss the appeal as inadmissible.[36] Waiver of the right to appeal can be applied to different types of legal remedies. According to Article 565, in conjunction with Article 515 of the German Code of Civil Procedure, the parties may also waive their right to a second appeal on points of law.[37]

4.4 Poland

In 2000, amendments[38] to the Polish Code of Civil Procedure introduced the possibility of waiving the right to appeal, but it is allowed only for small claims. Since 2019, the limit is approximately € 4,500. Article 505^8 states that a party that attends a hearing at which a judgment is announced may, after the judgment has been announced, declare that it waives the right of appeal. If both parties to the dispute waive the right of appeal, the judgment receives *res iudicata*. The parties may limit the waiver to selected parts of a judgment.[39] Still, only a few examples of such waivers can be found in Poland.

33 Gerhard Wagner, *Prozeßverträge. Privatautonomie im Verfahrensrecht* (Mohr Siebeck 1998) 48-49.

34 Hans-Joachim Musielak and Wolfgang Voit, *Kommentar zur Zivilprozessordnung* (18th edn, Franz Vahlen Verlag 2021) 515.

35 Ibid., 517.

36 Felix Maultzsch and Stefan Klingbeil, 'Contractualisation of Civil Litigation in Germany: A Development Towards More Party Autonomy' in Anna Nylund and Antonio Cabral (eds), *Contractualisation of Civil Litigation* (Intersentia 2023) 254.

37 Ibid., 255.

38 Code of Civil Procedure of Poland with amendments, Polish Journal of Law, 7 November 2019.

39 Andrzej Marcinak, *Kodeks Postepowania Cywilnego* (Beck 2020) 420; Sławomir Cieślak, Janusz Jankowski and Maciej Muliński, 'Contractualisation of Civil Litigation in Poland: The Admissibility of Procedural Agreements in Civil Proceedings' in Anna Nylund and Antonio Cabral (eds), *Contractualisation of Civil Litigation* (Intersentia 2023) 370.

4.5 *Taiwan*

There is no special legislation on the right to waive the right to appeal in Taiwan. Nevertheless, because the parties are entitled to the right of disposition under the Taiwanese Code of Civil Procedure law, they may agree on the right to exercise the right to appeal. However, there are different views regarding the exact scope of their freedom to agree on appeals. When a dispute is already subject to court proceedings, based on the legal logic of respect for the parties' right of procedural disposition, the parties should be allowed to waive their right of appeal.[40] If the dispute has not yet been subject to court proceedings – court proceedings have not yet been lodged – a more conservative view seems to prevail, arguing that the parties are not allowed to waive the right to appeal.

4.6 *ELI/UNIDROIT Model European Rules of Civil Procedure*

The ELI/UNIDROIT Model European Rules of Civil Procedure[41] introduces clear and detailed rules on waiver of the right to appeal. Rule 154 states that parties may waive their right of appeal. The waiver must be informed and explicit. It may be given to the court in writing before or during a court hearing or orally in a court hearing. The waiver may be effected before a first instance judgment, other decision or a first appeal judgment. Such a waiver may only be made where all the parties agree. The court must record all waivers in a judgment or other official record. It is stressed that such a waiver is not possible in consumer disputes.

The comments on the rules state that appeals waivers promote certainty and stability in the parties' relations. The reason is that both parties and the court are aware that an appeal will not be possible. From the court's perspective, this may also help reduce the duration of litigation, enabling it to manage its resources more effectively.

5 Future Perspectives on Appeals Waivers

There seem to be two distinct attitudes towards waiving the right to appeal. Some countries allow such agreements or waivers, and others have very strict jurisprudence on allowing parties to lodge an appeal. It could be agreed that party disposition with regard to the commencement, conclusion and the subject of proceedings – notions that are not as self-evident for Eastern European countries as for that part of Europe not

40 Kuan-Ling Shen, 'Contractualisation of Civil Litigation in Taiwan: Respecting Party Autonomy and the Right to Procedural Choice' in Anna Nylund and Antonio Cabral (eds), *Contractualisation of Civil Litigation* (Intersentia 2023) 387.

41 ELI/UNIDROIT Model European Rules of Civil Procedure (n 2).

affected by post-war socialism.[42] Thus, attitudes to other forms of contractualisation of civil proceedings could be reflected in the attitudes to waiving the right to appeal. In many countries, agreements to waive the right to appeal are still considered to be against public policy and are thus void. Still, the example of Poland shows that attitudes to appeals waivers are changing, also in Eastern and Central Europe. Thus, at least some of them will likely allow such waivers in the future. This shift has already occurred in Argentina and Brazil, where procedural agreements are allowed broadly. Currently, there are considerable differences among countries in this regard.

Even if some countries restrict appeals waivers in some types of cases, it is important to distinguish countries that allow appeals waivers and those that do not. These differences illustrate the broader attitude of legislatures and sometimes courts towards the flexibility of civil proceedings, the importance of respecting the will of parties to the dispute, and the principles of party disposition and cooperation in civil proceedings. Often, constitutional jurisprudence influences the degree of procedural flexibility in civil procedure.

It is difficult to find exact statistics on how often waivers of the right to appeal are applied in different countries and whether such waivers have any tangible influence on the number of appeals. It is said in Sweden that parties do not very often use the possibility of reaching an agreement not to appeal. One reason could be that parties generally do not consider such agreements to entail significant advantages. They want to retain the possibility to appeal until they know how the first instance court will rule and argue.[43] This kind of reasoning should be considered when drafting rules on appeal waivers. Some countries allow waiving the right to appeal before disputes have arisen, while others only allow it when the civil case is already pending or only the judgment of the first instance court has already been rendered. If the parties are allowed to waive the right to appeal during the early stages of the civil proceedings, they might want to change their mind once they have heard the content of the judgment. If the waiver of appeal has been concluded before the commencement of the court proceedings, it might not be applicable when the court of first instance has made a grave procedural error. In such cases, the fair trial rights of the parties should be protected, and the court of appeal should safeguard the main procedural principles, thus disregarding the appeal waiver. Arguably, according to the principles of civil procedure, there are not considerable objections against allowing appeals waivers, in general, as long as some safeguards are put in place. In most arbitration proceedings, appeals are not possible, and the arbitration awards can be challenged only on very limited grounds. Such rules

---

42 Stürner (n 9) 441.

43 Government of Sweden, SOU 2001:103, En modernare rättegång — reformering av processen i allmän domstol 309.

in arbitration proceedings are not regarded as a disadvantage of arbitration; on the contrary, they are considered to enhance procedural efficiency.

The most important form of procedural protection would be to require a waiver of appeal to be mutual. Allowing unilateral waivers of the right to appeal is more problematic than allowing mutual waivers. Unilateral waivers are allowed, for instance, in Germany, a country which has long been regarded as having a formalistic approach to procedural law. Moreover, appeals waivers should be expressly agreed upon in writing or orally, e.g. in a court hearing. Tacit waivers are problematic because they could trigger new disputes about the existence of the waiver and could jeopardise the interests of the parties.

Arguably, the ELI/UNIDROIT Rules exemplify a balanced view on the right to waive the right to appeal. These rules could set an example of how such a right could be implemented in jurisdictions that currently disallow or severely restrict appeal waivers. Also, the ELI/UNIDROIT Rules could trigger discussions about introducing a more flexible approach to civil proceedings in Eastern and Central European countries and could be used as an argument in cases before the constitutional courts. Overall, the ELI/UNIDROIT Rules take the view that procedural agreements should be allowed in other aspects of civil proceedings as well, and thus, they could propel the contractualisation of civil proceedings in European legal cultures in general.

It could be argued that the waiver of the right to appeal should not be allowed in consumer disputes. There could also be other types of cases in which the right to waive the right to appeal could be problematic and in breach of the central principles of civil procedure. This could be the case where one party is a natural person and the other is a trader or where one or both parties are not represented by a lawyer and in labour or housing disputes.

Party autonomy cannot be unlimited in civil proceedings. Nevertheless, it is likely that many countries will allow for well-informed, competent parties to waive their right to appeal. Whether the parties will choose to avail themselves of the opportunity in practice remains to be seen. The extent to which such waivers will become popular depends on many factors, for instance, on how the principle of the rule of law has been implemented and the extent to which citizens trust the courts.

Agreements Related to Alternative Dispute Resolution

Anna Nylund

1 Introduction

Alternative dispute resolution (ADR) covers a variety of dispute resolution processes, including (quasi-)adjudicative, evaluative, facilitative, and transformative processes, some of which are rights-based, others interest-based.[1] In allowing disputants to select and design the dispute resolution process and often also retain the power to determine the outcome, they epitomise the 'contractualisation' of dispute resolution, at least when the ties to court proceedings are minimal. As ADR processes are assumed to be faster and cheaper[2] and yield better outcomes, litigation is increasingly perceived as a last resort, reserved for cases in which ADR failed or which concern important questions of interpretation of the law.

Until recently, ADR processes, except arbitration, have had relatively weak regulation, which is likely to have had a cooling effect on their use in cross-border cases. Internationally, the 2018 UNICTRAL Model Law on International Commercial Mediation and International Settlement Agreements Resulting from Mediation (UNCITRAL Mediation Model Law)[3] and the 2019 United Nations Convention on International Settlement Agreements Resulting from Mediation (the Singapore Convention) form the main legal framework for mediation agreements and mediated settlement agreements. The 2008 EU Mediation Directive[4] has been seminal in regulating the interface between court proceedings and ADR in EU Member States. While these instruments apply only to mediation (broadly understood) in cross-border cases, they could serve and have served as a model for national rules for domestic cases[5] and for other modalities of ADR. They also illustrate some of the challenges in

1 See, e.g. Anna Nylund, 'Alternative Dispute Resolution' in Jan M. Smits, Jaakko Husa, Cathrine Valcke and Madalena Narsico (eds), *Elgar Encyclopedia of Comparative Law* (3rd edn, Edward Elgar 2023) 94-102.

2 E.g. Klaus J. Hopt and Felix Steffek, 'Mediation: Comparison of Laws, Regulatory Models, Fundamental Issues' in Klaus J. Hopt and Felix Steffek (eds), *Mediation. Principles and Regulation in Comparative Perspective* (Oxford University Press 2012), 97 99 and 103-104.

3 The 2002 UNCITRAL Model Law on International Commercial Conciliation was its predecessor.

4 European Parliament and Council Directive 2008/52/EC of 21 May 2008 on certain aspects of mediation in civil and commercial matters [2008] *OJ L136/281*.

5 E.g. Haris P. Meidanis, 'Enforcement of Mediation Settlement Agreements in the EU and the Need for Reform' (2020) 16 Journal of Private International Law 275, 281 ff.

regulating ADR in a manner that promotes its flexible and consensual nature while also protecting parties with limited resources and knowledge of the law.

The UNCITRAL Model Law and the Singapore Convention are designed primarily for commercial cases between medium to large enterprises and are rooted in international commercial law,[6] promoting private ordering. They tacitly assume that the parties to mediation make informed decisions regarding the dispute resolution process, the selection of the neutral(s) who assist them in resolving their disputes, and the outcome of the process. These beliefs also emanate from mediation theory. While this is probably correct for large commercial actors, research suggests that private individuals and small businesses often cannot make voluntary, informed decisions regarding the dispute resolution process and the outcome.[7] Thus, some modalities of ADR could reduce core democratic and fair trial values.

Because ADR is a panoply, three different modalities of ADR are interrogated: mediation as defined in the aforementioned norm sets, dispute boards as a widely used multi-tiered process, and the Norwegian public consumer dispute resolution (CDR) scheme, which is a highly institutionalised publicly funded multitiered process. The latter is specifically designed for private individuals and small companies, who are often self-represented, whereas dispute boards are for medium to large companies with legal representation. Considering the variation in ADR processes, this chapter posits that agreements for using ADR processes and settlement agreements concluded in such processes should be treated differently depending on the quality of procedural safeguards of the parties.

This chapter investigates two main intersections between ADR and court proceedings: whether and when courts enforce agreements to use ADR to resolve disputes in lieu of, or as a prerequisite to, court proceedings and whether and when agreements resulting from ADR should be enforceable and prevent a disputant from initiating litigation of the issues resolved in ADR.

Section 2 presents three forms of ADR processes and the procedural safeguards they offer: mediation, dispute boards, and the Norwegian public CDR process. Next, the civil procedural effects of agreements to use ADR (Section 3) and agreements resulting from ADR (Section 4) are discussed. Finally, Section 5 offers some concluding remarks.

6 E.g. Hopt and Steffek (n 2); Nadja Alexander, 'Introducing Regulatory Robustness Rating for Mediation Regimes in the EU' in Nadja Alexander, Sabine Walsh and Martin Svatos (eds), *EU Mediation Law Handbook* (Wolters Kluwer 2017) 1-2.

7 E.g. Nancy A. Welsh, 'Do You Believe in Magic? Self-Determination and Procedural Justice Meet Inequality in Court-Connected Mediation' (2017) 70 Southern Methodist University Law Review 721; Jacqueline Nolan-Haley, 'Does ADR's Access to Justice Come at the Expense of Meaningful Consent' (2018) 33 Ohio State Journal on Dispute Resolution 373, 383.

2 MEDIATION, DISPUTE BOARDS, AND CONSUMER DISPUTE RESOLUTION

2.1 Mediation as an Umbrella Term

Mediation is often used as an umbrella term encompassing a broad range of dispute resolution processes in which a third party (the mediator), who lacks the power to impose an outcome, assists the disputants in settling their dispute. This inclusive definition, which encompasses mediation, conciliation, (early neutral) evaluation, and so on,[8] is found in the Singapore Convention Article 2 (3), the UNCITRAL Mediation Model Law Article 1(3), and the EU Mediation Directive Article 3. Using a mediator distinguishes mediation from negotiation. The non-binding nature of the process, i.e. the fact that the mediator's recommendations do not bind the parties, separates it from inter alia arbitration and dispute boards.[9]

On a subordinate level, the role of the neutral distinguishes mediation from conciliation and evaluation. In mediation, the role of the neutral is purely facilitative (i.e. the mediator facilitates negotiation and problem-solving), while in conciliation, the neutral may also recommend a specific outcome, and in evaluation, the role of the neutral is to provide an assessment of, for instance, the likely litigated outcome, the value of the disputed issues (costs of repairing the damage or value of an object), and the strengths and weaknesses of the parties' cases.[10] Mediation in this narrower sense can be further divided into various modalities, including 'facilitative' mediation, in which the mediator seeks to improve communication, facilitate problem-solving, and promote interest-based outcomes; 'evaluative' mediation, which unfolds almost exclusively in separate meetings and in which the mediator assesses the strengths and weaknesses of the parties' cases and the likely litigated outcome or suggests 'prudent' outcomes; and 'haggling' or 'shuttle' mediation, also conducted in separate meetings while the mediator orchestrates the bargaining by pressing the parties to find a figure between their original offers.[11] The boundaries between the modalities are fluid: some resemble evaluation and conciliation more closely than mediation. The scope of

8 UNCITRAL Model Law on International Commercial Mediation and International Settlement Agreements Resulting from Mediation with Guide to Enactment and Use (2018) Note 9.

9 Nadja Alexander and Shouyu Chong, *The Singapore Convention on Mediation. A Commentary* (Wolters Kluwer 2019) 51-53; Nuria González Martín, 'Article 2: Definitions' in Guillermo Palao (ed), *The Singapore Mediation Convention* (Edward Elgar 2022) 101-105.

10 E.g. UNCITRAL Mediation Model Law Notes 10 and 11; ICC 2014 Mediation Rules Art. 1.

11 E.g. Alexander and Chong (n 9) 54-55; Anna Nylund, 'Alternative Dispute Resolution, Justice and Accountability in Norwegian Civil Justice' in Xandra Kramer, Jos Hoevenaars, Betül Kas and Erlis Themeli (eds), *Frontiers in Civil Justice. Privatisation, Monetisation and Digitisation* (Edward Elgar 2022) 82-84 with further references.

mediation varies from broad to narrow, from focusing mainly on the interests of the parties to a narrow legal focus.[12] The expected outcome of the process and the type of justice it serves depend on the procedure and the interventions (tools) the mediator uses.[13]

Mediation research suggests that mediators often practise another model than the one they purport to do and use interventions in a way that is not consistent with the mediation model.[14] The mediator's rationale for using them, rather than the presence or absence of an intervention in itself, influences the nature of the mediation process. Mediators are likely to deliver disparate processes depending on how they perceive their role and the purpose of mediation. For instance, mediators who perceive the assessment of the likely litigated outcome as indispensable because it sets the standard of a reasonable settlement are likely to treat such assessments as the culmination of the process and thus strive to elicit information to make the assessment. After delivering the assessment, they facilitate negotiations based on it. In contrast, mediators who believe that the assessment is only one component in an informed decision regarding settlement are likely to attempt to avoid the assessment from becoming a cognitive anchor that turns into a subconscious focal point of settlement negotiations.

Self-determination is a foundational value of mediation, yet mediation, as practised, often fails to live up to its promises. Considering the unclear definition of mediation, less resourceful parties might not fully understand which type of mediation process they have agreed to, the implications of various kinds of mediation on the process and outcome, the type of justice the process is likely to produce, and how to make informed decisions regarding the terms of the settlement. When mediators fail to deliver the process they purport to, the mediation process becomes even more perplexing for the less experienced parties. The combination of mediation's inherent values of self-determination, flexibility, and confidentiality, which serves 'repeat player' users of mediation well, is a toxic cocktail for the procedural safeguards of less experienced, less well-resourced disputants. Determining the standard for 'good mediation' is an insurmountable task considering the variation in mediation processes' scope, nature,

12 Leonard L. Riskin, 'Understanding Mediators' Orientations, Strategies, and Techniques: A Grid for the Perplexed' (1996) 1 Harvard Negotiation Law Review 7, 18-24.

13 Nancy A. Welsh, 'Bringing Transparency and Accountability (with a Dash of Competition) to Court-Connected Dispute Resolution' (2020) 88 Fordham Law Review 2449; John Lande, 'Moving Negotiation Theory from the Tower of Babel Toward a World of Mutual Understanding' (2017) Journal of Dispute Resolution 1.

14 ABA Section of Dispute Resolution, 'Report of the Task Force on Research on Mediator Techniques' (12 June 2017), https://www.americanbar.org/groups/dispute_resolution/resources/ (accessed 29 February 2024); James A. Wall and Kenneth Kressel, 'Mediator Thinking in Civil Cases' (2017) 34 Conflict Resolution Quarterly 331; Lorig Charkoudian, Christian de Ritis, Christian, Ramona Buck and Carrie L. Wilson, 'Mediation by Any Other Name Would Smell as Sweet—or Would It? The Struggle to Define Mediation and Its Various Approaches' (2009) 26 Conflict Resolution Quarterly 293.

and underpinning values.[15] Consequently, the threshold for considering the process 'undue' is exceedingly high.[16]

Private (ex parte) meetings are also considered an asset of mediation. However, private meetings increase the opacity of the process, making it a black box for disputants, not just outsiders. Disputants do not know what information the other disputants have presented in private meetings and cannot rebut it or correct false, misleading, or incomplete information.[17] Nor do the parties have a right to written documentation of the process and the grounds for the outcome. If the mediator makes evaluations, suggestions, or recommendations in private meetings, the disputants will not know whether the other disputant received an identical opinion. Stronger parties could attempt to spin the mediator to view their arguments more positively than is justified by providing inaccurate or incomplete information in private meetings;[18] encourage the mediator to stress the costs, duration, and risk of litigation; and insist that the mediator refrains from giving advice, even if the weaker party has need for more information to make informed decisions.

Research suggests that weak parties might be unable to make informed decisions regarding the process and the outcome. They often depend on the mediator providing information to arrive at a just result.[19] Parties with legal representation are sometimes deprived of the process and the outcomes they seek because their lawyers and the mediator frame the dispute as a matter of monetary compensation and fail to address the relational and psychological interests of the parties.[20] Because few, if any, of the procedural safeguards that apply in litigation and arbitration apply in mediation, these parties risk entering into and having to stay in a process that is neither fair nor produces just outcomes. Moreover, they lack access to appropriate forms of recourse and mechanisms for holding the mediator accountable for the process and the outcome.

Against this background, mediation should be treated as a bundle of processes rather than one distinct process. While the regulatory framework of the UNCITRAL

15 E.g. Erin R. Archerd, 'Evaluating Mediation's Future' (2020) Journal of Dispute Resolution 31; Mary Anne Noone and Lola Akin Ojelabi, 'Alternative Dispute Resolution and Access to Justice in Australia' (2020) 16 International Journal of Law in Context 108; Welsh (n 13).

16 Nancy A. Welsh, 'Dispute Resolution Neutrals' Ethical Obligation to Support Measured Transparency' (2019) 71 Oklahoma Law Review 823, 875; Jacqueline M. Nolan-Haley, 'Judicial Review of Mediated Settlement Agreements: Improving Mediation with Consent?' (2013) 5 Yearbook on Arbitration and Mediation 152, 154.

17 Nancy A. Welsh, 'You've Got Your Mother's Laugh: What Bankruptcy Mediation Can Learn from the Her/History of Divorce and Child Custody Mediation' (2009) 17 American Bankruptcy Institute Law Review 427, 445 and 448-449.

18 Ibid., 448-449.

19 Noone and Ojelabi (n 15); Jacqueline M. Nolan-Haley, 'Mediation, Self-Represented Parties, and Access to Justice: Getting There from Here' (2019) 87 Fordham Law Review 1, 6-7; Nolan-Haley (n 7); Welsh (n 7).

20 Tamara Relis, *Perceptions in Litigation and Mediation: Lawyers, Defendants, Plaintiffs, and Gendered Parties* (Cambridge University Press 2009).

Mediation Model Law and the EU Mediation Directive enables powerful parties to shape the process, small businesses and private individuals need a far more robust framework that might depart from the basic tenets of mediation to provide disputants with effective, not illusory, procedural safeguards.

2.2 *Dispute Boards: The Neutral Imposes an Outcome*

Engineering associations have developed dispute boards to prevent, manage, and resolve disputes in large-scale projects, such as the construction of bridges, large buildings, and factories.[21] Because challenging situations are inevitable in complex contracts, they must be addressed expediently, and the outcome should be technically, economically, and legally sustainable. To this end, dispute boards providing various dispute resolution services are often appointed for the entire duration of the project. The board attempts to prevent disputes from arising and escalating through negotiation and mediation. If early resolution is unsuccessful, the parties can request that the board either recommends a solution (Dispute Review Board, DRB) or makes a decision (Dispute Adjudication Board, DAB). Other set-ups include ad hoc boards, i.e. boards that are appointed to resolve a specific dispute rather than for the duration of the project, and unbundled dispute resolution services; i.e. mediation, expert evaluation, and adjudicative services are offered separately.[22] Typically, all or most of the dispute board members are engineers.[23] The 'engineering mindset' is very efficient because it focuses on identifying technological and logistical challenges and finding creative solutions to reduce disruptions and costs[24] rather than playing the 'blame game' of law.

Many organisations, including the International Chamber of Commerce (ICC) and the American Arbitration Association, offer dispute board services under the panoply of general ADR processes suitable for various disputes. Some jurisdictions, notably England and Wales, have integrated dispute boards into their civil justice system by enacting rules on so-called statutory adjudication (i.e. mandatory use of dispute boards for certain types of cases). Before resorting to litigation, parties in construction

---

21 Cyril Chern, *Chern on Disputes Boards. Practice and Procedure* (4th edn, Routledge 2020) 8-17; Shirley A. Shipman, Benjamin D. Waters William and Wood, *Brown & Marriott's ADR Principles and Practice* (4th edn, Sweet & Maxwell 2019) 112-114; Paul G. Taggart and Yasemin Çetinel, 'Dispute Board Rules Currently in Force: A Selective Overview, Comparison and Practical Considerations' (2016) 9 New York Dispute Resolution Lawyer 50.

22 Chern (n 21) 113-114.

23 Ibid., 187.

24 Marnie Jamieson and John Donald, 'Building the Engineering Mindset: Developing Leadership and Management Competencies in the Engineering Curriculum' Proceedings 2020 Canadian Engineering Education Association Conference, Paper 30, 1.

disputes must undergo a dispute board process or similar process involving exchanging information and meeting to discuss options for resolving their dispute.[25]

The ICC Dispute Board Rules of 1 October 2015 illustrates the set-up and regulation of standing dispute boards. In contrast to ad hoc dispute boards, standing dispute boards are appointed at the inception of the project, and their mandate ends after the project has been completed and all issues have been resolved. DRBs are regulated in Article 4, DABs in Article 5, and Combined Dispute Boards (CDBs), which are essentially DRBs with the right to render a decision at the parties' request, are regulated in Article 6 of the ICC rules. The discussion in this chapter is limited to the decision-making stage as this stage is distinct from processes falling under the panoply of mediation.

The ICC rules regulate inter alia the appointment of the dispute board members, their independence, access to information, remuneration, the beginning and end of their mandate, and their powers. Each of the three sub-processes is also regulated. Dispute avoidance is regulated in general terms (Art. 16). Informal assistance, which comprises services ranging from facilitating negotiations to mediation, providing the parties with an early neutral evaluation or any combination of these, is described in some more detail in Article 17. The rules on procedures for a formal referral in Articles 18-27 are more detailed. The rules stipulate the content and form of the statement of the case, the response, and additional documents, the content and conduct of hearings, time limits, and other formal and substantive rules. The decisions issued by DABs are immediately binding as a contract. However, by sending a notification of dissatisfaction within 30 days, a party can forestall the decision from becoming final. The recommendations issued by DRBs become binding (as a contract) and final unless a party sends a notification of dissatisfaction within 30 days of receiving the recommendation. A party filing a notice of dissatisfaction remains bound by the decision until a court or arbitral tribunal reverses the decision. The parties have agreed to refrain from commencing litigation or arbitration unless they have notified the other party of their dissatisfaction, the dispute board has not rendered its conclusion within 90 days, or the board is disbanded before it has rendered its conclusions pursuant to Articles 4 (6) and 5 (6).

The rules provide procedural safeguards by defining, among other things, the appointment and mandate of the board, the content of the statement of the case and the response, the principles for the hearings, the right of the board to request a party to submit additional written statements or documentation, and the duty of the board to state the reasons upon which its conclusions are based. There are also mechanisms for addressing breaches of procedural rules and principles and for ensuring that unlawful conclusions do not become binding.

25 Housing Grants, Construction and Regeneration Act 1996 Sections 108 and 108A, and the Pre-Action Protocol of Construction and Engineering Disputes, https://www.legislation.gov.uk/ukpga/1996/53/contents (accessed 29 February 2024).

Dispute boards are thoroughly regulated, particularly when the board renders a recommendation or decision. The nature of the outcome and the duration of the process are predefined, and the parties can oppose the decision by expressing dissatisfaction, thus remaining unbound by it.

2.3 *Norwegian Public Consumer Dispute Resolution*

The public Norwegian public CDR process is offered for all consumer disputes for which there is no sector-specific scheme and disputes concerning similar contracts concluded between private individuals. The process is two-tiered: if the combined investigation and mediation stage at the Norwegian Consumer Authority does not result in a settlement, one of the parties can file a claim within one month at the Consumer Dispute Board, a de facto adjudicative organ. The decision of the Consumer Dispute Board becomes binding and enforceable unless one of the parties initiates court proceedings within one month.[26] The process is free of charge for the consumer, but the consumer must pay for expert reports and similar documents when they are relevant and needed.

The Consumer Authority informs the parties on the legal norms applicable to their dispute to enable them to resolve their dispute without proceeding with the dispute resolution process and make informed decisions regarding the outcome. The Consumer Authority facilitates settlement when appropriate, and, if the parties do not settle, suggests an outcome. During the process, the Consumer Authority provides information to the parties to ensure that settlements are sufficiently informed. Any recommendations or suggestions must be recorded. The process is partly written. The parties must be given appropriate time to consider whether they wish to settle following the suggestion.[27] Once all relevant documents have been exchanged, the mediation process must be concluded within 90 days.[28] The Consumer Authority's role is incompatible with the principles of mediation in that the employees can give information on consumer law and typical outcomes, suggest outcomes, and, to some extent, give the parties advice.

In the Norwegian public CDR scheme, the principle of openness in public administration has substituted the principle of confidentiality. The 'mediator' must keep notes from all conversations, and all documents are public under Norwegian law. This allows Norwegian consumer and trader organisations to monitor the quality of services. The Consumer Authority must make information available on its website and

26 Consumer Complaints Act (Lov av 23. juni 2020 nr 98 om behandling av forbrukerklager i Forbrukertilsynet og Forbrukerklageutvalget (forbrukerklageloven).

27 Consumer Complaints Act Section 11.

28 Consumer Complaints Act Section 12.

its annual reports and monitor users' satisfaction regularly.[29] Both the parties to the dispute and consumer and trader organisations can then monitor the quality of the proceedings and the outcome for individual disputes and on the aggregate level.

If the parties do not settle, they can bring the case to the Consumer Dispute Board, which is, in practice, a publicly funded tribunal which renders a decision in written proceedings, applying the rules of consumer law. At this stage, the proceedings are no longer comparable to ADR but rather to court proceedings as the nature of the process is purely adjudicative. Accordingly, this stage will not be discussed in this chapter.

The parties are precluded from initiating court proceedings while the case is pending at the Consumer Authority, including the 30 days for filing for proceedings at the Consumer Dispute Board.[30] This is an exception to the main rule under Norwegian law that ADR agreements do not affect the right to file for court proceedings. In Norway, consumers are not bound by arbitration agreements.

3 Agreements to Use ADR

3.1 *The Nature, Duration, and Outcome of the Process*

Because ADR processes vary in scope, duration, set-up, outcome, and the obligations of the disputants and the neutral, pinpointing the obligations arising from an ADR clause and the outcome of the process could be difficult. Enforcing agreements to use ADR in place of or before litigation is a balancing act: if courts enforce such agreements too eagerly, they could unduly hinder access to court, and if they do not, the agreements are hardly worth the paper they are written on.[31] The balancing point depends on the type of ADR procedure the parties have agreed to and whether the parties are large or small enterprises or private individuals.

In deciding whether to enforce an agreement to use ADR, courts should consider both the ADR process that the parties have agreed on and who the parties to the dispute are, as well as the genesis of the ADR agreement.

ADR agreements as standard clauses are problematic because they do not necessarily reflect an informed decision; nevertheless, they should be upheld when standard contracts reflect business practices and the ADR process reflects the interests of both parties in a balanced manner. The clause should not disproportionately favour

---

29 Consumer Complaints Decree (Forskrift om behandling av forbrukerklager i Forbrukertilsynet og Forbrukerklageutvalget (forbrukerklageforskriften) FOR-2020-12-21-3084) Sections 7 and 8.

30 Consumer Complaints Act Section 23.

31 Ronán Feehily, *International Commercial Mediation. Law and Regulation in Comparative Context* (Cambridge University Press 2022) 66-68.

one party, particularly the more powerful party. Even if the ADR clause is individually negotiated, courts should be cautious when one party is a small business or private individual because they are less likely to fully understand the implications of the clause and make informed decisions regarding the process and participation.

The clearer the ADR process is defined, the more easily the court can assess whether the parties to the ADR agreement have fulfilled their obligations, whether the agreement stems from informed consent, and whether the process provides adequate procedural safeguards to the parties. Dispute boards, at least when the parties have defined the type of services, are well defined, the process is foreseeable, and the standard rules offer adequate procedural safeguards. Although a party could dispute the validity or applicability of the DAB or DRB clause or contest the appointment of the board, the likelihood of the process being a source of litigation is comparatively low because of the obligations arising from the process, and the procedural standards are reasonably clear.

The Norwegian public CDR process is more closely related to dispute boards than mediation because the process is regulated and described in detail, and the role of the neutral is clear. The duration of the mediation stage is also predefined. Because the Consumer Authority is a public body, the regular rules of openness, quality of services, impartiality, and so forth apply, which renders the body and its employees accountable for the quality of the services and provides adequate procedural safeguards for the parties.

A mediation clause, in contrast, could be very vague unless the parties have designated a specific form of mediation and outlined the process.[32] Hence, it might be challenging to establish what type of mediation process the parties have agreed to, what the scope of the process will be, what kind of outcomes are expected, and how to establish an appropriate threshold for good faith participation in the mediation process. The cost and duration of the procedure and the likely impact on the need for litigation might be challenging to assess, too. Considering the variation in the way in which mediation processes are delivered, weak parties, particularly self-represented parties, run the risk of finding themselves forced to participate in a process they do not desire. Weak parties also risk participating in a sub-standard process due to the lack of appropriate procedural safeguards.[33] Creating a process for accreditation of ADR services could facilitate making informed choices regarding ADR and courts enforcing agreements to use ADR: accredited ADR processes should be presumed to have minimum procedural safeguards. The EU Consumer ADR Directive[34] could serve as a blueprint for the registration process. However, the criticism against the lax

32 Ibid., 57-65.

33 Rachel Field and Jonathan Crowe, *Mediation Ethics* (Edward Elgar 2020) 150-151.

34 European Parliament and Council Directive 2013/11/EU on alternative dispute resolution for consumer disputes and amending Regulation (EC) No 2006/2004 and Directive 2009/22/EC (Directive on consumer ADR) OJ L165/63.

procedural safeguards the Directive affords, especially in conciliation proceedings, should be borne in mind.[35] Against this background, in the absence of an accreditation regime, courts should be cautious when enforcing agreements to use mediation when one party is a private individual or small business.

3.2 *Implications for Court Proceedings*

Courts enforce agreements to use ADR by dismissing the case or staying the proceedings. Alternatively, non-compliance could be sanctioned with costs or similar sanctions, i.e. the disputant would be allowed to bring the case but be liable.[36]

Considering that mediation is a consensual process and consent to mediation should not entail pressure to settle, parties should be allowed to exit mediation processes without fearing sanctions. This should be the case when the prospects of settling appear limited, the other party abuses the process, or the process fails to meet quality standards. In contrast, the parties should be required to participate throughout the dispute board and similar procedures culminating in an evaluation, recommendation, or decision unless the board or neutral fails to fulfil its duties. Courts should be particularly mindful of the fact that disputants might deplete their direct and indirect financial and emotional resources during mediation. Thus, they might relinquish their claim due to the additional tangible and intangible costs that litigation entails.[37] To avoid disputants being disadvantaged by the burdens of ADR and to ensure effective access to justice, courts should be mindful of these limitations. Moreover, courts should avoid litigation arising from the agreement to use ADR. The less clear the process and the requirements of good faith participation are, the more likely it is that disputes will arise from the ADR agreement.

---

35 Alexandre Biard, 'Impact of Directive 2013/11/EU on Consumer ADR Quality: Evidence from France and the UK' (2019) 42 Journal of Consumer Policy 109, 113; Andrea Fejos and Chris Willet, 'Consumer Access to Justice: The Role of the ADR Directive and the Member States' (2016) 1 European Review of Private Law 33; Marte Knigge and Charlotte Pavillon, 'The Legality Requirement of the ADR Directive: Just Another Paper Tiger?' (2016) 5 Journal of European Consumer and Market Law 155.

36 Feehily (n 31) 70-71, 73-76 and 166 ff. For a comparative overview, see Anna Nylund and Antonio Cabral, 'General Report: Contractualisation of Civil Procedure' in Anna Nylund and Antonio Cabral (eds), *Contractualisation of Civil Litigation* (Intersentia 2023) 30-31.

37 For examples of the detrimental impact of ADR clauses in various formats, see Helen Hershkoff and Judith Resnik, 'Contractualisation of Civil Litigation in the United States: Procedure, Contract, Public Authority, Autonomy, Aggregate Litigation, and Power: A View from the United States' in Anna Nylund and Antonio Cabral (eds), *Contractualisation of Civil Litigation* (Intersentia 2023) 463-481.

4 Agreements Arising from ADR

4.1 *Procedural and Substantive Effects of Agreements Arising from ADR*

The outcomes of ADR can be either imposed by the neutral or consensual, binding or non-binding. A binding outcome imposed by the neutral signifies that the neutral decides how the dispute is resolved, and the parties are bound by the decision as if it were a contract. It should be noted that except for arbitral awards, outcomes resulting from ADR, although contractually binding, are not quasi-judgments unless a provision renders procedural effect upon them. Evaluations and recommendations are examples of non-binding outcomes the neutral imposes because the parties use them to inform their negotiations. Consensual outcomes are binding as contracts if they fulfil the requirements of a valid contract and the parties decide so.[38]

Substantive law effects should then be separated from the procedural effects, that is, the access to direct enforcement and *res judicata* or estoppel effects of the agreement concluded in ADR. UNCITRAL Mediation Model Law Article 15 serves as an example of this distinction. Note 96 in the implementation guide of the Model Law states that Article 15 'stresses the binding and enforceable nature of settlement agreements', and then notes that '[t]he word "binding" reflects a contractual obligation between the parties' and that 'enforceable' refers to the obligation being 'susceptible to enforcement by courts' but does not refer to any specific type of enforcement.[39] In this context, the neutral's binding decision will also be characterised as an agreement since it binds the parties by contract, i.e. the ADR clause stating the outcome is binding.[40]

Proponents of giving agreements concluded in ADR procedural effects argue that those effects enable the parties to use the agreements as a sword and a shield.[41] Direct enforcement, the sword, creates a strong incentive to comply with the agreement and saves the parties from the costs, delays, and risks of obtaining an enforceable title. By refusing to abide by the agreement, a party could attempt to prompt a renegotiation when there is a considerable risk for a costly and time-consuming process to obtain an enforceable title. If agreements concluded in ADR have *res judicata* or estoppel effects,[42]

38 Feehily (n 31) 199-211.

39 UNCITRAL Model Law on International Commercial Mediation and International Settlement Agreements Resulting from Mediation with Guide to Enactment and Use (2018).

40 Feehily (n 31) 225-228.

41 Alexander and Chong (n 9) 69.

42 For a brief discussion of the differences between civil law and common law doctrines, see, e.g. Alexander and Chong (n 9) 72-74; Oscar G. Chase, Helen Hershkoff, Linda J. Silberman, John Sorabji, Rolf Stürner, Yasuhei Taniguchi and Vincenzo Varano, *Civil Litigation in Comparative Context* (2nd edn, West Academic 2017) 563 ff.

they function as shields protecting the parties from having to litigate or arbitrate disputes that have already been settled.

Opponents argue that giving procedural effects to agreements resulting from mediation, especially, would be contrary to the foundational values of interest-based, consensual dispute resolution. The outcome is the 'best possible' and balances tangible and intangible, short- and long-term interests of the parties. If the mediated agreements reflect the best realistic outcome, parties to such a contract should have strong incentives to comply, considering that it is superior to its alternatives.[43] When parties cannot fulfil their obligations, e.g. due to unforeseen circumstances, they should return to the mediation process to seek a realistic alternative outcome, not litigate.[44] Many users of dispute boards advocate non-enforceability because the parties can use the procedure to test their arguments and to receive a suggestion for the outcome and can then evaluate whether the proceeding to litigation or arbitration is worth it or whether they could attempt to negotiate some modifications to the recommendation or decision or comply with it.[45] There is no consensus on what type of procedural effects are the most advantageous.

Enforcement, the 'sword' function, of agreements resulting from ADR will be discussed next (Section 4.2), and then the 'shield' functions that protect the parties to the agreement from litigation of the issues settled will be analysed (Section 4.3).

4.2 *Enforcement of Agreements Arising from ADR*

We can identify three distinct approaches to the enforceability of settlement agreements or decisions arising from ADR.

The recommendations or decisions rendered by dispute boards are not enforceable as a judgment, but only binding on the parties as if they were contracts. Parties are nevertheless to comply with the recommendation or decision as soon as it is binding. Since decisions and recommendations are not enforceable, a party must obtain an enforceable title first.

Similar rules apply to settlement agreements concluded in the Norwegian public CDR mediation scheme: settlements are enforceable only as a contract. The reason is probably that drafting an enforceable quality settlement agreement would require considerable extra effort on behalf of the Consumer Authority. Time would be wasted in most cases because the parties comply with it voluntarily. The 'mediator' could alert the consumer if a trader repeatedly refuses to comply with settlements.

43 Linda Mulcahy, 'Mediation processes' in Maria F. Moscati, Michael Palmer and Marian Roberts (eds), *Comparative Dispute Resolution* (Edward Elgar 2020) 249.

44 Howard Raiffa, 'Post-settlement Settlements' (1985) 1 Negotiation Journal 9.

45 Chern (n 21) 9-11.

The Singapore Convention and the UNCITRAL Mediation Model Law take the opposite stance by facilitating direct enforceability of all international commercial mediated settlements, i.e. the parties can proceed directly to enforcement proceedings. The underpinning rationale is that enforceability is a prerequisite for mediation to become an attractive dispute resolution method. It reduces the risk of attempts to renegotiate the settlement or initiate arbitral or court proceedings.[46] To be enforceable, settlement agreements must fulfil the formal requirements in the Singapore Convention Article 4 and UNCITRAL Mediation Model Law Article 18.[47] A party can avoid the enforcement if a party is incapacitated; if the contents of the agreement are against public policy or the subject matter is not capable of being settled in mediation; if the agreement is null and void, inoperable, or incapable of being performed; if the agreement is not binding or final or if granting relief would be contrary to the settlement terms; if there was a severe breach of mediation standards; or if the mediator has failed to disclose issues that could raise justifiable doubts regarding the impartiality and independence of the mediator.

A middle ground is found in the EU Mediation Directive Article 6. The parties to a cross-border settlement agreement can jointly request that a competent organ, such as a court, makes the settlement enforceable by embodying it in a court settlement, notarial deed, or similar title.[48] The Directive does not specify the process for validation of mediated settlement agreements.[49] Agreements validated in one Member State are enforceable throughout the EU. The advantage of the EU system is that the parties decide whether the settlement agreement is enforceable at the time of the conclusion of the settlement or even at a later stage.

From the perspective of large enterprises, the direct enforcement model of the Singapore Convention is the most advantageous because in allowing parties to proceed directly to enforcement proceedings it expedites enforcement. Nevertheless, principles of dispute boards demonstrate how direct enforceability could also entail some disadvantages, especially if the neutral has the power to impose a solution.

The situation is different for small enterprises and individuals because they might not have been able to make informed decisions regarding the process and outcome

---

46 S.I. Strong, 'The Preamble to the Singapore Convention on Mediation: Identifying the Object and Purpose of the Treaty through Text, Content and Intent' 46 ff; Guillermo Palao, 'Article 3: General Principles', 107 ff, Mark T. Kawakami, 'Article 4: Requirements for Reliance on Settlement Agreements', all in Guillermo Palao (ed), *The Singapore Mediation Convention* (Edward Elgar 2022) 142 ff.

47 Singapore Mediation Convention Art. 5 and UNCITRAL Mediation Model Law Art. 19.

48 Instead of a mutual request, one party can file a request with the explicit consent of the other party. For a discussion of the limits of the current EU regime, see Esplugues, Carlos, and José Iglesias, 'Mediation and Private International Law: Improving Free Circulation of Mediation Agreements across the EU' in *The European Parliament and Directorate-General for Internal Policies, The Implementation of the Mediation Directive*. Workshop 29 November 2016 Compilation of In-depth Analyses. PE 571.395 (The European Union 2016).

49 For a discussion of various methods for granting enforceability, see Meidanis (n 5) 281 ff.

and have limited opportunities for rendering the neutral accountable for the process and outcome. However, when the ADR process is well defined and appropriate for the type of disputes and parties at hand, and sufficient procedural safeguards are in place, making agreements arising from ADR enforceable could be well justified. When a registration and quality monitoring process is put in place for providers of ADR services, enforceability could be limited to registered ADR providers who offer quality processes with adequate procedural safeguards.

Requiring a court or public notary to validate the settlement agreement to render it enforceable is time-consuming. Yet the delay can be outweighed by the additional safeguards the validation process provides. Moreover, rules that set a cooling-off period that allows the parties to withdraw from a settlement agreement could also be enacted to protect weaker parties from pressure to settle, as is done in the Norwegian public CDR scheme.

4.3 Res Judicata *Effects of Agreements Arising from ADR*

Res judicata effects or estoppel effects bar the parties from litigating (or arbitrating) a dispute or claim that has been settled in ADR proceedings. For simplicity, both effects are referred to as *res judicata* below and will be used to denote that the court will dismiss actions or claims that have been resolved in ADR.

Dispute board outcomes do not claim the effect of *res judicata*. However, courts in many jurisdictions could decide the case in simplified proceedings on procedural or substantive grounds: the parties manifestly lack interest in adjudicating the dispute as it has already been resolved. The claimant clearly lacks a reasonable prospect of success. These presumptions could be rebuttable under certain conditions, like those for challenging an arbitral award or because of new circumstances.

The Singapore Convention Article 3 (2) states that parties shall be allowed

> to invoke the settlement agreement in accordance with its rules of procedure and under the conditions laid down in this Convention, to prove that the matter has already been resolved.

The absence of direct references to recognition and *res judicata* can arguably be attributed to differences in rules and doctrines on *res judicata* and estoppel.[50] *Res judicata* can refer to the parties being barred from raising claims (claims estoppel), legal and factual issues (issue estoppel) that a court has already decided, or claims or issues that should have been raised in the course of the previous litigation. Moreover,

50 Alexander and Chong (n 9) 73-74; Palao (n 46) 43, 125-128.

the scope of *res judicata* varies among the states, depending on whether it is limited by the facts or law and facts. It should be noted that neither the EU Mediation Directive nor Article 59 of the Brussels Ibis Regulation on court settlements recognises *res judicata* effects of settlements. Even if settlements have *res judicata* or estoppel effects under national law, they do not have such effects in cross-border cases. The last rule is based on the reasoning of the ECJ in *Solo Kleinmotoren:* 'court settlements do not emanate from a judicial body ... deciding on its own authority on the issues between the parties' – they 'are essentially contractual in that their terms depend first and foremost on the parties' intention'.[51] Consequently, settlement shall not have *res judicata* effects.

Preventing costly litigation of settled disputes does not necessitate that agreements resulting from ADR have formal *res judicata* effects. In countries requiring litigants to have a genuine legal interest to litigate a claim, the defendant can avoid litigation by arguing that the dispute had ceased when it was settled in the ADR process.[52] This defence would then prompt the court to dismiss the action or claim. The presumption that the parties to agreements concluded in ADR lack a legal interest to litigate should be rebuttable. Alternatively, courts could find for the defendant based on a presumption that the action is manifestly without any prospect of success because the parties have already agreed to resolve it in a specific manner. Similarly, when one party is in breach of the settlement agreement, the other party is entitled to initiate litigation and has a legitimate interest to sue for breach of contract. Jurisdictions without rules or doctrines requiring a legal interest to litigate could benefit from introducing such rules, in addition to agreements arising from ADR, on a general basis to prevent abuse of litigation.

In this context, too, courts should be concerned with the quality of the ADR process and the outcome. Enforcing agreements, recommendations and decisions emanating from dispute boards should be unproblematic considering the presence of adequate procedural safeguards, and so should agreements resulting from the Norwegian public CDR scheme. In contrast, mediation is more problematic, considering how often the process lacks adequate procedural safeguards, including effective complaint mechanisms against inappropriate and unethical mediator behaviour.[53] Thus, there should be more leeway to relitigate the case.

51 Case C-414/92 *Solo Kleinmotoren GmbH v. Emilio Boch* (1994) ECLI:EU:C:1994:221, paras. 17-18. Marlene Brosch and Martina Mantovani, 'Article 2' in Marta Requejo Isidro (ed), *Brussels I Bis. A Commentary on Regulation (EC) No 1215/2012* (Edward Elgar 2022) 48.

52 Chern (n 21) 427-30.

53 Brian A. Pappas, 'Just Settlement? Rethinking the Mediator's Goals' in Art Hinshaw, Andrea Kupfer Schneider and Sarah Rudolph Cole (eds), *Discussions in Dispute Resolution: The Foundational Articles* (Oxford University Press 2021) 136-140; Welsh (n 17) 448-449.

5 Concluding Remarks

In enforcing agreements to use ADR instead of litigation and arbitration, agreements concluded in ADR courts must balance promoting ADR as an avenue to high-quality dispute resolution and protecting access to justice. The equilibrium between the two interests should be found by differential treatment of disputants and ADR processes. ADR agreements in commercial disputes between mid to large-size enterprises should be treated differently from those involving small enterprises and private individuals. When ADR is appropriately defined, designed, and regulated and the parties have a real opportunity to render the neutral accountable for the quality of the process, the outcome should have direct procedural effects. At the same time, caution is needed when enforcing agreements related to vague, opaque processes, particularly when these involve less resourceful parties. A tiered approach to ADR could spur the emergence of clearly defined ADR processes and the evolution of appropriate institutional frameworks to ensure fair ADR processes and just outcomes for each process. Rules should be tailored to each process to fit its characteristics and the strength of procedural safeguards it offers.

Ex Officio Application of Procedural Agreements in Consumer Contracts?

Alain Ancery and Bart Krans

1 Procedural Agreements: Options and Hurdles

Procedural agreements can help parties decide which procedural law regime, or parts of it, is applicable to them. The concept of procedural agreements is so broad that it can cover a wide range of procedural law topics. Parties can make agreements on various aspects of civil proceedings, but not all.

A rather common form of agreement in civil proceedings concerns the applicable forum. For example, parties can agree on which court has jurisdiction to decide a dispute. Such forum clauses or jurisdiction clauses are far from unknown in legal practice.[1] This type of clause can be purely national. Forum clauses may also have an international component.

Another type of procedural agreements are those that concern evidence. In that area alone, several variants and possibilities are conceivable. For instance, it may involve agreements on sharing the burden of proof. The question of which means of proof can be used to provide evidence on a possible point of dispute between the parties may lend itself to a contractual agreement. For example, can certain propositions only be proven by a written document? Magne Strandberg's chapter in this volume explores this further.[2] These evidentiary agreements concern an important example of procedural agreements in civil cases.

Arrangements on litigation can also be more specific or concern the course of proceedings or aspects that sometimes only become apparent at the end of an instance. Similarly, arrangements on the costs involved in civil proceedings are conceivable.[3] As regards the end of an instance, it is also possible to think about whether the proceedings between these parties will be continued in a higher court or whether the legal battle between the parties has been definitively decided with the judgment. Agreements are also possible on possible appeals.[4]

1 Florian Eichel and Rorick Tovar Galván, this volume.
2 Magne Strandberg, this volume.
3 Henrik Bellander, this volume.
4 Vigita Vėbraitė, this volume.

These types are not the only forms of litigation agreements. For example, can parties also agree that they will not raise a certain defence during any proceeding to which they are a party? In German law, procedural agreements are regularly constructed as agreements whereby parties commit to a certain litigation conduct.[5] In English law, attention has also been paid to whether litigation agreements can bind parties to certain conduct. This has focused on forum choices and arbitration clauses.[6]

One other example is agreements on arbitration and binding opinion proceedings. Arbitration or binding opinion agreements can also be seen as procedural agreements to some extent. After all, they imply that the state courts do not have jurisdiction. If parties choose arbitration, it implies that they also choose their own procedural regime (e.g. in accordance with the rules of the relevant arbitration institute). As far as binding advice is concerned, at least under Dutch law, such an agreement may also imply, for example, also temporarily sidelining the state courts.[7]

If there are so many options for procedural agreements, the question arises as to whether parties really have ample opportunity to shape the civil litigation they might pursue in the way they wish. One of the key questions is whether procedural agreements achieve their goal or whether there is some kind of obstacle to successful procedural agreements. The options for making valid agreements can and will vary from one jurisdiction to another, if only because contract law also varies from country to country. As with other contractual arrangements, procedural agreements can be subject to various types of restrictions.

Our hypothesis is that options for making valid agreements could and would vary from one jurisdiction to another, as contract law also varies from country to country. However, the similarity in restrictions for such agreements might be greater than expected for the EU countries, as they will often be found in fundamental rights stemming from Article 6 of the European Convention on Human Rights, consumer-protection EU directives or both.

Our focus in this contribution is on one specific possible hurdle for successful procedural agreements that, to our knowledge, has received little attention in the context of procedural agreements: the ex officio application of EU consumer law. This chapter, therefore, focuses on this specific barrier to the success of procedural agreements as far as such agreements are entered into by a consumer, on the one hand, and a professional party, on the other (B2C contracts). There is already extensive case law of the European

5 Gerhard Wagner, *Prozessverträge* (Mohr Siebeck 1998); cf. Marte Knigge, *De procesovereenkomst* (Kluwer 2014) Section 4.2.2.

6 Cf. Andrew Bell, *Forum shopping and venue in transnational litigation* (OUP 2003); Edwin Peel, 'Exclusive jurisdiction agreements: purity and pragmatism in the conflict of laws' [1998] Lloyd's Maritime and Commercial Quarterly, 182-227, cf. Knigge (n 5) Section 4.2.2.

7 *Van Delft/Van Boxtel* DSC 22 November 1985, NJ 1986/275 the Dutch Supreme Court has accepted this; cf. Knigge (n 5) Section 5.4.2.

Court of Justice (CJEU) on ex officio application of consumer law in B2C contracts. We will touch upon this case law in more detail later, but the general tendency is to protect the consumers unaware of their rights or unable to enforce them. That could apply across the board to B2C relations and, therefore, also to B2C procedural agreements, which happen to occur more often than one would think in the context of general terms and conditions (i.e. stipulating alternative dispute resolution (ADR) as a means of conflict settlement or the competent court outside the jurisdiction of the consumer). Could this case law of the CJEU on ex officio application of consumer law, in general, stand in the way of successful general terms and conditions used vis-à-vis consumers?

First, we will discuss the ex officio application of EU consumer protection legislation and provide an overview of the case law of the CJEU on the ex officio application of EU consumer protection law (Section 2). Then we will go into the ex officio review and more active courts (Section 3). In Section 4, we will explain the extent to which parties in B2C relationships could and should deviate from applicable procedural rules in view of the CJEU case law on ex officio application. We will discuss some procedural agreements in more detail (Section 5), before presenting concluding and closing remarks (Section 6).

2 Ex Officio Application of EU Consumer Protection Legislation

The Court of Justice of the European Union has ruled frequently on the ex officio application of EU consumer protection legislation. This has led to a vast amount of case law across various jurisdictions and types of interactions between consumers and professional counterparties (often referred to as B2C cases).[8] Although this case law

8 Joined Cases C-240/98-244/98 *Océano Grupo Editorial SA v. Rocio Murciano Quintero and others* [2000] ECLI:EU:C:2000:346; Case C-473/00 *Cofidis SA v. Jean Louis Fredout* [2002] ECLI:EU:C:2002:705; Case C-429/05 *Max Rampion and Marie-Jeanne Godard, née Rampion v. Franfinance SA and K par K SAS* [2007] ECLI:EU:C:2007:575; Case C-243/08 *Pannon GSM Zrt v. Erzsébet Sustikné Győrfi* [2009] ECLI:EU:C:2009:350; Case C-227/08 *Eva Martín Martín v. EDP Editores SL* [2009] ECLI:EU:C:2009:792; Case C-137/08 *VB Pénzügyi Lízing Zrt. v. Ferenc Schneider* [2010] ECLI:EU:C:2010:659; Case C-76/10 *Pohotovosť s.r.o. v. Iveta Korčkovská* [2010] ECLI:EU:C:2010:685; Case C-453/10 *Jana Pereničová en Vladislav Perenič tegen SOS financ spol. s r.o.* [2012] ECLI:EU:C:2012:144; Case C-472/10 *Nemzeti Fogyasztóvédelmi Hatóság v. Invitel Távközlési Zrt* [2012] ECLI:EU:C:2012:242; Case C-618/10 *Banco Español de Crédito, SA v. Joaquín Calderón Camino* [2012] ECLI:EU:C:2012:349; Case C-472/11 *Banif Plus Bank Zrt v. Csaba Csipai and Vikótria Csipai* [2013] ECLI:EU:C:2013:88; Case C-415/11 *Mohamed Aziz v. Caixa d'Estalvis de Catalunya, Tarragona i Manresa (Catalunyacaixa)* [2013] ECLI:EU:C:2013:164; C-92/11 *RWE Vertrieb AG v. Verbraucherzentrale Nordrhein-Westfalen eV* [2013] ECLI:EU:C:2013:180; Case C-397/11 *Erika Jőrös v. Aegon Magyarország Hitel Zrt* [2013] ECLI:EU:C:2013:340; Case C-488/11 *Dirk Frederik Asbeek Brusse and Others v. Jahani BV* [2013] ECLI:EU:C:2013:341; Case C-32/12 *Soledad Duarte Hueros v. Autociba SA and Automóviles Citroën España SA* [2013] ECLI:EU:C:2013:637; Case C-226/12 *Constructora Principado SA v. José Ignacio Menéndez Álvarez* [2014] ECLI:EU:C:2014:10; Case C-26/13 *Árpád Kásler and Hajnalka Káslerné Rábai v. OTP Jelzálogbank Zrt* [2014] ECLI:EU:C:2014:282; Case 169/14 *Juan Carlos Sánchez*

originated in mainstream consumer disputes, such as consumer sales, the case law has crept into areas of law that are usually to a lesser extent associated with consumer law matters, such as areas of financial law, and indirectly affected the ADR procedures as well.[9] The impact of this case law on national civil proceedings is noticeable.[10] Civil courts are required to take a more active approach in B2C cases, even if they are requested to review or ratify a decision resulting from an alternative dispute mechanism, which is only enforceable after it has been confirmed by a governmental court.

In the absence of concrete guidance by the CJEU on how to apply this case law in a national civil procedural environment, Dutch courts have set up a working group which provided practical recommendations to courts faced with case files in which the ex officio application of EU consumer law might become an issue.[11] The practical recommendations of one of the earlier reports of this working group were endorsed by the Supreme Court of the Netherlands in *Heesakkers v. Voets* and has since then become established case law in the Dutch legal order.[12]

Part of the ex officio review by civil courts is the contractual terms agreed between parties in a B2C relationship. In addition to parties being able to conclude contracts on substantive law issues, they are also, to a large extent, able to agree on procedural law issues, as mentioned in the previous paragraph.

National procedural autonomy is a basic principle in the interaction between EU law and the national civil procedure. The enforcement of substantive EU law is left to the national civil procedure of the Member State.[13] The EU law principles of equivalence,

---

Morcillo and María del Carmen Abril García v. Banco Bilbao Vizcaya Argentaria SA [2014] ECLI:EU:C:2014:2099; Case C-567/13 *Nóra Baczó and János István Vizsnyiczai v. Raiffeisen Bank Zrt* [2015] ECLI:EU:C:2015:88; Case C-479/13 *Froukje Faber v. Autobedrijf Hazet Ochten BV* [2015] ECLI:EU:C:2015:357; Case C-49/14 *Finanmadrid EFC SA v. Jesús Vicente Albán Zambrano and Others* [2016] ECLI:EU:C:2016:98; Case C-147/16 *Karel de Grote Hogeschool Katholieke Hogeschool Antwerpen VZW v. Susan Romy Jozef Kuijpers* [2018] ECLI:EU:C:2018:320; Joined Cases C-419/18 and C-483/18 *Profi Credit Polska S.A. v. Bogumiła Włostowska and Others and Profi Credit Polska S.A. v. OH* [2019] ECLI:EU:C:2019:930; Case C-453/18 *Bondora AS v. Carlos V.C. and XY* [2019] ECLI:EU:2019:1118.

9 Cf. Case C-168/05 *Elisa Mostaza Claro v. Centro Móvil Milenium SL* [2006] ECLI:EU:C:2006:675; Case-40/08 *Asturcom Telecomunicaciones SL v. Cristina Rodríguez Nogueira* [2009] ECLI:EU:C:2009:615.

10 Cf. Alain Ancery and Bart Krans, 'Consumer protection and EU-Driven Judicial Activism in the Netherlands' in Anna Nylund and Magne Strandberg (eds), *Civil Procedure and Hamonisation of Law* (Intersentia 2019) 125-193.

11 Latest report (in Dutch): *Ambtshalve toetsing III-Herzien rapport van de redactieraad van het LOVCK&T* www.rechtspraak.nl/Voor-advocaten-en-juristen/Reglementen-procedures-en-formulieren/Kanton#38b19954-3583-4ed8-ae7b-b087fafd0db031015c93-85fb-46ed-a947-d93867f4f45a3 (accessed 15 December 2023).

12 *Heesakkers/Voets* [2013] DSC 13 September 2013, ECLI:NL:HR:2013:691, NJ 2014/274, with case note H.B. Krans.

13 The existence of this concept is, however, disputed by some. For an overview: Anthi Beka, *The Active Role of Courts in Consumer Litigation* (Intersentia 2018) 24-25.

effectiveness and effective judicial protection limit national procedural autonomy.[14] Together, they create a framework in which the application and effectiveness of EU law can be ensured at a national level. Within this framework, an indirect effect on the national civil procedure is applied, which created the environment for the concept of ex officio application of EU consumer law to blossom.[15] The ex officio application of EU consumer law intends to ensure the effectiveness of consumer protection provisions[16] by not turning an imbalance in the contractual rights and obligations into a procedural imbalance.[17] To ensure national courts are able to apply EU consumer law ex officio, other national procedural provisions that could potentially hamper this ex officio application might need to be set aside. The CJEU has frequently ruled to open the option for national courts to apply EU consumer law ex officio. Examples of such provisions could be limitation periods or *res judicata*.[18]

Consumers are generally in a weaker position vis-à-vis the seller. Without national courts invoking or applying consumer protection provisions, there is a chance that consumers are deprived of consumer protection rules.[19] After all, consumers have limited legal knowledge, limited economic means and less information than their professional counterparties, which makes it difficult for consumers to identify consumer protection rules themselves or obtain legal representation. This should, however, not be used as an argument for why a more knowledgeable consumer with greater economic means should not be protected. In its *Rampion and Godard v. Franfinance SA and K par K SAS* ruling, the CJEU clarified that even if the consumer in a specific case is not in a weaker position vis-à-vis its professional counterparty, the case law of the CJEU on the ex officio application of consumer protection provisions still applies. The individual consumers do not have to specify that they meet the characteristics of a general consumer. This has

---

14 The case law on this started with the CJEU rulings in the C-33/76 *Rewe-Zentralfinanz eG and Rewe-Zentral AG v. Landwirtschaftskammer für das Saarland* [1976] ECLI:EU:C:1976:188, para. 5 and C-45/76 *Comet BV v. Produktschap voor Siergewassen* [1976] ECLI:EU:C:1976:191, para. 13.

15 Beka (n 13) 9; H.B. Krans, 'EU Law and National Civil Procedure Law: An Invisible Pillar' [2015] 23 European Review of Private Law 567-588.

16 Beka (n 13) 17; Michal Bobek, 'The Effects of EU Law in the National Legal Systems' in Catherine Barnard and Steve Peers (eds), *European Union Law* (OUP 2012) 166.

17 Vincenzo Zeno-Zencovich and Maria Cecilia Paglietti, 'Le droit processuel des consommateurs' [2014] Revue de droit internationale et de droit compare 321-355.

18 Cf. recent judgments of the CJEU: Case C-869/19 *Unicaja Banco SA v. L* [2022] ECLI:EU:C:2022:397; Case C-725/19 *IO v. Impuls Leasing România IFN SA* [2022] ECLI:EU:C:2022:396; Joined Cases C-693/19 and 831/19 *SPV Project 1503 Srl, Dobabank SpA, YB and others v. YX and ZW* [2022] ECLI:EU:C:2022:395 and Case C-600/19 *MA v. Iberbajo Banco SA* [2022] ECLI:EU:C:2022:394.

19 The protection of the weaker party has been identified by Reich as one of the general principles of EU civil law: Norbert Reich, *General Principles of EU Civil Law* (Intersentia 2014) 37-38. Cf. Case C-432/05 *Unibet (London) Ltd and Unibet (International) Ltd v. Justitiekanslern* ECLI:EU:C:2007:163 and Case C-243/15 *Lesoochranárske zoskupenie VLK v. Obvodný úrad Trenčín* ECLI:EU:C:2016:838 as well which empowers national courts to ensure the effective judicial protection of EU law rights for EU citizens.

led the CJEU to endorse a more active approach for national courts in B2C cases.[20] The mere fact that an individual qualifies as a consumer is sufficient.[21]

3 Ex Officio Application and a More Active Court

The ex officio application of EU consumer protection legislation is a two-step approach. The court first investigates whether a term in a B2C contract, which is the subject of a dispute before it, falls within the scope of a consumer protection EU directive and, if it does, assesses whether such a term is compliant with the rules of that directive (as implemented in national legislation), provided that the court has available to it the necessary legal and factual elements to carry out this examination. The principle of hearing both sides – *audi alteram partem* – needs to be observed, not only for its sake but also to ensure that both parties have equal opportunity to bring forward their views. This constitutes another fundamental right, i.e. equality of arms. This is settled case law since *Pannon GSM Zrt. v. Erzsébet Sustikné Győrfi* and *VB Pénzügyi Lízing Zrt. v. Ferenc Schneider*.[22]

The duty to carry out the examination of necessary legal and factual elements arises when the factual and legal elements are available to the court. For some jurisdictions, that will be when parties have explicitly relied on these factual elements; for others, also when the factual elements somehow became part of the proceedings, because, for example, they were included by one of the parties in the case file, which was submitted to the court. As a general principle of civil procedure, the court applies the law to the facts that are presented to it by the litigating parties.[23] Over the past decades, there has been a shift towards a more active approach of courts, where courts, although not infringing upon the right of the parties to define the subject matter of the dispute, do ask for additional documents, reasons for not referring to certain factual elements in the case file and question the legal basis of the claim.[24] We would think that this practice is not contrary to fundamental principles of civil procedure, as it rebalances the civil procedure in such a way as to make it much more focused on the material conflict between the parties with courts seeking to do justice to both parties and acknowledging that governmental adjudication is funded out of the general resources. To the extent that the parties' right to a fair trial is respected, courts can find such a

20 Cf. Case C-110/14 *Horațiu Ovidiu Costea v. SC Volksbank România SA* [2015] ECLI:EU:C:2015:538.

21 A recent example of *ex officio* application concerning the Directive (EU) 2015/2302 on package travel can be found in Case C-83/22 *TukTuk Travel SL* [2023] ECLI:EU:C:2023:664.

22 Case C-243/08 *Pannon* (n 8); Case C-137/08 *VB Pénzügyi Lízing Zrt.* (n 8).

23 Beka (n 13) 79, with reference to (among others) Rolf Stürner, 'Procédure Civile et Culture Juridique' (2004) 4 Revue Internationale de Droit Comparé 797-824, in which the liberal underpinning of the adversarial principle is described.

24 A.G.F. Ancery, *Ambtshalve toepassing van EU-recht* (Kluwer 2012) 76-77.

new balance.[25] In the Netherlands, for example, the passivity of the courts has tended to reduce since 2002, for which a fundamental review of civil procedure rules, a shift in the thinking of the (public) function of civil procedures and the related costs, and court rulings have functioned as a catalyst.[26] Similar tendencies can also be identified in the civil procedural systems of other EU Member States.[27]

The case law of the CJEU had to be construed as allowing national courts to adopt a more active approach and fit within these principles of the civil procedure. EU consumer law should, for the purpose of the ex officio application of it, be considered as rules of public order,[28] which allows courts in most civil law systems (and theoretically in common law systems as well) to take on a more active role, beyond the ambit of the dispute. In a recent case,[29] the CJEU seems to expect national courts to apply inquiry powers to ensure it will receive the factual elements necessary to assess the fairness of potentially unfair contract terms.[30] In other words, a more active use of inquiry powers appears to be available to courts in civil law systems, although the extent to which the court uses these differs. The German *Frage- und Hinweispflicht* (Art. 139 Zivilprozessordnung (GZPO)) enables courts to take substantive control over the civil procedure by providing guidance to parties on material points that they overlooked, as long as the principles of inter partes proceedings are guaranteed. It is not a tool courts can use to conduct their own factual inquiry but a means to further debate on topics raised but not followed up on by the parties.[31] Although it enables courts to actively point the consumer towards overlooked aspects of consumer law, the German Supreme Court does not allow courts to use these powers to bring parties to claims or defences that have not yet been raised.[32]

French courts have similar powers in that they are not restricted to factual elements that parties have explicitly brought to their attention (Art. 7 *Code de la procédure civile* (French CPC)) and in that they can make active use of inquiry powers. Dutch courts

25 Such scaling is done by Jolowicz (J.A. Jolowicz, 'Adversarial and Inquisitorial Models of Civil Procedure' [2003] 52 International & Comparative Law Quarterly 281-295).

26 Cf. W.D.H. Asser, H.A. Groen, J.B.M. Vranken and I.N. Tzankova, *Uitgebalanceerd. Eindrapport Fundamentele herbezinning Nederlands Burgerlijk Procesrecht* (Boom 2006).

27 Cf. Beka (n 13) 313ff.

28 Which impression seems to arise from Case C-40/08 *Asturcom Telecomunicaciones* (n 9), where the CJEU considers the relevant consumer protection provisions equal to provisions from public order, and was reaffirmed in Case C-479/13 *Froukje Faber* (n 8). If an ex officio application is not allowed, even on public order grounds, national courts can still be obliged to ex officio apply consumer protection provisions, as shown by Case C-618/10 *Banco Español de Crédito* (n 8).

29 Joined Cases C-419/18 and C-483/18 *Profi Credit Polska* (n 8).

30 On this case and ex officio application of consumer law, in general, on which parts of this contribution are based as well: A.G.F. Ancery, 'Consumer Credit Contracts and *Ex Officio* Application: A Dutch Perspective' (2021) 4 Journal of European Consumer and Market Law 160-164.

31 Beka (n 13) 108 ff.

32 BGH 2 October 2003, BGHZ 156, 269. Cf. AC van Schaick, *Mr. C. Assers Handleiding tot de beoefening van het Nederlands Burgerlijk Recht. Procesrecht 2, Eerste aanleg* (Wolters Kluwer 2022) 93 as well.

cannot look beyond the ambit of the dispute but do have considerable inquiry powers to incentivise parties to substantiate missing factual elements. And, not unimportantly, parties are obliged to provide facts in accordance with the truth (*waarheidsplicht*; Art. 21 Dutch CCP). If they do not comply with this obligation, the court can take the measures it deems required.[33]

4 Procedural Agreements and Ex Officio Application of EU Consumer Law

The ex officio review of B2C contracts could add an extra layer to the discussion on the ex officio application of consumer law, as the review of such contracts could result in the conclusion that one or more contract terms infringe upon EU consumer law rules. Is a court obliged or permitted to take actions to mitigate such infringements without parties taking actions themselves?

If courts are allowed to make use of inquiry powers beyond the ambit of the dispute in order to determine whether a contract falls within the scope of a consumer protection EU directive, if courts can apply consumer-protective rules to these factual elements, then the next step could be that it could also disapply or annul terms of the contract that are non-compliant with EU consumer law. Given that the reason for the annulment would be non-compliance with *consumer protection* rules, the annulment would have to be to the benefit of the consumer.

The vast amount of CJEU case law, as mentioned in Section 2, is far from unnoticed in several European countries. It has, inter alia, drawn attention in the Netherlands from district courts, courts of appeal, the Supreme Court and scholars.[34] The Dutch courts of first instance have established a working group tasked with providing recommendations on the ex officio application of EU consumer law. The presumption at the heart of its recommendations is that Dutch courts are required to ex officio apply the full corpus of EU consumer law along the lines of the established case law of the CJEU (as discussed in Sections 2 and 3).[35] The working group has set out such ex officio

33 Cf. C.J.A. Seinen, 'De gevolgtrekking die hij geraden acht. Sancties op schending van de waarheidsplicht' (2014) 3 TCR 84-95.

34 E.g. District Court of Amsterdam, 11 November 2015, ECLI:NL:RBAMS:2015:7848, District Court Midden-Nederland, 21 June 2017, ECLI:NL:RBME:2017:2980, Court of Appeal Arnhem-Leeuwarden 10 September 2013, ECLI:NL:GHARL:2013:6635, Court of Appeal Den Bosch 29 August 2017, ECLI:NL:GHSE:2017:374, DSC 12 February 2016, ECLI:NL:HR:2016:236, NJ 2017/282 and DSC 26 February 2016, ECLI:NL:HR:2016:340, NJ 2017/214, H.J. Snijders, 'New developments in national rules of ex officio raising of points of community law by national courts' in A.S. Hartkamp, C.H. Sieburgh, L.A.D. Keus, J.S. Kortmann and M.H. Wissink (eds), *The influence of EU Law on National Private Law* (Kluwer 2014) 95-117, J. Hijma, *Algemene voorwaarden* (Wolters Kluwer 2016) 72-76 (nr. 44a-44b); Ancery (n 24).

35 Report *Ambtshalve toetsing III Herzien rapport van de redactieraad van het LOVCK&T* 10-16.

application in much detail. We will first address the recommendations of the Dutch working group and then address some possible procedural agreements and the impact that the case law on the ex officio application of EU consumer law might have on those agreements (Section 5).

Dutch courts are required to first consider whether EU consumer law is indeed applicable. It is, therefore, important to establish whether one of the contracting parties operates in the capacity of a consumer. Such capacity would usually be apparent from all the circumstances of the case, but if that is not the case, the working group advises the courts in default cases to assume that a natural person (usually the defendant) acts in the capacity of the consumer unless stated otherwise by the claimant.[36]

If it has been established that the case at hand concerns a B2C relationship, the court should consider whether there are relevant consumer protection provisions that might be applicable and that the consumer has not yet invoked. After all, the ex officio application presumes that a consumer has not invoked a relevant consumer protection provision. Indications that there might be a problematic balance between the parties, which could most likely be corrected by applying a consumer protection provision, would be a large amount that is being charged to the consumer and that cannot be explained by (the nature of) the contract or the application of a penalty clause.[37]

If a court suspects that there might be an imbalance between parties that needs to be corrected to benefit the consumer, it should start assessing whether the relevant facts are available. That does not mean that the parties should have referred to these facts or that they are already in the case file. The Supreme Court of the Netherlands requires courts to apply their inquiry powers in search of the facts to apply consumer protection provisions if they have reason to assume that a consumer protection provision should have been invoked by the consumer.[38] This goes well beyond what is standard practice in the Netherlands, where civil courts are generally required to remain within the ambit of the dispute unless there is a prevailing reason of public interest why they should do otherwise.[39]

The right to be heard should be applied in all cases, including default cases. That would mean that a claimant has the option to amend its claim or arguments following the court's intention to ex officio apply consumer law provisions. It also means that if a consumer appears in court and states that he or she refuses consumer law provisions to be applied, courts should refrain from such an application.[40]

The last step is the actual effectuation of the ex officio application. It is important to consider whether the agreement can remain without the to-be annulled or disapplied

36 Ibid., 20-21.
37 Ibid., 21-22.
38 [2013] ECLI:NL:HR:2013:691.
39 Cf. Arts. 24 and 149 Dutch CCP.
40 Report *Ambtshalve toetsing III Herzien rapport van de redactieraad van het LOVCK&T* 24-25.

term or whether the annulment or misapplication affects the remainder of the contract as well.

5 Some Procedural Agreements in More Detail

Parties can generally enter into a wide variety of procedural agreements, as set out in the introductory part. When these are entered into between consumers and professional parties, such agreements can become problematic because of existing consumer-protective EU directives and the need for courts to apply consumer-protective provisions ex officio. An example would be the jurisdiction clause in the terms of the contract between Sustikné Györfi and the Hungarian mobile telephone provider Pannon, which specified that potential conflicts needed to be settled by the court in the place of incorporation of Pannon. That required the consumer to have the case adjudicated by a court 275 km away from their hometown. The CJEU considered the following:

> that, in a contract concluded between a consumer and a seller or supplier within the meaning of the Directive, a term, drafted in advance by the seller or supplier – which was not subject to individual negotiation – the purpose of which is to confer jurisdiction in respect of all disputes arising under the contract on the court in the territorial jurisdiction of which the seller has his principal place of business, satisfies all the criteria necessary for it to be judged unfair for the purposes of the Directive.[41]

As per the settled case law of the Supreme Court of the Netherlands cited previously, such unfairness needs to be ex officio applied by the court, and if found unfair, the clause needs to be disregarded. That is in line with the advice of the Dutch working group that considers jurisdiction clauses in B2C contracts to the detriment of the consumer to be unfair terms.[42]

Another procedural agreement that could be problematic from an EU consumer law perspective is an arbitration clause, which requires consumers to have their disputes settled in arbitration proceedings instead of by a governmental court. These clauses are, to a large extent, considered unfair by the CJEU, although they could still be considered fair in case certain conditions are fulfilled[43] and are indeed considered unfair in the Netherlands unless the consumer is at liberty to opt for adjudication by a governmental

41 Case C-243/08 *Pannon* (n 8); Case C-137/08 *VB Pénzügyi Lízing* (n 8).

42 Report *Ambtshalve toetsing III – Herzien rapport van de redactieraad van het LOVCK&T* 25-26 and 30.

43 Cf. Case C-168/05 *Mostaza Claro* (n 9); Case C-40/08 *Asturcom Telecommunicaiones* (n 9).

court within one month after the professional party has indicated that it wants the conflict to be settled via an arbitration procedure.[44]

Procedural agreements that shift the burden of proof from the professional party to the consumer are also a type of agreement that can easily create an imbalance to the detriment of the consumer and is, therefore, a clause that is often considered problematic. An example of this is the *CA Consumer Finance SA v. Ingrid Bakkaus, Charline Bonato and Florian Bonato* case that led to a CJEU ruling in 2014. The consumers had signed a statement indicating that Consumer Finance SA fulfilled all its precontractual obligations, therefore de facto containing a shift in the burden of proof to the detriment of the consumer. The CJEU ruled as follows:

> It should, however, be stated that compliance with that principle would be undermined if the burden of proving the non-performance of the obligations laid down in Articles 5 and 8 of Directive 2008/48 lay with the consumer. The consumer does not have the means at his disposal to enable him to prove that the creditor, first, did not provide him with the information required under Article 5 of that directive and, secondly, did not check his creditworthiness.[45]

Although not a case on the EU Unfair Terms Directive, it can be noticed that the CJEU is quite vigilant when it comes to terms that create procedural imbalances between consumers and professional parties and that, therefore, might hamper the effectiveness of EU consumer-protective directives. National civil procedural law provisions often prohibit deviation from rules on the burden of proof to the detriment of the consumer. For example, Article 7:23 Dutch Civil Code provides for a presumption of deficiencies that arise within six months after a consumer sale to be present at the moment of sale, and deviations from this presumption are void (cf. Art. 7:6 (1) Dutch Civil Code).

Does this mean that procedural agreements are not at all possible when entered into in a B2C context? We think not as long as the rationale for the case law of the CJEU is kept in mind when agreeing on such terms. If the terms are intended to create a further imbalance between the consumer and the professional party (to the detriment of the consumer, of course), then it would most likely not be acceptable from a consumer protection perspective. However, if there are good and valid reasons for agreeing on a deviation from the generally applicable procedural regime, not creating a further imbalance but merely further streamlining the procedural regime, it might hold a stand. There would then be clauses that might be agreed to, although still to be approached with caution. An example of this is agreements on the applicable law, which

---

44 Art. 6:236(n) Dutch Civil Code.

45 Case C-339/13 *CA Consumer Finance SA v. Ingrid Bakkaus, Charline Bonato and Florian Bonato* [2014] ECLI:EU:C:2014:2464.

are not prohibited but can only be applied under the condition that consumers are informed that they are still entitled to the consumer protection as conferred on them by EU consumer law.[46]

6 Concluding Remarks

Procedural agreements come in various shapes and sizes. They can involve several types of procedural issues, varying from jurisdiction to evidence and appeals. If those agreements are entered into by a professional party and a consumer, European case law on ex officio application may be relevant. It is by no means excluded that such procedural agreements may be capable of being affected without the parties being able to rely on them in court. We see no reason why the CJEU's extensive case law would not also cover procedural agreements. That does not mean, however, that consumers and professional parties could never enter into such agreements but that careful thought should be given to restoring the procedural balance between consumers and professional parties and to respecting fundamental rights. In short, there must be sufficient and valid grounds for entering into such agreements, and it should not create a further imbalance to the detriment of the consumer.

If this European line in case law of the CJEU holds true, it could, at least in theory, also concern default cases to which consumers are parties. And it need not be limited to the first instance either. It is also argued that complaint boards, when dealing with European consumer law, are obliged to deal with the line of reasoning of the CJEU as well. It should be borne in mind, however, that this line of CJEU case law obviously applies only to the law of EU Member States and not outside it.

Will the applicability of this CJEU case law on procedural agreements lead to further Europeanisation of procedural law by the back door? That remains to be seen. The rationale of the Directive on general terms plays an important role in the CJEU's case law on ex officio application. Some harmonisation could be addressed via that link. Nevertheless, it will come down to national courts. Will national courts apply the CJEU's line of reasoning in more or less the same degree and with more or less the same intensity? Or will there be differences? That procedural agreement can fall under the regime of European case law on ex officio application seems clear to us.

46 Case C-191/15 *Verein für Konsumenteninformation v. Amazon EU Sàrl* [2016] ECLI:EU:C:2016:612.

International Commercial Courts: Drivers of Contractualisation, Hobby Horses of Politicians or Apocalyptic Riders of Civil Justice?

Wolfgang Hau

1 Introduction

Since ancient times, judges and courts have been dealing with controversies between merchants and/or business enterprises. As trade has almost always and everywhere been international, it is in the very nature of commercial disputes that such courts also hear cases with cross-border implications – and probably far more frequently than normal civil courts. A more recent development in the 21st century, however, is that some states are setting up specialised courts or court divisions for international commercial matters. The term 'international commercial courts' (ICCs) has become established for this phenomenon and is used here, although this can not only lead to confusion with the ICC (i.e. the International Chamber of Commerce) International Court of Arbitration but is also misleading: because the cases dealt with are 'international', not necessarily the laws applied, and the courts as such are not 'international' either but rather part of the respective national court system.[1]

In terms of the type of disputes dealt with, the parties involved and the usually very high amounts in dispute, ICCs target cases that would also principally lend themselves to commercial arbitration. Notwithstanding the different economic backgrounds of the various ICCs (see Section 2), to varying degrees, they can even be considered hybrids between state judiciary and international arbitration. The most obvious commonality is the strong emphasis on party autonomy and the flexible procedural design. This

1 Therefore, the topic here is not 'transnational commercial courts', although there is intensive discussion, particularly at the level of the European Union, as to whether the creation of 'European Commercial Courts' might make sense. While the European Parliament is clearly in favour of this project (European Parliament resolution of 13 December 2018 with recommendations to the Commission on expedited settlement of commercial disputes, OJ 2020 C 388, 692), the European Commission remains reserved. For support from an academic perspective, see Giesela Rühl, 'The Resolution of International Commercial Disputes – What Role (if any) for Continental Europe?' (2021) 115 American Journal of International Law 11, 15-16; Selina Domhan, *Internationale private Streitschlichtung: Impulse für die Errichtung eines Europäischen Handelsgerichts* (Duncker and Humblot 2022).

aspect makes a closer analysis particularly interesting with regard to the phenomenon of contractualisation (or 'consensualisation') of civil procedure, to which this book is devoted. The aim of this chapter is not to provide a comparative study on the procedural regimes of the various ICCs or to consider to what extent ICCs and arbitration tribunals are competitors or rather complements[2] but to examine by means of examples whether a degree of party autonomy is emerging that goes beyond what is known from litigation in ordinary state courts and is more in line with arbitration standards.[3] For this purpose, the UNCITRAL Model Law on International Commercial Arbitration[4] can be used as a yardstick, as it has been accepted around the world and may thus claim to reflect global consensus on key aspects of arbitration practice.

2 Landscape of International Commercial Courts

In recent years, a number of ICCs have been created in several states, either as stand-alone new courts or as mere divisions of existing courts,[5] and much has already been reported and discussed about this phenomenon.[6] However, this chapter will not be about

2 On this often-discussed question, see, for example, Quentin Loh, 'The Rise of International Commercial Courts – A Threat to Arbitration?' in Martin Gebauer, Thomas Klötzel and Rolf A. Schütze (eds), *Usus Atque Scientia – Festschrift für Roderich C. Thümmel zum 65. Geburtstag* (De Gruyter 2020) 501; Luca G. Radicati di Brozolo, 'Competition between Cross-Border Dispute Settlement Mechanisms: Domestic Courts, Arbitration and International Commercial Courts' in Christoph Benicke and Stefan Huber (eds), *National, International, Transnational: Harmonischer Dreiklang im Recht – Festschrift für Herbert Kronke zum 70. Geburtstag* (Gieseking 2020) 447, 455-457; Marta Requejo Isidro, 'International Commercial Courts in the Litigation Market' (2019) 9 International Journal of Procedural Law 4, 34-41; Dorothee Ruckteschler and Tanja Stooss, 'International Commercial Courts: A Superior Alternative to Arbitration?' (2019) 36 Journal of International Arbitration 431; Stephan Wilske, 'International Commercial Courts and Arbitration — Alternatives, Substitutes or Trojan Horse?' (2018) 11 Contemporary Asia Arbitration Journal 153.

3 For a similar approach, see Georgia Antonopoulou, 'The 'Arbitralization' of Courts: The Role of International Commercial Arbitration in the Establishment and the Procedural Design of International Commercial Courts' (2023) 14 Journal of International Dispute Settlement 328.

4 For the text of the UNCITRAL Model Law on International Commercial Arbitration 1985 (with amendments as adopted in 2006) and the Explanatory Report by the UNCITRAL Secretariat, see https://uncitral.un.org/en/texts/arbitration/modellaw/commercial_arbitration.

5 On both organisational models and their consequences under European Union law, see Pietro Ortolani and Bas van Zelst, 'International Commercial Courts and EU Law: Easing the Tension' (2023) 14 Journal of International Dispute Settlement 76.

6 Particularly interesting collections of country reports and comparative analyses can be found in the following books: Xandra Kramer and John Sorabji (eds), *International Business Courts: A European and Global Perspective* (Eleven 2019); Stavros Brekoulakis and Georgios Dimitropoulos (eds), *International Commercial Courts – The Future of Transnational Adjudication* (Cambridge University Press 2022); see also Man Yip and Giesela Rühl (eds), *New International Commercial Courts: A Comparative Perspective* (Intersentia 2024). The following German-language monographs should also be mentioned: Domhan (n 1) 62-82; Nicole Grohmann, *Internationalisierung der Handelsgerichtsbarkeit: Eine Frage des Managements* (Mohr Siebeck 2022); Adriaan den Hertog, *Große internationale Wirtschaftsstreitigkeiten und staatliche*

ICCs in general but specifically about the issue of contractualisation. For this purpose, it seems useful to distinguish between two constellations.[7]

On the one hand, there are countries that want to establish themselves as centres for international business activities, especially in the financial sector or as stock exchanges, and attract foreign investors and traders. Then the establishment of an ICC is simply part of the infrastructure that such states make available to potential market participants as a confidence-building measure. Examples include the Astana International Financial Centre (AIFC) in Kazakhstan, the Dubai International Financial Centre (DIFC) and the Qatar Financial Centre (QFC), each of which has at least one ICC (AIFC Court,[8] DIFC Courts,[9] Qatar International Court[10]). Similarly, the two new China International Commercial Courts[11] (CICC) are obviously intended to gain the confidence of foreign parties who are likely to have reservations about litigation in ordinary Chinese courts.[12]

On the other hand, some traditional industrialised countries, especially in Western Europe, have always had established court systems but now find themselves in an international competition for litigation business.[13] For reasons that are not always clear, such jurisdictions, especially since Brexit, are trying to attract some of the cases previously heard mainly in the London Commercial Court (LCC[14]). To this end, new

Gerichte im 21. Jahrhundert: Plädoyer für einen Commercial Court Germany (Nomos 2021); Bernhard Klose, *Justiz als Wirtschaftsfaktor: Rechtsfindung im Spannungsfeld von Effizienz und Planbarkeit* (Nomos 2020).

7 For a slightly different typology of ICCs, see Georgios Dimitropoulos, 'The Design of International Commercial Courts: From Organizational Hybridity to Functional Interoperability' in Brekoulakis and Dimitropoulos (n 6) 254, who proposes to distinguish between 'special economic zone courts', 'stand-alone international commercial courts' and 'international chambers within ordinary courts'.

8 Homepage: https://court.aifc.kz. Cf. Lord Woolf CH and Christopher Campbell-Holt, 'The Emergence of International Commercial Courts and Dispute Resolution Centres in Frontier Markets: A Perspective from Kazakhstan' in Brekoulakis and Dimitropoulos (n 6) 489; Nicolás Zambrana-Tévar, 'The Court of the Astana International Financial Center in the Wake of Its Predecessor' (2019) 13 Erasmus Law Review 122.

9 Homepage: www.difccourts.ae. Cf. Tareq Na'el Al-Tawil and Hassan Younies, 'DIFC: Courts of the Future' in Kramer and Sorabji (n 6) 205.

10 Homepage: www.qicdrc.gov.qa. Cf. Andrew Dahdal, 'International Commercial Courts: The Qatari Experience' in Kramer and Sorabji (n 6) 235.

11 Homepage: https://cicc.court.gov.cn. Cf. Julien Chaisse and Xu Qian, 'The China International Commercial Court: Architecture, Pitfalls and Promises' in Brekoulakis and Dimitropoulos (n 6) 468; David Holloway, 'The New Chinese International Commercial Court and the Future of Dispute Resolution in the Belt and Road Initiative' in Lei Chen and André Janssen (eds), *Dispute Resolution in China, Europe and World* (Springer 2020) 51; Ning Zhao, 'The CICC: An Endeavour towards the Internationalization and Modernization of Chinese Courts' in Kramer and Sorabji (n 6) 159.

12 Cf. Wei Cai and Andrew Godwin, 'Challenges and Opportunities for the China International Commercial Court' (2019) 68 International & Comparative Law Quarterly 869, 902 ('improve the credibility of the judicial system').

13 For an overview of the situation in Europe, see Sonja A. Kruisinga, 'Commercial Courts in the Netherlands, Belgium, France and Germany: Salient Features and Challenges' (2019) 39 Praxis des Internationalen Privat- und Verfahrensrechts 277; Marieke Witkamp, 'Internationalizing Domestic Courts in Europe: A Comparative Analysis on Procedure, Function, Organization' in Brekoulakis and Dimitropoulos (n 6) 278.

14 Homepage: www.gov.uk/courts-tribunals/commercial-court.

divisions of existing courts are being set up specifically for international commercial matters, with English as the working language. Prominent examples of such 'forum selling' are the Netherlands Commercial Court (NCC District Court and NCC Court of Appeal),[15] the International Chamber of the Commercial Court in Paris (ICCP) and, more recently, the International Chamber of the Court of Appeal in Paris (ICCP-CA).[16] A notable and apparently successful example outside Europe is the Singapore International Commercial Court (SICC),[17] whose special feature is that it emerged not from the traditional court system but as an extension of the already existing arbitration hub.

However, there are not only success stories.[18] In Belgium, the Brussels International Business Court (BIBC), despite being met with great expectations, is considered a failure.[19] In Germany, although there are already specialised court divisions for international cases in some states (*Bundesländer*),[20] a Federal legislative reform to finally create an ICC worthy of the name has still not materialised. In fact, the Federal Government (*Bundesregierung*) has not adopted the proposals that have been repeatedly put forward by the Federal Council (*Bundesrat*) for many years[21] but has now presented

---

15 Homepage: www.rechtspraak.nl/English/NCC. Cf. Eddy Bauw, 'Commercial Litigation in Europe in Transformation: The Case of the Netherlands Commercial Court' (2019) 13 Erasmus Law Review 15; Harriët Schelhaas, 'The Brand New Netherlands Commercial Court: A Positive Development?' in Kramer and Sorabji (n 6) 45; Jeroen van der Weide, 'The Netherlands Commercial Court (NCC): Its Challenges and Perspectives' in Chen and Janssen (n 11) 81.

16 Homepages: www.tribunal-de-commerce-de-paris.fr/en/home and www.cours-appel.justice.fr/paris/presentation-generale-ccip-ca-iccp-ca. Cf. Alexandre Biard, 'International Commercial Courts in France: Innovation without Revolution?' (2019) 13 Erasmus Law Review 24; Emmanuel Jeuland, 'The International Chambers of Paris: A Gaul Village' in Kramer and Sorabji (n 6) 65.

17 Homepage: www.sicc.gov.sg. Cf. Man Yip, 'The Singapore International Commercial Court: The Future of Litigation?' in Kramer and Sorabji (n 6) 129.

18 There is certainly no recipe for success, but there are some minimum requirements, which Hugh Mercer ('The English Commercial Court' (2020) Zeitschrift für Internationales Wirtschaftsrecht 200, 202) aptly names: 'Dispute resolution is an eco-system which requires at least the following: a critical mass of potential clients; judges of very high legal calibre but with a commercial mindset; a mix of available courts and arbitration; a flexible and adaptable legal profession serving the court; rules of procedure in constant evolution in the search for best practice; all the acteurs de la justice working together.' See also Erlis Themeli, 'International Commercial Courts Competition in Europe: A Litigation Experience Approach' in Kramer and Sorabji (n 6) 273.

19 On the background and reasons, see Geert van Calster, 'The Brussels International Business Court: A Carrot Sunk by Caviar' in Kramer and Sorabji (n 6) 107; Erik Peetermans and Philippe Lambrecht, 'The Brussels International Business Court: Initial Overview and Analysis' (2019) 13 Erasmus Law Review 42.

20 Note, for example, the recent field report from Stuttgart (Baden-Württemberg) by Graf von Westphalen, 'Da verändert sich was – Ein Jahr "Commercial Court" in Stuttgart' (2022) 7 Zeitschrift für Internationales Wirtschaftsrecht 96.

21 Latest attempt: Federal Council's Draft of 27 April 2022 on a Law to Strengthen the Courts in Commercial Disputes (Bundesratsentwurf für ein Gesetz zur Stärkung der Gerichte in Wirtschaftsstreitigkeiten), Bundestags-Drucksache 20/1549. On this draft, see, on the one hand, Hermann Hoffmann, 'Stärkung der Gerichte in Internationalen Wirtschaftsstreitigkeiten' (2022) 55 Zeitschrift für Rechtspolitik 108, and, on the other hand, clearly more sceptical, Thomas Riehm and Quirin Thomas 'Specialized Commercial Courts and Their Role in Cross-Border Litigation' in Martin Schmidt-Kessel (ed), *German National*

its own (and probably more promising) draft bill,[22] which differs considerably from the Federal Council's plans in some respects. Finally, it is remarkable that initiatives to create an ICC have not yet been taken up at all in, for example, the USA or Australia.[23]

3 Choice of Court

3.1 *Consensual Foundation of Court Activity*

Typically, the activity of an ICC requires an agreement between the parties. This is particularly important in countries with an established court system where ordinary courts conduct proceedings in accordance with detailed rules in the national language concerned. If there is a deviation from this in the sense that the case is to be heard by a special court or court division (the ICC) applying special procedural rules and a different language, this requires a justification, which can, in principle, be seen in both parties' consent. It is more of a mere technical question whether this consensus was reached by the parties before the commencement of the proceedings[24] or whether the plaintiff turned to the ICC on its own motion and the defendant then submitted to the proceedings before that court.

Reports on the 21st International Congress of Comparative Law (Mohr Siebeck 2022) 673, 701-704, remarking that 'perhaps in the end it boils down to wanting to show that Germany is part of the movement to set up International Commercial Courts and thus has its finger on the pulse of times'. For accounts of earlier versions of the draft in the English language, see Burkhard Hess and Timon Boerner, 'Chambers for International Commercial Disputes in Germany: The State of Affairs' (2019) 13 Erasmus Law Review 33; Gerhard Wagner and Arvid Arntz, 'Commercial Courts in Germany' in Chen and Janssen (n 11) 3.

22 Federal Government Draft of 6 October 2023 of a Law to Strengthen Germany as a Litigation Centre by Introducing Commercial Courts and English as a Court Language in Civil Litigation (Act to Strengthen Germany as a Centre of Justice) (Entwurf der Bundesregierung vom 6. Oktober 2023 eines Gesetzes zur Stärkung des Justizstandortes Deutschland durch Einführung von Commercial Courts und der Gerichtssprache Englisch in der Zivilgerichtsbarkeit [Justizstandort-Stärkungsgesetz]), Bundestags-Drucksache 20/8649. On this draft, see Markus Burianski and Lisa Fleckenstein, 'Commercial Courts und Schiedsverfahrensreform: Gelingt die Aufholjagd zugunsten des Justizstandorts Deutschland?' (2023) 56 Zeitschrift für Rechtspolitik 162; Hannah Eckhoff, Leane Meyer and Paul Schiering, 'Die Attraktivität Deutschlands als Forum internationaler Streitbeilegung' (2023) Recht der Internationalen Wirtschaft 804; Hilmar Raeschke-Kessler, 'Von der Schieflage zum ausbalancierten System – Schiedsgerichte und Commercial Courts' (2023) 76 Neue Juristische Wochenschrift 3558.

23 Cf. S.I. Strong, 'International Commercial Courts in the United States and Australia: Possible, Probable, Preferable?' (2021) 115 American Journal of International Law 28.

24 If there is a contractual relationship between the parties and a common willingness to invoke an ICC in the event of a dispute, it certainly makes sense in terms of an early forum planning to already include a corresponding clause in the contract.

The detailed requirements for a case to be accepted by the ICC depend on the national procedural law concerned.[25] No provisions in this regard can be derived from international treaties and European law: Article 5 of the 2005 Hague Convention[26] or Article 25 Brussels Ibis Regulation,[27] for example, stipulate the conditions under which the parties may conclude a choice of forum agreement. However, these provisions only concern the international jurisdiction of the forum state and, depending on the wording of the parties' agreement, local jurisdiction within that state. In contrast, they do not regulate the conditions under which the subject matter jurisdiction of a special court or a court division is given.[28] For instance, if the parties wish to bring their case before the NCC, it is not sufficient to agree on the jurisdiction of the Amsterdam District Court under Article 25(1) Brussels Ibis Regulation, even though, technically speaking, the NCC is only a division of that court.[29] Although it might be said that the activity of an ICC is based on a 'jurisdiction agreement',[30] it is important to keep in mind that different formal requirements may apply: An explicit written agreement of the parties is often required in order to bring the case before an ICC,[31] whereas for an agreement to confer international jurisdiction on the forum state under Article 25(1) Brussels Ibis Regulation, it is sufficient if this agreement is merely evidenced in writing or in a form which accords with practices that the parties have established between themselves.[32]

---

25 For an instructive overview, see Janet Walker, 'A Comparative Perspective on International Commercial Courts: Jurisdiction, Applicable Law and Enforcement of Judgments' in Brekoulakis and Dimitropoulos (n 6) 128-132 (both parties choose the court), 132-135 (defendants accepts the plaintiff's choice).

26 Convention of 30 June 2005 on Choice of Court Agreements.

27 Regulation (EU) No 1215/2012 of 12 December 2012 on jurisdiction and the recognition and enforcement of judgments in civil and commercial matters (2012) OJ L351/1.

28 On this aspect in the context of the 2005 Hague Convention, see Art. 5(3) ('the preceding paragraphs shall not affect rules (a) on jurisdiction related to subject matter or to the value of the claim; (b) on the internal allocation of jurisdiction among the courts of a Contracting State') and the comments on this in the Explanatory Report by Trevor Hartley and Masato Dogauchi, para. 135. As regards Brussels Ibis, see Ulrich Magnus and Peter Mankowski, *Brussels Ibis Regulation* (Sellier, 2nd edition 2023), Art. 25, para. 166c.

29 For the situation in the Netherlands and further examples from other jurisdictions, see Eva Lein, 'Jurisdiction and Choice of Court Clauses in Favour of International Commercial Courts' in Brekoulakis and Dimitropoulos (n 6) 158, 167-171. The NCC model clause can be found here www.rechtspraak.nl/English/NCC/Pages/clause.aspx.

30 Cf, for example, in Man Yip, 'The Battle for Jurisdiction through Jurisdictional Requirements: Comparing the Commercial Court of England and Wales, the Singapore International Commercial Court and the Chinese International Commercial Court' in Brekoulakis and Dimitropoulos (n 6) 197.

31 See, for example, Art. 1.3.1(d) NCC Rules 2020, www.rechtspraak.nl/SiteCollectionDocuments/NCC-Rules-second-edition.pdf which requires that 'the parties to the proceedings have expressly agreed in writing for proceedings to be before the NCC District Court in English'.

32 For a closer analysis of such differences, see Georgia Antonopoulou, 'Requirements upon Agreements in Favour of the NCC and the German Chambers – Clashing with the Brussels Ibis Regulation?' (2019) 13 Erasmus Law Review 56.

3.2 Party Autonomy with Regard to Admissible Cases

The types of disputes for which a state makes its ICC available are related to the purpose of establishing such a court (see above Section 2): If a state is primarily concerned with promoting its own national economy as an attractive business location, it will only admit cases that have a sufficient connection to the country. This is true, for example, for the CICC, which can only take on the case if there is not only an agreement between the parties but also an actual connection to China.[33]

On the other hand, if a state aims to attract litigation business as such, it will define the group of admissible cases *ratione personae* and *ratione materiae* much more generously. Singapore goes particularly far in this respect: in principle, the SICC can hear and try a case if there is a written 'jurisdiction agreement' and the case is of an 'international and commercial nature' (SICC Rules 2021 Order 2 Rule 1(1)). However, for being international in nature, it is sufficient that the parties have expressly agreed that the subject matter of the action relates to more than one state (Order 2 Rule 1(3)(a)(ii)). This provision corresponds almost verbatim to Article 1(3)(c) UNCITRAL Model Law. Furthermore, parties are also free to agree that the subject matter of the action is commercial in nature (Order 2 Rule 1(3)(b)(iii)). In this respect, Singapore goes even further than the UNCITRAL Model Law, which recommends a generous interpretation of the term 'commercial' but does not explicitly take into account the parties' wishes.[34]

3.3 Party Autonomy with Regard to the Composition of the Court

It has already been pointed out that it is not the ICCs that are 'international' but typically the matters they deal with. However, some new ICCs, especially in Asia, have a genuinely international bench, including judges from other jurisdictions who have already completed a judicial career there and who are, therefore, particularly experienced.[35] It is important, however, to bear in mind that the preferences of the parties may differ:

33 Art. 34 Civil Procedure Law of the People's Republic of China (Revised in 2017): 'The parties to a contractual dispute or any other property dispute may agree in writing to be subject to the jurisdiction of the people's court at the place having connection with the dispute, such as where the defendant is domiciled, where the contract is performed, where the contract is signed, where the plaintiff is domiciled or where the subject matter is located, etc.'

34 See footnote 2 to Article 1 and the Explanatory Report by the UNCITRAL Secretariat, para. 12.

35 For illustrative examples, in particular, on the career paths of retired English judges in foreign ICCs, see Christopher Grout and William Blair, 'The Role of International Commercial Courts in Commercial Dispute Resolution' in Brekoulakis and Dimitropoulos (n 6) 29, 41-42; Alyssa S. King and Pamela K. Bookman, 'Traveling Judges' (2022) 116 American Journal of International Law 477; Anselmo Reyes, 'The SICC, International Judges and International Commercial Dispute Resolution' in Anna Dziedzic and Simon Young (eds), *The Cambridge Handbook of Foreign Judges on Domestic Courts* (Cambridge Univerity Press 2023) ch. 5.

sometimes, a judge's experience with cross-border disputes is particularly important, while sometimes expertise in a very specific area of law seems more valuable.[36] This leads to the question of whether the parties can be allowed to select their judges, as in the field of international commercial arbitration[37] – an idea that would be inconceivable in an ordinary state court.

As far as can be seen, party autonomy does not extend to the composition of the bench in ICCs either, so it falls short in comparison to arbitration. In Germany, for example, it is argued that constitutional law precludes a rule that would leave the parties free to choose among the professional and lay judges of the court or at least to determine which chamber should decide their case.[38] Nevertheless, there are certain peculiarities compared to standard procedural law: according to the recent drafts, the parties can agree that if their case exceeds a certain amount in dispute, it will be heard directly by a higher regional court, which normally only sits as a court of appeal. This, at least indirectly, gives the parties some leeway when it comes to choosing the judges responsible for their dispute.

4 Procedural Framework

4.1 *Arbitration as a Model*

The leitmotiv of procedural design in international commercial arbitration is laid down in Article 19(1) of the UNCITRAL Model Law: 'Subject to the provisions of this Law, the parties are free to agree on the procedure to be followed by the arbitral tribunal in conducting the proceedings.' As the Explanatory Report points out, autonomy of the parties in determining the rules of procedure is of special importance in international cases since it allows the parties to select or tailor the rules according to their specific wishes and needs, unimpeded by traditional and possibly conflicting domestic concepts, thus obviating the […] risk of frustration or surprise.[39]

If state courts want to prove themselves to be serious competitors to arbitration by setting up ICCs, they will have to offer their potential 'customers' more than good

36 For general observations on the varying degrees of specialisation in ICCs, cf. Marta Requejo Isidro, 'International Commercial Courts: Specialised Courts?' in Xandra Kramer, Alexandre Biard, Jos Hoevenaars and Erlis Themeli (eds), *New Pathways to Civil Justice in Europe: Challenges of Access to Justice* (Springer 2021) 257.

37 See Art. 10(1) and Art. 11(2) UNCITRAL Model Law.

38 On this discussion, see Grohmann (n 6) 350-353; Riehm and Thomas (n 21) 685-686.

39 Explanatory Report by the UNCITRAL Secretariat, para. 36.

technical equipment[40] and the possibility to hear cases in English:[41] since the Covid pandemic, even in normal state courts, the IT infrastructure has been improved in many countries,[42] and the obligation to use only the official language in court no longer seems self-evident.[43] Therefore, it is understood as a selling point of the ICCs that their organization and procedure show flexibility in ways that are more characteristic of arbitration in allowing greater space to party autonomy in the dispute resolution process than in the regular court setting.[44]

4.2 *Flexibility as an End in Itself?*

The question arises as to how far national legislatures will be willing to give parties a say in the design of the procedure before ICCs. In this respect, Belgium went particularly far with its 2018 draft for the BIBC.[45] However, it is noteworthy that this initiative was met with much criticism and probably failed precisely because it wanted to open up too much freedom for the parties and push back the applicability of the Belgian procedural law too far.[46] In Belgium, political reasons, in particular, suspicion against favouring rich litigants, may ultimately have been the decisive factor: there were considerable reservations about the creation of a 'caviar court', and this has sealed BIBC's fate for the time being.[47]

But one can also ask, in general, whether too much flexibility regarding the procedural framework is attractive for the 'demand side' of ICCs: after all, litigants usually do not want a particularly creative procedure, but, above all, an appropriate decision on the merits.[48] In many cases, this can probably be achieved fastest if the court

40 On this aspect, see Pietro Ortolani, 'The Use of Technology at International Commercial Courts' in Brekoulakis and Dimitropoulos (n 6) 335.

41 Cf. Mercer (n 18): 'the notion that setting up a court in the English language makes an international commercial court is a rather limited and inadequate perspective'.

42 For instructive country-reports on this development, see Bart Krans and Anna Nylund (eds), *Civil Courts Coping with Covid-19* (Eleven 2021).

43 Cf. Rule 19 ELI/UNIDROIT Model European Rules of Civil Procedure (MERCP): 'Proceedings, including documents and oral communications, must as a general rule be in a language of the court. The court may permit all or part of the proceedings to be conducted in other languages where doing that would not prejudice the parties or the right to a public hearing.'

44 Dimitropoulos (n 7) 269. See also Georgia Antonopoulou, 'Procedure before International Commercial Courts and Ordinary Courts: A Comparative Perspective' in Brekoulakis and Dimitropoulos (n 6) 421, 439: 'arbitration features' that distinguish ICCs from ordinary courts.

45 For details, see Peetermans and Lambrecht (n 19) 52-54.

46 See Antonopoulou (n 44) 441-442.

47 On this discussion, cf. van Calster (n 19) 113-114.

48 Cf. Michael Patchett-Joyce, 'Private Autonomy in International Commercial Dispute Resolution: International Commercial Arbitration and International Commercial Courts' in Brekoulakis and Dimitropoulos (n 6) 388, 396-397: 'Business is business; disputes are a sideshow. Business also craves certainty. It wants laws that are clear, intelligible and uniformly applied. It wants those mechanisms to

and attorneys simply apply the standard procedural rules with which they are most familiar. The energy that would be spent on setting modified rules will often be better spent in negotiating a compromise on the substance of the dispute. For lawyers, in particular, procedural routine means reliability and thus minimisation of liability risks. It therefore seems sensible for the ICCs in France and the Netherlands, for example, to apply a set of rules that are somewhat more flexible than standard procedural law, but pre-formulated.[49]

4.3 *Party Autonomy with Regard to Evidence Rules*

It is fair to assume that practitioners – both judges and lawyers – typically see the greatest need for more flexibility vis-à-vis standard procedural law and the greatest potential for saving time and costs in the field of evidence. The ICC rules already take this into account by opening up possibilities that the normal procedural law of the forum may not provide for but which are common in other legal systems and do not meet with any fundamental constitutional concerns. Examples of this are the cross-examination of witnesses and experts or the complete recording of testimonies.

In some states, however, more specific evidentiary agreements play an important role. Article 8.2 of the 2020 NCC Rules,[50] for example, validates an agreement between the parties by which they elect to depart from the statutory rules of evidence, provided that such an evidentiary agreement is submitted to the court early and does not concern facts to which the law attaches consequences that are beyond the parties' autonomy. The German Federal Council's draft law proposes the following rule: The parties may, by express written agreement, make binding provisions for the court on the distribution of the burden of proof, on the need for evidence and on the limitation to certain means of evidence. Guidelines for the court on the assessment of evidence, in particular on the standard of proof, are excluded.[51]

At first glance, this sounds like a sensible balance between party autonomy, on the one hand, and the conformation of procedural minimum standards, on the other. Nevertheless, the proposal is not entirely unproblematic. In particular, one must not forget that the question of the extent to which the parties can influence the burden of proof by agreement is not decided by the *lex fori* but by the *lex causae*. In the EU, this

---

be good (reliable), cheap (i.e. cost-effective) and quick (in relative terms). It may also want to protect legitimate commercial confidences. It wants effective enforcement of decisions made (either awards or judgments). In short, business wants to dispose of disputes – including international disputes – as quickly, cheaply and effectively as possible.'

49 On the situation in France and the Netherlands, see Witkamp (n 13) 290-293.

50 See 2020 NCC Rules (n 31).

51 Federal Council's (n 21) draft version of Section 284(3) Code of Civil Procedure.

follows from Article 18(1) of the Rome I Regulation[52] and Article 22(1) of the Rome II Regulation,[53] which are binding on the national legislature.

4.4 Public Proceedings versus in Camera Proceedings

In state courts, at least in principle, hearings are held in public, and court decisions, including the reasoning, are announced in public.[54] Against this background, confidentiality is an important reason that typically speaks in favour of arbitration from the perspective of many parties: it is obvious that companies in dispute shy away from disclosing business secrets and having their reputation tarnished by media reports.

On the other hand, public proceedings are of great importance for democracy and the rule of law: judges, unlike arbitrators, have the function not only of deciding individual disputes but also of serving the development of the law by means of publishing judgments.[55] When it comes to the demand for confidentiality, the legislature must, therefore, balance conflicting interests, and the outcome must not depend solely on the wishes of the parties.[56] When a state sets up an ICC, it should not simply be a matter of competing with private arbitration institutions but of ensuring its own courts' influence on important areas of commercial law. Of course, the state cannot force anyone to take legal action, but when a party turns to the state courts, it should not be up to the plaintiff or the parties to decide whether it makes sense for a public judgment to be issued in order to set a precedent. Where, exceptionally, there are convincing reasons for proceedings in camera, these reasons should be taken into account regardless of whether the procedure takes place before an ICC or an ordinary court. Preferential treatment of ICCs and their 'customers' can hardly be justified.

4.5 Appeals

It is often claimed that arbitration proceedings can be concluded more quickly than proceedings before state courts. This may be true on average but is not least due to the fact that there are usually no appeal mechanisms within arbitration (but possibly the

52 Regulation (EC) No 593/2008 of 17 June 2008 on the law applicable to contractual obligations (Rome I) [2008] OJ L177/6.

53 Regulation (EC) No 864/2007 of 11 July 2007 on the law applicable to non-contractual obligations (Rome II) [2007] OJ L199/40.

54 See, for example, Rule 17 MERCP (n 43).

55 Cf. Patchett-Joyce (n 48) 404: 'It is in a court's DNA to put legal reasoning in the public domain whereas arbitral tribunals are hardwired to keep such analysis for the parties' eyes only.'

56 See, for example, Gerhard Wagner, *Rechtsstandort Deutschland im Wettbewerb: Impulse für Justiz und Schiedsgerichtsbarkeit* (C.H. Beck 2017) 226-228.

right of a party to challenge the award before a state court). In some ICCs, which are designed as mere divisions of courts of first instance, there is a counterpart also in the second instance: noteworthy are the Netherlands Commercial Court of Appeal and the International Chamber of the Paris Court of Appeal. This seems consistent, considering that the ICCs are part of the national court system and that it is the task of the higher courts to ensure uniformity of judgments. However, it also remains the case that, just as in ordinary proceedings, the parties may waive their right to appeal against the judgment of an ICC.[57]

5 Recognition and Enforcement

Basically, one would think that enforcement has no particular significance for the topic at hand: if the activity of the ICC is based on an agreement of both parties, one may expect that an amicable solution will also be reached on the merits, or that if a judgement is given, it will be followed voluntarily. Nevertheless, the commitment of the parties naturally depends on the ICC having the authority to issue a binding and, if necessary, enforceable decision. In this respect, enforceability outside the forum state of the ICC is important because the parties often will not have any enforceable assets there. Moreover, it will be relevant for them that the judgment is also recognised in other jurisdictions.

In terms of quasi-worldwide recognition and enforcement, arbitration has an enormous head start thanks to the New York Convention.[58] But judgments of ICCs whose jurisdiction is based on a choice of forum agreement can also hope for wide acceptance today: be it under European law, bilateral or multilateral conventions or autonomous national rules.[59] It is remarkable, however, that private autonomy can prove to be an obstacle to recognition and enforcement. For example, as already mentioned, in Singapore parties are allowed to contractually determine whether their case is 'international' and 'commercial in nature' and can thus be decided by the SICC. However, this does not ensure that the decision of the SICC is to be recognised and enforced in other contracting states to the 2005 Hague Convention:[60] for Article 1 of the Convention determines, according to autonomous standards and without regard to the will of the parties, whether its scope of application is open.[61] Furthermore, it is at least theoretically conceivable that party autonomy in the proceedings before an ICC was so

57 On the requirements for a waiver of the right to appeal, in general, cf. Rule 154 MERCP (n 43).

58 New York Arbitration Convention of 10 June 1958 on the Recognition and Enforcement of Foreign Arbitral Awards: www.newyorkconvention.org.

59 For overviews, see Anselmo Reyes and Kevin Tan, 'Recognition and Enforcement of International Commercial Court Judgments' in Chen and Janssen (n 11) 31; Walker (n 25) 147-156.

60 See n 26.

61 Antonopoulou (n 44) 424, also points to this conflict.

extensive that the courts of other states refuse recognition and enforcement because they assume that the ICC did not act as a 'court' but as a mere ADR institution or even that the proceedings before the ICC were not in accordance with the rule of law and therefore do not comply with public policy.

Against this background, it may be attractive to give the judgment creditor the opportunity to enforce its success by relying on well-established arbitration mechanisms. The Dubai International Financial Centre model, which allows a judgment of its court under certain preconditions to be converted into an arbitral award, seems to be particularly innovative in this respect.[62]

6 Effects on Non-Consenting Parties

Complex commercial cross-border cases often involve more than just the two parties to the original contract from which the dispute arose. As the decision-making power of an arbitral tribunal is based solely on the consensus of the parties, it traditionally causes considerable problems in the field of arbitration to include third parties in the proceedings who have not signed an arbitration agreement.[63]

Apparently, legislation in some states assumes that such problems do not exist if an ICC, rather than an arbitral tribunal, handles the case: The ICC's power to join a third party is imputed under the same rules as those which apply to ordinary state courts when they hear cases under general procedural rules and in the language of the state.[64] This position seems doubtful, however, if it means that a joined but non-consenting third party has to accept all the consensual peculiarities that apply in proceedings before the ICC.[65] Therefore, it falls short, for example, if the recent German drafts allow third parties to insist on a German translation of the third-party notice if they do not have sufficient knowledge of English, but then, if the translation is provided, do not grant any special protection of the third parties in the further proceedings. In contrast, Dutch law is much more willing to give due consideration to the interests of a non-

62 Cf. Amended DIFC Courts Practice Direction No 2 of 2015 – Referral of Judgment Payment Disputes to Arbitration: 'If parties who have submitted (or have agreed to submit) to (or are bound by) the jurisdiction of the DIFC Courts wish further to agree that any dispute arising out of or in connection with the non-payment of any money judgment given by the DIFC Courts may, at the option of the judgment creditor (as defined below), be referred to arbitration under the Arbitration Rules of the DIFC-LCIA Arbitration Centre, they may to that end adopt an arbitration clause in the terms of the recommended arbitration agreement set out below by reference to the Referral Criteria as defined.' For details, see Antonopoulou (n 44) 442-444.

63 Cf. Radicati di Brozolo (n 2) 456: 'one of arbitration's most obvious weaknesses'.

64 On such provisions, see Walker (n 25) 135-138.

65 For a critical analysis, see Drossos Stamboulakis and Blake Crook, 'Joinder of Non-Consenting Parties: The Singapore International Commercial Court Approach Meets Transnational Recognition and Enforcement' (2019) 13 Erasmus Law Review 98.

consenting third party.[66] One should always bear in mind that in ICC proceedings, as in arbitration, the will of the parties cannot, in principle, affect the procedural rights of a third party who has not voluntarily submitted to the procedure with its special rules of play. Thus, there are definitely limits to contractualisation, even before the ICCs.

7 Conclusion

The emergence of ICCs is a fascinating phenomenon because it proves that states are willing to learn from arbitration. In principle, open-mindedness towards innovation is to be welcomed, especially if it is accompanied by a willingness to invest in the infrastructure of the courts. ICCs can be seen as a field of procedural experimentation where practitioners and academics explore which new features prove useful and what conclusions can be drawn for litigation before ordinary national courts. In this respect, the new catchphrase 'arbitralisation of courts' is just as unhelpful as the earlier warnings against a 'judicialisation of arbitration'.

However, there are limits, not only in terms of transferability of the results to general procedural law but also already for the design of ICC regimes: ICCs are, after all, state courts to which the general constitutional requirements apply, and this inevitably restricts the autonomy that parties may wish for. Consequently, the yardstick for establishing and designing an ICC should not be solely whether it meets the needs of the 'demand side', i.e. potential parties and their lawyers, but whether it succeeds in ensuring an appropriate balance between flexibility and the rule of law. This may sound self-evident, but it shall nevertheless be recalled here, especially since there is a risk that states may be too willing to make concessions precisely because they see themselves in an obscure competition with other jurisdictions.[67] While it may make sense to conceive

66 See Art. 2.2.2 of the NCC Rules (n 31): 'If a third party, by motion and with the court's permission, is added in the action as a claimant or a defendant, the third party is bound by the other parties' agreement in respect of the language of the proceedings. This does not apply in the event of a claim for contribution or indemnity, or where a third party is given notice under Art. 118 CCP, or where a third party has intervened. The court will only allow a party to be added to the action for contribution or indemnity, or under Art. 118 CCP, or as an intervening party, where the party to be added has consented in writing to English being the language of the proceedings, or where the other parties agree that the entire action will be dealt with in Dutch.' For further details, see den Hertog (n 6) 122-123, 169-170.

67 The questionable basis for the discussion about this alleged competition between national court systems becomes apparent when it is seriously pointed out that attracting more proceedings is also about strengthening the gastronomy and hotel industry; this argument was mentioned, for example, by Hermann Hoffmann, *Kammern für internationale Handelssachen: Eine juristisch-ökonomische Untersuchung zu effektiven Justizdienstleistungen im Außenhandel* (Nomos 2011) 157. Of course, this reasoning is proven invalid given that it is a significant competitive advantage for an ICC to offer online hearings, thus saving the parties and lawyers time-consuming and cost-intensive journeys to the court.

of ICCs as a forward-looking product, arbitration must not unquestioningly become the new benchmark for the judiciary if one does not want to risk selling out civil justice.

Moreover, states must be aware that their courts, unlike arbitral tribunals, not only have to decide individual cases but also have an important role in confirming and developing the entire legal system. For society, an adequate dispute resolution system for standard cases is far more significant than first-class adjudication of relatively few cross-border cases with enormously high amounts in dispute in favour of parties who normally also have access to arbitration. The point is not to stir up envy[68] but to ask the legitimate question of whether the financial means and human resources that a successful ICC requires would be better invested in the infrastructure and judiciary of civil justice, in general.[69]

Insofar as a sober cost-benefit calculation shows that ICCs are but an expensive legal prestige object, basically a hobby horse for some politicians and senior judges, they are a luxury that should be dispensed with. The same applies to an ICC, which even makes a profit through high court fees but whose attractiveness is essentially based on the confidentiality of the proceedings, so that it fails as an effective instrument for the further development of the law: such an ICC may be a lucrative business model, but states should rather leave such business to private arbitration institutions and focus on their core tasks.

68 In this respect, Patchett-Joyce (n 48) 398, correctly remarks that 'it is easy to stigmatise (as some have) an ICommC as a "caviar court", a "court for the super rich", a "VIP court" or a "luxury item"'.

69 On this line of reasoning, see, for example, Riehm and Thomas (n 21) 704: 'If the main reason for the establishment of Commercial Courts therefore is to promote the quality of German law and the German judiciary, then this gives a whole new twist to the subject: why not invest in the substance of German law and the German judiciary to create a better product that can then be promoted on an international level?'

Flexible Proceedings and Procedural Contracts

Alan Uzelac

1 Introduction: Flexibility and Civil Procedure in Continental Europe

Flexibility and civil procedure do not always go hand in hand. Procedural law has always been proud of its formality. In Europe, the procedural codes of the 19th and 20th centuries extensively elaborate formal rules of procedure in many technical rules. Until today, a typical code of civil procedure is a big and heavy book which comprises thousands of lengthy articles.[1]

At least in Continental Europe, the proceduralists used to be proud of the fixed nature of legal rules from their codes. They were supposed to provide the best - and, in principle, invariable - rules for dispute resolution. Even though civil procedure deals largely with disputes regarding rights and duties that parties may freely dispose of, even now, the rules of civil procedure are, per se, not regarded as dispositive. On the contrary, most rules of civil procedure are mandatory for both the parties and the court, with only rare exceptions.

In history, the traditional justification for the mandatory nature of procedural formalities used to be the avoidance of arbitrariness. As Rudolf Jhering stated in his famous quote about procedural law as formal law, '[t]he form is the sworn enemy of arbitrariness, the twin sister of freedom.'[2] Invariable formal rules not only protect the parties against the abusive discretion of judges but also safeguard public interests, preventing the parties from abusive behaviour that hurts public interests. By its nature, civil procedural law is considered to be a part of public law, and, therefore, unless otherwise provided, both for the parties and for the court, the rules of civil procedure are strict law.[3]

Such a perspective on procedural rules naturally impairs flexibility. The process which would be determined by an agreement of the parties for each litigation (so-called

1 See, e.g. the French *Code de procedure civile* (CPC) with its current 1,582 articles and German *Zivilprozessordnung* (ZPO) with 1,120 articles; even the 'short' codes such as the Swiss Code or Croatian CCP have 400 to 500 articles.

2 'Die Form ist die geschworene Feindin der Willkür, die Zwillingsschwester der Freiheit.' Rudolf Jhering, *Geist des römischen Rechts* (Breitkopf und Härtel 1858) 497.

3 See Hans W. Fasching, *Zivilprozeßrecht* (Manz 1990) 71-73.

Konventionalprozeß, 'conventional proceedings') has generally been rejected within the boundaries of state civil justice already in the second half of the 19th century, and this has been presented as an achievement of modern civil procedural doctrine ever since.[4] Many Central and Eastern European procedural textbooks have been following that approach for decades, emphasising that procedural law is *ius cogens* and arguing that, unless expressly provided by procedural law, any procedural action that differs from legal rules is, in principle, not admissible.[5] Therefore, from a classic civil law European perspective – at least within the countries which adhere to Germanic models – within the ambit of judicial civil proceedings, a system of procedural rules agreed by the parties, and to be applied before the state courts, is a *contradictio in adiecto.*

Indeed, not every provision regulating civil litigation is mandatory. Even in more restrictive jurisdictions of Continental Europe, there is limited number of exceptions, which need to be expressly provided. Within a relatively narrow ambit, forum selection clauses (e.g. prorogation clauses) allow for the contractual selection of a local jurisdiction different from the default one. By their agreement, parties to a dispute may be allowed to suspend the proceedings for a certain period while pursuing an out-of-court settlement option. Ultimately, the parties can discontinue the court proceedings by withdrawing their claims or concluding a court settlement approved by a judge. However, a number of issues that deal with the constitutive elements of litigation and its progress have been more or less beyond the limits of party autonomy. Among such issues are the composition of the tribunal, selection of adjudicators, application of different procedural rules or specific procedural tracks for the conduct of the proceedings, selection of the language of proceedings, order of submissions and development of procedural stages, procedural preclusions, form of decisions made in the proceedings, means of recourse against judgments, and many other matters. Unless procedural law expressly provides that a certain agreement related to the procedure is valid and binding, a traditional civil law view has been that any 'contract' concluded by the parties concerning the progress of litigation would be, at best, a nonbinding recommendation for the court which could disregard it and decide otherwise; in the worst-case scenario such a 'contract' would be regarded as harmful and illegal.

4 For the reasons for rejecting a 'dispositive civil procedural law', see Oskar Bülow, 'Dispositives Civilprozeßrecht und die verbindliche Kraft der Recthsordnung' (1881) 64 Archiv für die civilistische Praxis 1, 1.

5 For textbooks of former Yugoslavia and its successor states, see Siniša Triva and Mihajlo Dika, *Građansko parnično procesno pravo* (7th edn, Zagreb 2004) sec 7/3; Jože Juhart, *Civilno procesno pravo FLR Jugoslavije* (Ljubljana 1961) 35; Lojze Ude, *Civilno procesno pravo* (Ljubljana 2002) 91; Borivoje Poznić and Vesna Rakić Vodinelić, *Građansko procesno pravo* (17th edn, Beograd 2015) 73-74; Branko Čalija and Sanjin Omanović, *Građansko procesno pravo* (2nd edn, Sarajevo 2000) 17-19.

2 Abandoning the Inflexibility – or Not

2.1 *Should Litigation Import Freedom of Choice Inherent to Arbitration?*

The same parties that cannot escape mandatory rules of civil procedure still have a way to evade the inflexible framework of court proceedings entirely. While conventionally agreed rules in the court proceedings are traditionally rejected, by agreeing on arbitration, the parties, in theory, allow themselves almost total flexibility because their dispute resolution agreement may depart from almost any procedural provisions fixed by law or other authority, as far as the procedure agreed upon by the parties is still fundamentally fair.

A feature of arbitration often accentuated for its promotion has been that, in arbitration, 'the parties have ultimate control of *their* dispute resolution system,' i.e. that '[p]arty autonomy is the ultimate power determining the form, structure, system and other details of arbitration.'[6] A principal factor differentiating litigation and arbitration has been identified as the 'rigidity of national court procedures'.[7]

Indeed, arbitration courts as private or DIY ('do-it-yourself') courts offer a much greater span of options. On a contractual basis, the parties are free to construct all building blocks of the dispute resolution process by their arbitration agreement and create from scratch an adjudication mechanism as a special-purpose vehicle for fulfilling their interests. While the source of arbitrators' authority to decide (*iurisdictio*) is exclusively a private empowerment of private adjudicators and not the state power to regulate conflicts (*imperium*),[8] the fundamental principle is that any meaningful consensus about the dispute resolution process is acceptable and contractually binding, unless specifically excluded by law.

Contractual design of dispute settlement in the realm of arbitration is thereby old (but nevertheless still useful) news. Contractual determinations may take the form of an arbitral clause contained in the contract that originated years before the dispute has arisen; they can be made in the form of a *compromise* – an agreement concluded to deal with an already existing legal problem. By majority opinion, the right to contractually depart from adopted procedural arrangements does not stop with establishing a dedicated dispute resolution body. It continues to exist during the arbitration proceedings until the end of the arbitral process.

It is hard to imagine a broader spectrum of procedural flexibility than the one awarded to the parties to an arbitration agreement. Parties may consensually fix the

---

6 Julian D.M. Lew, Loukas A. Mistelis and Stefan M. Kröll, *Comparative International Commercial Arbitration* (Kluwer 2003) 4.

7 Ibid., 5.

8 See Emmanuel Jeuland, *Droit processuel général* (LGDJ 2012) 372-374.

composition of the tribunal; determine the qualities of adjudicators, e.g. their nationality and profession; and even appoint by name 'their' arbitrators. The assisting bodies, from institutions administering arbitration to administrative secretaries, also depend on the parties' agreement. In principle, the procedure is also subject to any agreement made by the parties, from issues such as language or languages of the proceedings to detailed case management matters.

Has the time come to abandon this dualism, the black-and-white picture of two worlds – the flexible world of arbitration and the rigid (inflexible) world of judicial civil procedure?

Several recent developments indicate that the old dogma of anti-conventionalism in civil procedure is being questioned. On the one hand, there is a spike in interest in one domain which was the least inflexible – the domain of *Prozessleitung* (Austro-German notion for the active judicial steering of the litigation process) – this time in the guise of case management (its Anglo-Saxon counterpart). Addressing the problems of slow, overburdened and inefficient civil justice systems, it became essential to improve the overall control of judicial proceedings and their progress, both at the level of management of individual cases and at the level of court administration.[9] The optimisation of resources needs a more proactive approach and flexibilisation of judicial proceedings. Case management movement in civil law jurisdictions questions the view that statutory norms must amply regulate procedure and, instead, argues that it should be made more flexible and adjusted to particular circumstances of the case. On the other hand, in common law jurisdictions, case management questions the adversarial and reactive nature of litigation, in which the judge is turned into a spectator of lawyers' tactical battles before the court.[10]

On the other hand, the reduction of court caseloads and the newly found competitiveness of some national justice systems opened the trend of creating international commercial tribunals as optional, rent-a-court venues adjusted to the special demands of the parties. The specialised commercial courts established in Amsterdam, Brussels, Cologne, Düsseldorf and Paris (in Europe), as well as some others elsewhere (Kazakhstan, Dubai, Qatar, Singapore etc.), started to market their activities

9 See C.H. van Rhee (ed), *Judicial Case Management and Efficiency in Civil Litigation* (Intersentia 2008) 11-25; Peter Chan and C.H. van Rhee (eds), *Civil Case Management in the Twenty-First Century: Court Structures Still Matter* (Springer 2021). For Latin America, see Ramón Garcia Odgers, 'El surgimiento del case management y la superación del juez director del proceso: el proceso como reflejo de las exigencies y problemas de nuestra época', *Revista de derecho* (Concepción 2020) 113-147; Álvaro Pérez Ragone, 'An Approach to Case Management from the Horizontal and Vertical Structure of Court Systems' (2018) 23 Zeitschrift für Zivilprozess 345-375.

10 This negative impact of a purely adversarial model became commonplace in the US, so '[m]any American lawyers recognise that judicial management holds the key to more expeditious and less expensive litigation.' Richard Marcus, 'The Litigation Superpower's Case Management Cure for Adversarial Ills' in Chan and van Rhee (n 9) 121.

to parties irrespective of their domicile, offering inter alia some services which were so far reserved for arbitration, for example, proceedings in foreign (mostly English) language.[11] While the success of these initiatives has been limited, they prove a trend of cultural change in the approach to litigation within national civil justice systems. From the once-dominant repellent tactics and 'get out of my court' attitude, now at least some jurisdictions wish to convert (some) state courts into optional, attractive and efficient dispute resolution centres which desire to be competitive and recapture 'clients' from other jurisdictions and prominent arbitral institutions.

Finally, the contemporary focus on civil courts as a user-friendly service for citizens and businesses inevitably raises the question of whether user satisfaction can be reached without empowering the users to (co)design the procedure.[12] The arguments for that are strong: if the parties have the right to freely enter into legal relationships governed by substantive law and have the right to select a forum, why would their voice not be heard with respect to the organisation of the dispute settlement procedure? If civil justice is not conceived as an unquestionable, God-given institution with authoritarian powers but as a system of service providers (online or offline) which cater for the interests of their users, they have the right to be consulted and at least receive plausible explanations for the selected methods and procedures used to dispense justice.

The main topic of this chapter is, however, devoted to flexibility in the context of another movement in the doctrine of civil procedure, which is currently gaining traction.

The latest voices for flexibilisation of litigation proceedings also start from the dilemma: 'Is it necessary for us to remain in the duality of rigid litigation versus flexible arbitration?'[13] This time, the key submission is that the methods of private justice (arbitration and mediation) need to be transposed in the world of state justice, abolishing the inherent distrust in procedural contracts and promoting a renaissance of *Konventionalprozeß* in the form of contractualisation of civil procedure.

Being convinced that civil procedure as it currently functions in many countries does not provide an appropriate level of speed, quality and adjustability to the demands of the present time, I will, however, in this chapter, further explore whether the desired flexibility can indeed be best achieved by a 'contractualisation'. After discussing some questions on the meaning of procedural contractualisation, I will conclude that more

11 On this topic, see Erlis Themeli, *Civil Justice System Competition in the European Union. The Great Race of Courts* (Eleven 2018); Xandra Kramer and John Sorabji, 'International Business Courts in Europe and Beyond: A Global Competition for Justice?' (2019) 12 Erasmus Law Review 1-9; Xandra Kramer and John Sorabji (eds), *International Business Courts. A European and Global Perspective* (Eleven 2019).

12 On the change in understanding where courts would not be conceived as a place, but as a service, see Richard Susskind, 'The Future of Courts' (July/August 2020) The Practice 6, see https://clp.law.harvard.edu/knowledge-hub/magazine/issues/remote-courts/the-future-of-courts/ (accessed 3 March 2024).

13 Antonio Cabral, 'Designing Procedure by Contract: Litigation Agreements in Contemporary Civil Procedure' (2019) 9 International Journal of Procedural Law 368.

participation of the parties in the design of the proceedings is indeed desirable but that, at the same time, the notion of contractualisation is a less-than-perfect response to new challenges.

2.2 *Is Procedural Contractualisation a Guarantee of Flexibility?*

There is a certain seductive flair in the notion of procedural contractualisation. Arbitration has been 'stealing' cases from the state courts' jurisdiction for decades. It has been argued that arbitration is superior to litigation as it provides more freedom and more choice in shaping the dispute resolution process. And with a good reason: arbitration has often demonstrated that a process not regulated by thousands of complex technical rules can be much better organised and much more efficient and flexible than judicial proceedings. As the cornerstone of every proper arbitration is a contract – the arbitration agreement, it is logical that the idea of 'contractualisation' deserves attention and further exploration also in civil procedure in general.

However, the prima facie attractiveness of the contractualisation notion should not stop us from a closer examination of its meaning. As I will show, further exploration reveals some important problems, both from the perspective of court proceedings and the perspective of the analogy with arbitration practice.

To clarify, 'procedural contractualisation' is sufficiently broad to cover many different topics. In preparing this contribution, the editors suggested that 'contractualisation' may be used as 'a panoply to cover procedural contracts, procedural agreements, and consensual decision-making in civil litigation'.[14] Much of that is not the topic of this text. I will limit my remarks to the issues that deal with flexibility *within* the litigation process, i.e. issues related to consensual departure from prescribed procedural rules among the parties who have resorted to litigation. Within litigation, I will mainly focus on the core of the flexible judicial process – the management of cases before the first instance court. The right of the parties to opt out of the litigation process and resort to other alternative dispute resolution methods is a well-established right, and I will not discuss it here. Neither will I deal with prorogation or other choice of forum agreements. The main issue of this chapter is not how to replace a less flexible court procedure with a more flexible arbitration (or mediation) procedure, but whether court proceedings should be made more flexible and whether a 'contractualisation' (modelled after arbitration and ADR practices) is the right method to achieve such a goal.

The answer to the first question is generally positive: inflexible models of civil procedure arising out of 19th-century legal doctrine cannot withstand the test of modern times. The societal and technological changes call for a transformation of

14 Editors' Letter to Contributors, June 2022.

civil justice, and this process is already ongoing.[15] Rigid procedural forms are hardly acceptable in a dynamic environment. In the context of digitisation, many traditional rules and routines will have to be re-examined and replaced. Indeed, fewer and more open-ended rules allow for more flexibility than an environment in which hundreds of legislatively prescribed procedural provisions need to be constantly adjusted to the changed (and/or changing) circumstances. The quick reaction of those involved in concrete judicial proceedings and their ability to address concrete issues in real time are much more appropriate for optimising speed and resources. It is much closer to the modern ideal of fair, cooperative and proportionate civil proceedings, which has been globally promoted since Woolf's reforms in England and Wales.[16]

Responding to the second question is more difficult. Apparently, an agreement made by the parties on the conduct of the proceedings may create a flexible procedural design adjusted to the particulars of the concrete case, provided that several conditions are fulfilled: parties must be cooperative, act in good faith, have sufficient expert knowledge and experience in (designing of) dispute resolution mechanisms and be sufficiently close to the dispute, i.e. be able to address and regulate problems as they arise. How realistic is that all these conditions will be fulfilled? In reality, dispute resolution clauses are often drafted under a veil of ignorance years before a dispute arises. Would detailed litigation agreements drafted well in advance provide a desired flexible procedural regulatory network? It is not very likely. This submission will later be further corroborated by the experiences from arbitration practice, showing that arbitration's real source of flexibility is not in the broad use of contractual freedom to design the procedure (see Section 2.4).[17]

Admittedly, litigants designing the procedure may be advantageous for some standard sorts of disputes that occur regularly and have similar features. But rarely are the contractual parties equally prepared and equally motivated to regulate their uncertain future disputes. If yes, the forging of procedural clauses is often motivated by the interest of one of them, usually the one who dictates the content of the main contract. The result is not a flexible procedure but a procedure tilted in favour of one party. The consequences of unlimited contractual freedom to regulate dispute resolution have already been plastically visible after the US Supreme Court decision in the AT&T case:[18] instead of a flexible procedure, the outcome is a binding clause which provides a contractually blessed denial of justice.

15 On its various aspects, see Alan Uzelac (ed), *Transformation of Civil Justice. Unity and Diversity* (Springer 2018).

16 See John Sorabji, *English Civil Justice after the Woolf and Jackson Reforms* (Cambridge University Press 2014).

17 See Section 2.3.

18 *AT&T Mobility LLC v. Concepcion* 563 U.S. 333 (2011).

The very form of contract can, in fact, be problematic. As such, contracts are a feature which formalises relationships. In that sense, the contract is a kind of invitation to rigidity and litigiousness – to blind insistence on the *pacta sunt servanda* principle instead of a continuing cooperative relationship which jointly reframes the rules and makes decisions favourable to all participants. Further examples of potential inflexibility a 'contractualisation' may bring will be provided below.

Before entering into an analysis of arbitration practice, another fundamental question needs to be asked. If a contract is an agreement on the conduct of proceedings concluded between two private parties, should they have an *exclusive* right to design procedure? Can they *alone* forge procedural rules for cases that they submit to state courts and do it in a way which would regulate the process in a binding way, i.e. in a way which is mandatory for the justice system, courts and individual judges entrusted with their case?

2.3 *Should Parties Have an Exclusive Right to Design Procedure for Their Case?*

In principle, a contract is an agreement between two or more persons who assume, each with respect to the other, certain rights and obligations.[19] In case of a violation of contractual terms, sanctions will apply. How would this definition work in the context of civil litigation?

Who are the parties to a 'procedural contract'? If a parallel to arbitration is used, the parties to a dispute are those who agree on a way how their dispute would be handled; for example, what substantive law should be applicable? What forum would be competent to resolve the merits of the case? What would be the language of proceedings, and, in particular, who would be the adjudicator(s)? What would be the procedure under which the competent body would proceed? Following this model, the procedural contract in a court procedure would be the contract between the parties to a dispute, whereby the parties would determine one or several specific features of the dispute resolution process.

An interesting example of procedural contracts recognised in a rather general form is found in the 2015 Brazilian Code of Civil Procedure. Its Articles 190 and 200 allow procedural agreements and provide for the immediate effectiveness of procedural legal acts and legal transactions signed by the parties.[20] In addition to some forms

---

19 Compare *Black's Law Dictionary* (6th edn, 1990) 322 ('an agreement between two or more persons which creates an obligation to do or not to do a particular thing').

20 Antonio Cabral and Pedro Henrique Nogueira, 'Contractualisaiton of Civil Litigation in Brazil: Party Autonomy and Procedural Agreements' in Anna Nylund and Antonio Cabral (eds), *Contractualisation of Civil Procedure* (Intersentia 2023) 82.

of agreements (e.g. jurisdictional agreements) already specified by law, it seems that Brazilian law also allows for other, non-specified or atypical procedural agreements.[21] Thus, as such, procedural agreements ('contracts') can be concluded prior to or after initiating litigation and contain in principle any procedural agreement except those expressly excluded by law, and they are very similar to arbitration agreements. This position, rather different to the traditional European approach, is probably the most far-reaching example of 'arbitralisation' of litigation and a clear case of a bilateral private law agreement by which two private parties, with no participation of other persons or authorities, shape litigation rules. However, it is also the most consequent example of 'contractualisation' that results in a 'litigation agreement', which, just like an arbitration agreement, is a binding private transaction between the two parties.

What would be the role of the court in such procedural contracts? In arbitration, arbitrators or arbitration institutions are not the parties to an arbitration agreement. Nevertheless, it is generally considered that the parties' will expressed in the arbitration agreement binds the arbitrators who accept to arbitrate.[22] While not being the parties to such a contract, they are at best authorised to help execute it in a way that is faithful to the parties' intentions.

In litigation, the role of contractual arrangements in connection with procedural issues cannot be uniformly assessed. Again, a difference is generally made between some agreements expressly recognised by law and whose validity, mandatory nature and legal effects are provided by law. Certain effects can be reached by parties' action or inaction, and they are often interpreted as tacit agreements and voluntary acceptance of negative inferences. However, these types of agreements are mostly limited to issues of jurisdiction, as in jurisdictional clauses and prorogation agreements (including some forms of *prorogatio tacita*). Settlement agreements concluded before a court are also viewed as specific mixed-type contracts with both substantive and procedural effects. Again, in such agreements, the principal actors are the parties, but the court also has a strong supervisory role. Apart from formal checking of legal requirements for their validity, in the case of court settlements, the participation and supervision of the court may be more proactive, suggesting formal and substantive modifications and rejecting to approve the agreement if it is unclear, inoperative, incapable of being performed, adverse to third parties or contrary to public policy.

---

21 Ibid., 83.

22 Yet, arbitrators may refuse the offer to arbitrate under rules selected by the parties if they deem those rules to be unsuitable. In particular, arbitration institutions often limit the right of the parties to depart from the selected institutional rules. See, e.g. Rule 19 (Rules Governing the Proceedings) of the ICC Rules of Arbitration (2021), according to which the parties can only depart from the rules not stipulated by the default regime of the ICC Rules: ('...arbitral tribunal shall be governed by the Rules and, *where the Rules are silent*, by any rules which the parties or, failing them, the arbitral tribunal may settle on...').

But these types of procedural contracts are fundamentally different from the agreements which deal with the conduct of the proceedings in a narrow sense – the procedural agreements regarding various issues of case management. These agreements are the most pertinent for our topic – flexibility of the proceedings. Therefore, let us focus on the court's role regarding eventual agreements on the progress of litigation. Such agreements may, e.g. decide whether a court hearing will be suspended or adjourned, whether proceedings are deemed terminated, when and where the next hearings will take place, in what form and at what time the parties submit their statements, declarations and evidence. Such decisions on the management of proceedings, including the setting of procedural calendars, belong to a set of procedural actions which determine the formal course of proceedings, known in German and Austrian theory as *formelle Prozeßleitung.*[23] To a great extent, efficient and flexible judicial proceedings depend on a well-considered, well-planned and proactive approach to the organisation of litigation. The same is true for the organisation of the fact-finding process and gathering of evidence and other material needed for adjudication (so-called substantive case management or *materielle Prozeßleitung*), albeit parties do have, in this respect, a greater margin of influence which arises from their authority to dispose of their substantive rights, either directly or indirectly.

Naturally, the decision-making on such case management issues may be subject to an agreement of the parties or a decision by the court. It is common in the history of comparative civil procedure that the progress of litigation, which solely depends on parties' dispositions (according to the old theory about the parties as *domini litis*), generates an inefficient, slow and overly formalistic process. Such a process was not regarded as helpful for ascertaining the facts of the case and providing effective remedies for the breaches of parties' substantive rights. From the end of the 19th century, when Franz Klein drafted the reform of civil procedure in Austria, the model of civil proceedings governed by uncontrolled actions of the procedural adversaries that turn litigation into a selfish playground of the litigants is denounced as undesirable. In the words of Klein, litigation should not be 'a war without a Red Cross'.[24] From that time onwards, many reforms in Europe and elsewhere strengthened the role of the judge, seeking to create an efficient yet flexible procedural regime where '[p]rocedural formalities were to be pushed back as much as possible, and the judge was given an active role in the conduct of the action.'[25] The strengthening of the role of the judge in

23 See, e.g. Fasching (n 3) 412.

24 Franz Klein, *Pro futuro. Betrachtungen über Probleme der Civilproceßreform in Österreich* (Deuticke 1891) 39.

25 C.H. van Rhee, 'The Development of Civil Procedural Law in Twentieth-Century Europe: From party Autonomy to Judicial Case Management and Efficiency?' in C.H. van Rhee (ed), *Judicial Case Management and Efficiency in Civil Litigation* (Intersentia 2008) 11-25.

case management has been a strong national and international trend, although present in different manifestations and different intensities.[26]

Indeed, the idea of 'procedural contracts' may be a different and, in theory, a more cooperative way of influencing litigation than the adversarial model of litigation in which a battle of litigants is observed and tolerated by a passive judge. But both modalities have a common element. Express procedural agreements and implied 'agree to disagree' adversarial style of proceedings equally root on the idea of litigation being in the ownership of the litigating parties. However, history has shown that, without active control of the proceedings, the parties can easily hijack them and steer them in a socially and economically undesirable direction.[27] Blind faith in the good intentions of the parties and their alleged common interest in speedy and efficient litigation that almost never materialises in practice does not produce effective and just results. Trust is good, but control is better; thus, an active collaboration of the parties is welcome and desirable, but only if it is accompanied by effective supervision and strong institutional incentives to act in conformity with the main goals of civil procedure.

For this reason, the current state-of-the-art consensus among civil proceduralists in Europe, formulated in the ELI/UNIDROIT Model European Rules of Civil Procedure,[28] roots on the idea of joint and shared responsibility of the court and the parties who need to cooperate in order to achieve a fair, efficient and speedy resolution of the dispute.[29] In case management, the role of the court is even more highlighted: the court is responsible for active and effective case management.[30] The parties, on the other hand, do not assume a passive role – they have an obligation for 'careful conduct of litigation' under which they must

> present their claims, defences, factual allegations and offers of evidence as early and completely as possible and as appropriate to the careful conduct of litigation in order to secure procedural expedition.[31]

---

26 Walter Rechberger and Daphne-Ariane Simotta, *Grundriss des österreichischen Zivilprozessrecht. Erkenntnisverfahren* (Manz 2009) 204-205.

27 Criticism of an exclusively party-driven procedure was not only expressed by Franz Klein; also in Germany, the 'liberal attitude' of 1877 CCP 'gave the parties unlimited freedom in conducting civil proceedings', and it was therefore 'an almost ideal instrument for delaying the proceedings by dilatory tactics'. Peter Gottwald, 'Defeating delay in German civil procedure' in C.H. van Rhee (ed), *The Law's Delay* (Intersentia 2004) 121-122. Once it was reformed, the German model of active judicial management became the role model for American critics of a 'lawyer-dominated system of civil procedure'; see most notoriously John H. Langbein, 'The German Advantage in Civil Procedure' (1985) 52 *University of Chicago Law Review* 823-866.

28 *ELI/UNIDROIT Model European Rules of Civil Procedure* (Oxford University Press 2021).

29 See Rule 2 (Principle of Cooperation).

30 See Rule 4 (Role of the Court – the General Case Management Duty).

31 Rule 47.

From this perspective, a reinvented 'contractualisation' of civil litigation, unless combined with the active participation and supervisory role of the court, essentially does not bring flexibility. On the contrary, it may be a return to the past, ineffective forms of civil litigation, where the proceedings have been abducted by the parties (or, more often, their lawyers) who have been staging their procedural tactics in front of a passive judge who could not do anything but helplessly observe their procedural manoeuvres.

2.4 *Is Arbitration Really Conducted According to Tailor-Made Rules Designed by the Parties?*

Some may say, but what about arbitration? Is it not proof that parties' agreements on the course of the process can make arbitration more effective and better suited to the specificities of each individual dispute than most civil litigations?

Asking such questions is logical but demonstrates a usual misconception about how the arbitration process works. While urban legends and professional advertisements glorify parties' autonomy, arbitration practice shows relatively few successful instances of parties' procedural inventiveness. On the contrary, worst-case scenarios often materialise when innovation is attempted – in the form of pathological arbitration clauses.[32] Namely, the prevailing form of arbitration agreements is arbitration clauses inserted in the main contract before the dispute has arisen. Due to their superficial drafting and low level of attention devoted to them, arbitration clauses have often been labelled 'champagne clauses' or 'midnight clauses'. Designing procedural rules on dispute resolution only minutes before the bottles are opened to celebrate the conclusion of the (main) contract reached after lengthy negotiations naturally invites trouble. Thus, the general advice of arbitration professionals is to refrain from inventing new rules and stick to short and fool-proof standard model clauses of a few reputable arbitration institutions (e.g. ICC, LCIA, VIAC). Still, arbitration practice is permeated with examples of incredibly clumsy and stupid arbitral clauses, which regularly cost a lot of time and expenses and can rarely be saved even by the most pro-arbitration courts and tribunals.

To note just a few of such examples of failed references to the selection of dispute resolution bodies and methods: 'the American Arbitration Association or any other US court'; 'disputes will be referred to arbitration if the parties so determine'; 'arbitration

32 For the origin of this expression, see Fréderic Eisemann, 'La clause d'arbitrage pathologique' in *Commercial arbitration – essays in memoriam Eugenio Minoli* (Unione tipografico-editrice torinese 1974) 129; for a series of examples, see Fourchard Gaillard Goldman, *On International Commercial Arbitration* (Kluwer 1999) 264-272.

in a county other than that of the each of the parties'.[33] These and many other examples which regularly occur show the level of care and/or knowledge regarding dispute resolution agreements in voluminous international transactions concluded by professionals armed with high-level legal support. The outcome of procedural innovativeness at the lower and local levels may only be worse. Considering that litigation covers a much broader span of (non-commercial and non-international) disputes than does arbitration, and eventually also includes unrepresented lay parties, it is to be assumed that litigation agreements, if used on a bigger scale, would have a much bigger margin of error compared to pathological arbitration agreements.

Yes, arbitration is, in most comparable cases, more flexible, more efficient and faster than civil litigation. But the reasons for that are not in an a priori abstract right of the parties to exert creativeness in procedural agreements, i.e. to impose their own rules on arbitrators and arbitral institutions. On the contrary, effective arbitrations have their roots in the selection of short and open-ended standard arbitration clauses, which allow experienced arbitrators to communicate with the parties and jointly select the best options for the case at hand in the preparatory stage of the proceedings. Constant communication with the parties, open discussions at the first case management hearing, and the joint setting of the procedural calendar, as well as numerous email exchanges of various proposals and draft decisions, in the end, make an effective arbitration proceeding.

While, in theory, arbitration proceedings are governed by the parties' agreement adjusted to the particulars of the case, in reality, many arbitrations (especially international commercial ones) feature a stunning harmonisation of procedural forms and practices. While not codified, best practices of international commercial arbitration find their place in many specialised books, papers and journals.[34] They are disseminated at many conferences and practised at massive moot competitions.[35] Multinational law firms regularly have their arbitration departments follow successful practices from their previous cases. In most cases, this practice boils down to avoiding normative experiments and, instead, focusing on selecting efficient arbitrators. They, in turn, regularly follow tested methods of successful case management (e.g. chess clock arbitration), prefer the flexible use ('as a guidance') of soft-law instruments (e.g. IBA Rules on Taking of Evidence)[36] and generally organise the proceedings in a way which

33 Goldman (n 32).

34 The interest in planning started already in the 1990th – see the papers collected at ICCA 12th Congress in Albert Jan van den Berg (ed), *Planning Efficient Arbitration Proceedings* (Kluwer 1996).

35 Among them, the best example is the Willem C. Vis International Commercial Arbitration Moot, sponsored by UNCITRAL and VIAC. With an annual attendance of almost 400 student teams and 1,000 arbitrators from over 80 jurisdictions, in the last 30 years, it has played a major role in promoting a uniform approach to modern arbitral procedure.

36 For IBA Rules on Taking of Evidence in International Arbitration and other practice rules and guidelines, see https://www.ibanet.org/resources.

is not only cooperative but also flexible. This, in practice, means that good arbitrators always consult the parties on the proposed course and methods of proceedings, seeking to obtain their agreement – but not an agreement which will be drafted as a formal and binding document, a 'contract'. Reaching an express or implied consensus regarding draft procedural orders issued by the arbitral tribunal is regularly sufficient and more practical. Relying on a signed 'contract' may be too tempting for one or both parties (i.e. their lawyers) to try various objections and legal strategies of its (mis)interpretation and challenge. Therefore, to avoid sidecar proceedings and secure a focus on the main proceedings, experienced arbitrators insist on consensual decision-making with respect to the conduct of the proceedings but without a formalisation that would amount to a 'contractualisation'.[37]

With the spreading of arbitration practice, the number of experienced arbitrators may, of course, become insufficient to maintain uniformity, except in a limited number of ad hoc arbitrations. But another trend with the same effect is visible: institutionalisation of arbitration. As noted by commentators, this trend 'is not entirely in keeping with the principle of the primacy of the parties' intentions' as '[i]t is becoming increasingly rare for the parties to choose their arbitrators and organise their procedure directly.'[38] It is argued that 'the vast majority of international commercial arbitrations in the world now' are handled by permanent arbitral institutions under their pre-set rules – just like in the state courts. The full circle is thereby drawn: some describe what is going on as the 'judicialisation' of arbitration, this time in a private setting.[39]

In short, a closer study of arbitration practice reveals that the situation with consensual conduct of procedure is much more complex and that a simplistic analogy that advocates replacing a 'rigid' litigation style with a 'flexible' arbitration approach simply does not work. Certainly, a cross-fertilisation between arbitration and litigation does happen, and it is desirable. The state system of civil justice has much to learn from the practice of alternative dispute resolution methods, which have been developing quicker, and offer more modern, user-friendly and flexible case management methods. However, the actual practice of arbitration also teaches us to avoid excessive 'contractualisation' and formalisation of procedural rules and resort to alternative ways

37 Effective management of arbitration is regularly undertaken jointly by both the parties and the arbitral tribunal, and the central place for the determination of the procedure is case management conferences. See, e.g. ICC Rules of Arbitration, Art. 22(1), which requires the arbitral tribunal and the parties to make every effort to conduct the arbitration in an expeditious and cost-effective manner. Under the ICC Guide on Effective Management of Arbitration, issued for In-House Counsel and Other Party Representatives (ICC 2017), 'in practice, after receiving the case file, the arbitral tribunal may invite the parties to make case management proposals,' and 'after listening to the parties, will adopt procedural measures that it deems to be appropriate for the case at hand', taking into account the 'complexity and value of the dispute', seeking to realise 'a cost-effective and expeditious arbitration ... in which the time and cost devoted to resolving the dispute is appropriate in light of what is at stake.' ICC Guide, 13-14.

38 Goldman (n 32) 33.

39 Ibid.

of securing a cooperative but efficient and flexible procedural environment. While agreements are always welcome, 'procedural contracts' – when they get formalised and put on paper – may become a straitjacket which forces all participants to concentrate on their interpretation rather than on the effective course of litigation.

3 Effective Flexibility: From Bipartisan Contractualisation to Multilateral Procedural Cooperation

Be it as it may, contemporary civil litigation is certainly not flexible enough. Nevertheless, 'litigation contracts' that regulate the course of litigation are only a small element in a big puzzle and must be used cautiously. Insofar as the notion of 'contractualisation' of procedure is concerned, it should also be handled with care. In addition to the criticisms of the 'contractualisation' concept that have already been presented, let me add another, which points to this notion's symbolic dimension and connotations. Namely, a 'contract' is a static, finalised agreement in a legal universe. It is the result rather than the process. It is the notion that looks backwards; it is retrospective and not prospective.

Efficient case management, on the other hand, needs to be future-oriented. It must be apt to quick changes in the case management decisions depending on circumstances, so it is dynamic and ongoing. It needs to focus on benefits and goals and not on the assignment of blame and sanctions for the non-observance of the formal terms of the contract – which is how lawyers often perceive and use contracts. Therefore, I would say that the notion of 'contractualisation' is the notion that divides and not the notion which unites.

On the contrary, the best practices in effective dispute resolution teach us that we need notions that unite and focus on the continuing communication process. The eyes need to be focused on the road, not fixed on the milestones along the road. In the same vein, effective dispute resolution cannot be limited to one actor in the judicial arena alone, be it the parties and their agreements ('litigation contracts') or the court and its authoritarian rulings.

An approach that has been developed on the basis of these best practices, an approach that unites the parties and the court in pursuing the common goal that transcends their individual interests, is developed in the already mentioned ELI/UNIDROIT Model Rules. Among the key intentions of these rules was to create 'uniform flexible rules for first instance proceedings' and allow 'flexible application of the uniform rules'.[40]

The principle of loyal cooperation of all key players in litigation – the parties, their lawyers and the court – shares with the idea of 'contractualisation' the aspiration to

40 Preamble, ELI/UNIDROIT Model Rules (n 28) 9.

'foster instruments of cooperation, consensus, negotiation, a less authoritarian legal system that emancipate individuals, giving them room to self-regulate'.[41] However, as the parties do not have exclusive ownership over the litigation process, the genuine consensus needs to be broader and include not only the parties (i.e. their lawyers) but also those called to adjudicate the dispute. The key role of the adjudicator is not only recognised in litigation but also – as already demonstrated – in the most private and contractual form of dispute resolution, in arbitration. It has been the element of national reforms and various progressive model rules, from the Storme Project in the 1980s to the 2006 Principles of Transnational Civil Procedure.[42]

The principle of cooperation differs from the idea of 'contractualisation' not only with respect to broadening the circle of those involved in the attempts to reach a consensus regarding the organisation of the civil proceedings but also with regard to the orientation towards the purpose of such consensus. The parties do have the freedom to influence or even regulate civil procedure: yes, but for what cause? While 'procedural contracts' emphasise the rights of the parties, the cooperation principle accentuates the obligations of the parties (as well as that of all other participants in civil proceedings) to use their rights in a way that contributes to the common goal of the procedure: a fair, efficient, speedy and proportionate resolution of civil disputes.[43]

Having set the goal, it is easier to proceed. 'Flexibility' is defined as 'being characterised by a ready capability to adapt to new, different, or changing requirements'.[44] The best way to steer the ship through the rough sea of uncertainty is to orientate it towards the lights emitted from bright lighthouses of principles. The basis of procedural flexibility is the adjustment to new and ever-changing circumstances based on a *dialogue* and not a *contract*. In this dialogue, there should be a moderator, and that moderator in judicial proceedings – the pilot of the ship – naturally is the judge, who should not be stripped of their management powers. But continuous loyal cooperation among all participants needs a cooperative helmsman. Thus, '[t]he court must use its management powers on a dialogical basis, i.e. it must hear the parties before issuing case management orders.'[45]

Another distinctive element of flexible, multilateral, procedural cooperation that distinguishes it from radical 'contractualisation' is its safeguards against abuse.

---

41 Cabral (n 13) 371.

42 On this development, see C.H. van Rhee 'Towards Harmonised European Rules of Procedure: Obligations of the Judge, the Parties and their Lawyers' (2020) 1(6) Access to Justice in Eastern Europe 6-33. Regarding the cooperation principle in Principle 11 of the ALI-UNIDROIT Transnational Principles, see C.H. van Rhee, 'Obligations of the Parties and Their Lawyers in Civil Litigation' in J. Adolphsen et al. (eds), *Festschrift für Peter Gottwald zum 70. Geburtstag* (Beck 2014) 669-679.

43 See Alan Uzelac, 'Towards European Rules of Civil Procedure: Rethinking Procedural Obligations' (2017) 58 Hungarian Journal of Legal Studies 1, 3-18.

44 https://www.merriam-webster.com/dictionary/flexible.

45 Preamble, ELI/UNIDROIT Model Rules (n 28) 11.

> The flexibility built into first instance case management, and proceedings generally, must not, however, be abused by lawyers or the court adopting a piecemeal approach designed to prevent concentrated proceedings taking place.[46]

A key precondition for useful flexibility is effective sanctions and incentives preventing the actors, be it the parties, the lawyers or the court, from being non-cooperative and from resorting to or adopting abusive procedural tactics to delay the arbitration proceedings. The notion of 'sanctions' in this context is not identical to legal enforcement of individual rights, as it covers various types and forms, from negative inferences and procedural preclusions to cost orders, disciplinary proceedings, contempt-of-court rulings and fines for procedural abuse.[47]

For all these reasons, I am convinced that a meaningful concept of procedural flexibility is better served by a broad teleological framework of procedural cooperation than by binding procedural contracts. Indeed, in modern civil procedure, the parties must be involved in managing their case. They have a right to be consulted, and their voice must be heard. Their will regarding the choice of forum and venue for the resolution of their civil disputes as well as their agreements regarding the use of alternative dispute resolution methods must be recognised and obeyed. But, if the litigants have opted for the package of services of state litigation providers, the best option for them is to loyally participate in a flexible process managed by skilful adjudicators who are ready and willing to hear the parties' suggestions and engage in a dialogue regarding all important issues of case management. Relying excessively on pre-existent 'litigation contracts' may be as helpful for the flexibility of judicial proceedings as the heavy armour was helpful for the mobility of the Teutonic Knights.

In conclusion, let me add that this contribution deliberately reduced the discussion on procedural agreements to issues of case management, which are most pertinent to the flexibility of the first instance of litigation. Zooming out to further issues, we will see that comparative civil procedure knows hundreds of shades of grey with respect to various agreements between the parties regarding some elements of judicial procedure. Whether and when the parties may waive their right to resort to appeals and other means of recourse; whether and to what extent may the parties exclude provisional measures or conclude various agreements relating to evidence – these and similar issues are subject to a wide variety of national specificities. Some of them (e.g. agreements on the admissibility of evidence and burden of proof) are more closely connected to substantive law issues, while the others deal with incidental and appellate proceedings. While the reasoning presented in this chapter may also apply to some of these issues, their more detailed discussion is left for some other occasion.

46 Ibid.
47 See more in Uzelac (n 43) 6-15.

Increasing Complexity, Adaptation of Proceedings and Litigation Agreements

Shusuke Kakiuchi

1 Introduction

The title of this chapter, which was suggested by this book's editors, has three components: 'Increasing Complexity', 'Adaptation of Proceedings' and 'Litigation Agreements'. This title suggests the hypothesis that civil litigation procedures need to be adapted to an increasing complexity and that litigation agreements can be effective tools for this. In this chapter, I will exhibit the plausibility of this hypothesis and try to draw some implications from it.

In Section 2, I will discuss the concept of complexity, which may give rise to the need to adapt proceedings. Then, in Section 3, I will discuss the challenges that litigation agreements may face in providing a solution to the problem: the issues of effectiveness and legitimacy.

2 Complexity and the Role of National Courts

2.1 Complexity

2.1.1 Complexity of Individual Cases

The term 'complexity' can be used in relation to a variety of subjects. When one speaks of complexity in the context of civil justice, the first thing that comes to mind would be the complexity of litigation. Indeed, 'complex litigation' is an oft-discussed topic in the field of civil procedure. Although what it means is not unequivocal,[1] according to a general understanding, it is generally understood as having the following characteristics:

1 See for example Federal Judicial Center, *Manual for Complex Litigation, Fourth* (2001) 1, which states that the term 'complex litigation' is not 'susceptible to any bright-line definition'. See also Jay Tidmarsh and Roger H. Transgrud, *Complex Litigation and Its Alternatives* (2nd edn, Foundation Press 2018) 1, which states that '[a]lthough judges, lawyers, and scholars all agree that "complex civil litigation" exists, there is no commonly agreed[sic] meaning of the term.'

(a) a large number of parties and claims, (b) a large quantity of information and issues and (c) difficulty in providing effective redress.[2] As can be seen from this explanation, complexity of litigation refers primarily to complexity in the subjective sense (the large number of interested parties) and, secondarily, to complexity in the objective sense (the complexity of the issues to be dealt with).[3]

Whether litigation is complex in a subjective or objective sense, its complexity adds a burden to civil proceedings. Indeed, if there are many potential plaintiffs and defendants who may assert claims and defences that are closely related, difficult issues may arise: can the cases of all parties be dealt with simultaneously in a single procedure and, if so, how can the different interests of those parties be taken into account in that procedure? If the cases of all the parties cannot be dealt with in a single procedure and many cases are pending before the court, is some coordination between the many procedures necessary? Similarly, if the issues in dispute are complex and require a great deal of information and thorough examination for their clarification, the proceedings are likely to be more time-consuming and expensive. This is true particularly when the information required is of a highly specialised or technical nature.

Thus, in the context of civil justice, complexity poses a burden or challenge to proceedings.[4] This is because complexity implies a departure from the simplest form of procedure: that with one plaintiff, one defendant and one (simple) claim. This characteristic of complexity will become more apparent by contrasting it with its opposite – the simple case. In the context of civil procedure, the simplicity of a matter means that the matter is not complicated and is easy to handle because it raises no difficult question of law or fact.[5] Thus, the need for inexpensive and quick proceedings is common in such matters.[6] Conversely, in complex cases that deviate from such a simple model, the proceedings are likely to be more time-consuming and expensive. In short, the complexity of a case is a symptom of its irregularity, which causes various difficulties for the proceedings.

2 See Tidmarsh and Transgrud (n 1) 4-5.

3 In addition, complexity with regard to parties generally increases complexity with regard to issues because the multiplicity of parties usually means a multiplicity of claims, which usually also means a multiplicity of issues to be determined.

4 This is the reason why voluminous manuals, such as the *Manual for Complex Litigation*, are written.

5 For an analysis of the simplicity of a case, see Xandra Kramer and Shusuke Kakiuchi, 'Relief in Small and Simple Matters in an Age of Austerity' in Hakan Pekcanitez, Nur Bolayir and Cemil Simil (eds), *XVth International Association of Procedural Law World Congress, Istanbul* (Oniki Levha Yayıncılık 2016) 131-132.

6 This connection can be explained from both the demand- and supply-side perspectives, ibid 136-138. See also Xandra Kramer and Shusuke Kakiuchi, 'Austerity in Civil Procedure and the Role of Simplified Procedures' (2015) 4 Erasmus Law Review 139, 140.

2.1.2 *Complexity of Docket*

Another related but different issue is the complexity of the court's docket as a whole. This can be understood in two ways. First, if the court is required to deal with many complex cases, it may add a burden to the court as a whole. Second, more importantly, complexity of docket can be understood as diversity. For example, even if individual cases are complex, if they are similar to each other, the docket as a whole is highly homogeneous and not necessarily diverse. Conversely, even if the individual cases are simple, if they are highly heterogeneous, they will impose diverse duties on the court. Thus, again, this type of complexity may pose a challenge to the proceedings and the courts.

When the degree of the second type of complexity is high, the question of whether it is justifiable to apply uniform procedural rules to all cases arises. For example, speed may be particularly required in some types of cases, whereas confidentiality is required in others. Legislators can address this problem by creating special rules or proceedings for some types of cases.[7] However, when the degree of diversity is very high, it is not possible to establish special rules in advance for all types of cases.

2.1.3 *Complexity of Socioeconomic Conditions*

Whether it is the individual cases or the entire docket that is complex, it is likely that the complexity reflects the conditions existing outside the court system. Indeed, behind complex cases, there must be certain socioeconomic conditions that create them, and the same is true for a complex docket. As Loïc Cadiet put it, '*c'est toute la complexité sociale que l'action en justice fait entrer dans le prétoire* [it is the whole complexity of society that the lawsuit brings into the courtroom].'[8] In other words, it is the complexity of social life that causes the complexity of individual cases or of the entire docket. This is particularly important when considering *increasing* complexity because the primary cause of the increase must be sought in socioeconomic conditions outside the judicial system.

2.2 *Increase in Complexity*

2.2.1 *Increase in Complex Cases*

Complexity, regardless of which type among the aforementioned, may increase. This can happen, at least logically, in a variety of ways. For instance, an increase in the complexity of individual cases may mean an increase in the number of complex cases, an increase in the degree of complexity of individual complex cases or both. The same applies basically to the complexity of the overall docket. Rather, to be more exact, both an increase in

---

7 This corresponds to what is called '*pluralisme du système judiciaire*' by Loïc Cadiet. See Loïc Cadiet, 'Le défi du nombre et de la complexité – La justice face aux défis du nombre et de la complexité' (2010) 13 Les cahiers de la justice, para. 24.

8 Ibid., para. 4.

the number of complex cases and an increase in the degree of complexity of individual cases can be understood as an increase in the complexity of the overall docket. However, an increase in the diversity of cases draws more attention from the perspective of the overall docket. This is because if there is an increase in the number of a particular type of complex case, rules tailored to such cases may be developed, but this response will be difficult if every individual case is different from the others.

Whatever the meaning of increased complexity, whether such a phenomenon occurs in real life is a matter best left to empirical research. However, some signs of change can be pointed out.

For example, the recent introduction in many countries of class action procedures and similar procedures, formerly unknown outside the United States, accounts for the increasing importance worldwide of cases involving the claims of a large number of victims.[9] The European Union's Directive 2020/1828 on representative actions for the protection of the collective interests of consumers, which was adopted in November 2020, was a milestone for developments in this direction on the European continent. Similar developments can also be found in other jurisdictions, such as Brazil,[10] China[11] and Japan.[12]

These trends can be understood as reflecting the increasing number of cases involving a large number of parties and claims.[13] Indeed, Recital 1 of the above-mentioned directive clearly points out its background by stating that '[g]lobalisation and digitalisation have increased the risk of a large number of consumers being harmed by the same unlawful practice'. If this statement is correct, it would mean an increase in the number of complex cases, among other things.

9 For recent developments, see, e.g. Alan Uzelak and Stefaan Voet (eds), *Class Actions in Europe: Holy Grail or Wrong Trail?* (Springer 2021). See also Xandra Kramer, Jos Hoevenaars and Erlis Themeli, 'Frontiers in Civil Justice – Privatising, Digitising and Funding Justice' in Xandra Kramer and others (eds), *Frontiers in Civil Justice: Privatisation, Monetisation and Digitisation* (Elgar 2022) 2-3.

10 See for example Hermes Zaneti Jr, 'Collective Redress in Brazil: Success or Disappointment?' in Uzelak and Voet (n 9) 345 ff.

11 See for example Yulin Fu, 'Class Actions and Public Interest Litigation in China' in Uzelak and Voet (n 9) 369 ff.

12 In Japan, the Consumer Contract Act (Act No. 61 of 2000) was amended in 2006 to introduce a consumer collective action mechanism under which consumer organisations can demand an injunction against a business. This was followed by a law enacted in 2013 (Act on Special Measures Concerning Civil Court Proceedings for the Collective Redress for Property Damage Incurred by Consumers [Act No. 96 of 2013]), which introduced a special procedure under which a consumer organisation can file an action seeking a declaratory judgement determining the company's liability based on factual and legal causes common to a large number of consumers.

13 See Section 2.1.1.

2.2.2 *Increase in the Complexity of Docket*

As for the question of whether the complexity of docket is increasing, it is noteworthy that interesting changes in the number of civil litigation cases and their contents have been observed in recent years in several jurisdictions.

In some jurisdictions, a decrease in the number of civil litigation cases has been noted in recent years. A prominent example of this is Germany, where approximately 420,000 civil actions were filed in regional courts (*Landgerichte*) and 1.45 million in local courts (*Amtsgerichte*) in 2000, whereas in 2021, only approximately 330,000 and 750,000 cases, respectively, were filed.[14] There is some debate on the causes of this decline in the number of civil litigation cases.[15] Although it seems that no clear causes have been established, one hypothesis is that, particularly in simple cases, disputes may be avoided or resolved outside the courts.[16] If this hypothesis – which appears to be consistent with the fact that the decline in the local courts is significantly greater than in the regional courts – is correct, it would imply an increase in the proportion of more complex and harder cases in the courts' dockets.

A similar phenomenon can also be observed in Japan. As a result of the reform of its judicial system initiated in 2001, the number of lawyers increased by approximately 2.5 times between 2000 and 2021,[17] but the number of civil litigation cases did not increase at all during that period.[18] Moreover, interestingly, while the number of cases in district courts even decreased,[19] the average duration of civil proceedings in those courts became slightly longer during that period.[20] Of particular importance is the fact that the average length of proceedings has been shortening since 2000 and was as short as 6.5 months in 2009, when the maximum number of cases was reached, but it has since lengthened while the number of cases has decreased.

---

14 See Statistisches Bundesamt, *Fachserie. 10, Rechtspflege. Reihe 2, Gerichte und Staatsanwaltschaften. 1, Zivilgerichte*, Tables 1.1 and 4.1.

15 The German Federal Ministry of Justice has set up a research project for this issue, the results of which will be published by the end of 2023. See Monika Nöhre, 'Ursachenforschung nach dem Rückgang der Zivilklagen' (2021) 6 Deutsche Richterzeitung 220 for a description of the project.

16 An interesting remark in this regard is that simple debt collection, which used to be a large proportion of the work in small- and medium-sized German law firms, has become much less common today. See Michael Dudek, 'Rückgang der Fallzahlen – Änderung der Konfliktkultur' (2020) 18 Juristenzeitung 886.

17 The numbers of lawyers in 2000 and 2021 were 17,126 and 43,206, respectively.

18 The total number of new civil litigation cases received by district and summary courts was 460,642 in 2000 and 463,939 in 2021. More precisely, the number of cases increased once, reaching approximately 900,000 in 2009, but then declined to the same level as in 2000. This was due to a temporary surge in the number of so-called actions for recovery of overpaid interest against credit companies triggered by several Supreme Court decisions.

19 The number of new cases received by district courts was 162,589 in 2000 and 141,264 in 2021. The figure for 2021 includes the number of family cases, which were originally under the jurisdiction of the district courts, but were placed under the jurisdiction of the family courts in 2004.

20 The average length of proceedings in 2020 was 9.9 months, longer than 8.8 months in 2000. See Supreme Court of Japan, *Saiban no Jinsokuka ni Kakaru Kenshô (dai9kai) ni Kansuru Hôkokusho* [Report on the 9th Review of the Speeding up of Court Proceedings] (2021) 58, Figure 5.

The question of what causes the aforementioned increased delays naturally arises. One of the main suspected causes is the increase in the number of cases requiring new expertise, atypical cases and cases involving high emotional conflict.[21] According to the Japanese Supreme Court, the number of traditionally typical cases brought before the courts, such as those relating to moneylending and land registration, is decreasing, whereas the number of claims for various types of damages, including atypical ones, is increasing.[22] As for the reasons for this, it is argued that with the increase in the number of lawyers, more lawyers are involved in pre-litigation negotiations, at which stage typical cases are resolved.[23] It is also observed that the contracts that are brought to court are becoming increasingly diverse and individualised as well as specialised and complex.[24] Various software development contracts are often discussed as prime examples of such complex contracts.[25]

An increase in the number of atypical cases would mean an increase in diversity in the courts' dockets. It can thus be seen as a sign of the increasing complexity of the courts' dockets, suggesting that the courts can no longer adequately fulfil their duties by dealing only with classic disputes as traditionally envisaged.

2.2.3 Background: Increase in Complexity of Socioeconomic Conditions

If the complexity of individual cases or the entire docket reflects the complexity of socioeconomic conditions, as suggested in Section 2.1.3, an increase in the complexity of the former must reflect an increase in the complexity of the latter. Although it is difficult to demonstrate an increase in the complexity of socioeconomic conditions with clear parameters, an increase in the number of multiparty cases and atypical cases, as described earlier, can be regarded as indicating an increase in the complexity of social life, which gives rise to such cases.

---

21 See Supreme Court of Japan, *Saiban no Jinsokuka ni Kakaru Kenshô (dai7kai) ni Kansuru Hôkokusho* [Report on the 7th Review of the Speeding up of Court Proceedings] (2017) 67. See also Supreme Court of Japan, *Saiban no Jinsokuka ni Kakaru Kenshô (dai8kai) ni Kansuru Hôkokusho* [Report on the 8th Review of the Speeding up of Court Proceedings] (2019) 72.

22 Supreme Court of Japan, *Saiban no Jinsokuka ni Kakaru Kenshô (dai7kai) ni Kansuru Hôkokusho* [Report on the 7th Review of the Speeding up of Court Proceedings] (2017) 71. For the changes in caseload over the past 20 years in Japan, see also Shusuke Kakiuchi, 'How Should We Understand the Current Cumber of Civil Litigation Cases in Japan?' in Daniel H. Foote et al. (eds), *Hô no Keiken teki Shakai Kagaku no Kakuritsu ni Mukete* [Festschrift for Prof. Masayuki Murayama: Towards the Establishment of an Empirical Social Science of Law] (Shinzansha 2019) 251 ff, which argues that in money claims cases, which account for two-thirds of the local court caseload, there has been a decline in typical claims, such as claims for payment of sales prices and loans, and an increase in unclassifiable, miscellaneous claims for damages.

23 Ibid., 71.

24 See, e.g. Legal Training and Research Institute, *Minji Soshô ni Okeru Jijitsu Nintei: Keiyaku Bun'ya betsu Kenkyû (Seisaku oyobi Kaihatsu ni Kansuru Keiyaku)* [Fact-finding in Civil Litigation: A Study Based on Different Contract Types, in Particular Contracts for Development of a Product] (Hôsôkai, 2014) 1.

25 Ibid., 3 and 91.

While the increasing complexity of social life may have various causes, perhaps one of the most important among them is the development of technology. Indeed, technological developments have been greatly expanding the possibilities for human activity, giving rise to new types of conflicts in society that may be brought before the courts. The disputes arising from software development contracts are a good example of the direct impact of technological developments on the complexity of disputes. In addition, the easier and more active movements of people and trade across borders are likely to lead to diverse attributes and mentalities of the parties to a dispute. The increasing rapidity of such changes should also not be overlooked. Today, people's attitudes are changing rapidly, resulting in ever-increasing diversity in society.

2.3 *Litigation Agreements as a Response to Increasing Complexity*

2.3.1 Need to Adapt Proceedings to Increasing Complexity

As already suggested in Section 2.1.2, the increasing complexity, particularly of the docket, raises questions about the appropriateness of applying uniform procedural rules to all cases. As increasing complexity of the docket means increasing diversity of cases, this leads to a diversity of needs for proceedings, to which the responses must also be diverse.[26] In addition, it should be noted that the development of information technology has created procedural options that did not exist in the past, such as hearings using web conferencing systems; thus, we now have more procedural choices at our disposal than before. The fact that more procedural options have become available may stimulate a further diversification of needs. In short, there is an increasing diversity of conflicts in society and an increasing diversity of demands for how to resolve them. The question, then, is how to answer these diverse needs and provide procedures suitable for them.

The first possible approach is to create special rules or procedures in advance by law, according to the characteristics of each type of case. This approach has two major advantages: predictability and legitimacy. If the rules are set out in advance by law, interested parties will be able to foresee the applicable rules in advance, negotiate their rights and obligations and decide whether to file a lawsuit based on such information. At the same time, the legitimacy of the rules' content will be guaranteed when they are embodied in laws enacted by Parliament or equivalent authorities. However, lack of flexibility is a serious disadvantage of this approach. As already suggested, if the degree of diversity is very high, special rules cannot be established in advance for all types of cases.

26 As Cadiet argued some years ago, complexity invites the consideration of a reform introducing '*sur mesure*' proceedings instead of '*prêt-à-porter*' proceedings. See Cadiet (n 7), para. 27.

A second possible approach is to leave the adjustment to individual cases to the discretion of the judge on a case-by-case basis. The main advantage of this approach is, of course, its flexibility. Indeed, this approach would make it possible to adapt the procedure more or less to the needs, however diverse they may be. However, this approach is not without serious problems, as it does not guarantee the predictability of such adjustments to the parties. Moreover, under this approach, the legitimacy of specific measures cannot be taken for granted. While it is true that the discretionary powers of judges are becoming increasingly important in many jurisdictions, the issue of how to control them has been a much-discussed topic in recent years.[27]

As seen so far, both the first and second approaches have their own problems that are difficult to solve, and it is in this context that litigation agreements draw particular attention. Thus, it is argued that the contemporary model of the procedure should be based on permanent cooperation between the judge and the parties and rely on the use of a contract as a management tool where necessary, which implies a 'contractualisation of the procedure'.[28] Indeed, litigation agreements do not appear to suffer from any of the disadvantages of the first and second approaches. They are flexible, at least insofar as freedom of contract applies to their contents. As the parties themselves know their needs the best, it would be reasonable to leave them to specify the details of the procedures to meet those needs. Litigation agreements are also predictable, at least insofar as they are agreed upon prior to the dispute.[29] They should be regarded as legitimate because they are based on the free will of the parties. As Cabral argues, litigation agreements are considered powerful tools to overcome uncertainties in lawsuits, affording greater efficiency and adaptability to proceedings.[30] From this perspective, parties should be able to agree on rules concerning the service of process, number of witnesses, choice of expert, cost allocation, waiver of the right to appeal, and conditions of enforcement, among other things.[31]

2.3.2 Complexity and the Role of National Courts

Even if coordinating proceedings through party agreements has many advantages, some may doubt its appropriateness for proceedings before national courts. Indeed, litigation is not the only means of dispute resolution. There are other dispute resolution mechanisms

27 As a tentative study from the perspective of the basic structure of the procedure, see Shusuke Kakiuchi, 'Struktur des Zivilprozeßverfahrens und "Rechtsangleichung"' in Karl Riesenhuber and Kanako Takayama (eds), *Rechtsangleichung: Grundlagen, Methoden und Inhalte* (De Gruyter 2006) 541 ff.

28 Cadiet (n 7), para. 27.

29 On the advantages of litigation agreements in providing certainty and predictability, see Antonio Cabral, 'Designing Procedure by Contract: Litigation Agreements in Contemporary Civil Procedure' (2019) 2 International Journal of Procedural Law 363, 375.

30 Ibid., 368.

31 Ibid., 364. See also Cadiet (n 7), para. 17, which mentions agreements suspending the proceedings to pursue an amicable solution and those fixing the timetable for the preparatory proceedings.

based on the parties' agreement, such as arbitration, where the parties are allowed a wide range of dispositions regarding the proceedings. Could arbitration, then, not be an adequate alternative option? One may argue that because the use of arbitration is left at the disposal of the parties, parties who wish to customise their proceedings can do so by using arbitration, so that court proceedings would not need to meet their needs.

The question of whether arbitration could be an adequate alternative option to litigation is closely related to the questions of what role national courts should play and how to evaluate the existence of arbitration as a legal institution. Thus, one may perhaps argue that not all disputes arising in society need to be resolved through litigation and that diverse needs could be met through other dispute resolution mechanisms, including arbitration, mediation and various forms of online dispute resolution (ODR), which have recently been developing rapidly. According to this view, court proceedings can maintain their classical form and deal only with disputes that suit them. Even if – as is the case in some jurisdictions – the use of litigation declines as a result, there should be nothing to lament.

However, some issues can be raised against the aforementioned argument. First, as Cabral has argued, arbitration is not applicable in all cases because some substantive rights are not waivable and, therefore, not 'arbitrable',[32] and, even if the subject matter is legally arbitrable, arbitration is often so expensive that a large proportion of the population cannot afford it.[33]

Second, there may be other factors that make it difficult for the parties to enter into an arbitration agreement. Of course, such an agreement is possible only if both parties are willing to agree on how to resolve their current or future disputes, but, even if they are ready to agree,[34] it does not follow that they would always prefer arbitration. Indeed, if at least one of the parties is willing to use the national courts, an arbitration agreement cannot be expected, even if both parties have the intent to make some changes to the proceedings. Such a preference for a state court may result from a number of reasons, including the concerned party's trust in the state courts, the superiority of state court proceedings in terms of quality, and lower costs of state court proceedings.

Third, even if there are no obstacles to the parties' use of arbitration, it can be problematic from the public interest perspective if the use of the national courts is avoided in too many cases. This could undermine the important functions of the court system: to provide precedents in the form of publicly accessible judgements and to

32 See for example Art. II(1) and V(2)(a) of the United Nations Convention on the Recognition and Enforcement of Foreign Arbitral Awards (New York Convention), which require the subject matter to be capable of settlement by arbitration for it to be arbitrable.

33 See Cabral (n 29) 363, 377.

34 It is not always easy to reach an agreement on the dispute resolution process between parties with conflicting interests. It should be noted, however, that for parties who are able to make use of litigation agreements, it should not be too difficult to reach a certain agreement.

ensure the development of legal rules in response to social changes.[35] Of course, this does not mean that parties should be barred from using arbitration or other dispute resolution mechanisms and forced to litigate. As long as the self-determination of the parties is adequately guaranteed, a failure to use judicial proceedings is not, in itself, to be blamed even if it will reduce the courts' functions. However, it would be problematic if the rigidity and inflexibility of the national court proceedings would prevent parties from using litigation in the national courts to resolve their disputes despite their willingness to do so. In such a situation, the parties would be more or less forced to use alternative dispute resolution (ADR) mechanisms instead of litigation, which would undermine their self-determination. Thus, this would also be problematic from the perspective of access to justice.

In view of the aforementioned considerations, the existence of arbitration proceedings does not justify the idea that national court proceedings need not be responsive to diverse needs. Rather, court proceedings should be flexible enough to accommodate a greater variety of disputes and should continue to play an important role in society.

This conclusion reaffirms the importance of litigation agreements as powerful tools for adapting court proceedings to a wide variety of cases and parties' needs.

3 Challenges for Litigation Agreements

3.1 *Overview*

Even if expectations for litigation agreements are high, there are still challenges that such agreements have to handle so that they can perform their expected functions fully.

First, although agreements are flexible in nature, this does not mean that any content can be validly determined. There must be certain limits to the contents of litigation agreements.

Second, even within the sphere where agreements are legally admissible, it is not certain that litigation agreements can be expected to be concluded in many cases. This puts the effectiveness of litigation agreements as tools in question. Their effectiveness will depend on the incentives to enter into agreements and the associated costs of doing so. Taking these factors into account, some issues emerge that need to be addressed.

Third, from a normative perspective, the issue of the legitimacy of litigation agreements needs to be considered.

---

35 As is well known, this is one of the issues that Fiss raised against the promotion of settlements. See Owen M. Fiss, 'Against Settlement' (1984) 93 Yale Law Journal 1073, 1085.

3.2 *Limits of Litigation Agreements*

Although the traditional, strict position against litigation agreements, according to which all litigation agreements that are not expressly provided for by law are inadmissible, can no longer be maintained today,[36] it does not mean that litigation agreements of whatever contents are permissible. Thus, flexibility, which is the main advantage of litigation agreements, has certain limits.

Some of the procedural rules specified by law embody fundamental values, typically identified by the Constitution, and may not be changed by parties' agreements. For example, in Japan, the principles of publicity and orality of the trial are provided by an article of the constitution.[37] Consequently, an agreement that all proceedings shall be conducted non-publicly or that the proceedings should be fully written would be contrary to this provision and would have no effect.[38]

As this example shows, not all rules of procedural law can be subject to modification through litigation agreements. Thus, the key question is where the boundary should be drawn from the viewpoint of public policy, within which parties should be free to make agreements.[39] As will be seen later, this is not always an easy task.

It should be added that even if some parts of the procedure can be changed through litigation agreements, the changes must be within the framework of the litigation procedure. In other words, it is not possible to create a procedure that can no longer be regarded as litigation. As long as it is a 'litigation' agreement, however flexible it may be, it can make only minor modifications within the boundaries of the litigation procedure.[40] Litigation agreements are not magic wands that address all needs.

---

36 The validity of the traditional principle of the prohibition of arbitrary or conventional procedure (*Verbot des Konventionalprozesses*) is questionable today. See Cabral (n 29) 369-371. Similar criticisms of this principle can also be seen in Japan. See Hajime Kaneko, 'Soshô ni kansuru Gôi ni tsuite' [On Agreements Relating to Legal Proceedings] (1935) 53 Hôgaku Kyôkai Zasshi 2277. This article was subsequently included in a book containing a collection of Professor Kaneko's writings. Hajime Kaneko, *Minji Hô Kenkyû* [Studies on Civil Law] (Vol. 1, Kôbundô 1940) 239 ff.

37 Art. 82 of the Constitution of Japan provides that '[t]rials shall be conducted and judgment declared publicly.' 'Trial' here is understood to mean the hearing for oral arguments in the case of civil procedure. Combined with Art. 87 of the Code of Civil Procedure, which provides that the parties shall, in principle, conduct oral arguments on their case before the court, this provision establishes the principle of publicity and orality in the civil procedure.

38 Although it is possible for parties only to submit written documents and not to appear in the hearing for oral arguments, there will be a risk that the action will be deemed to have been withdrawn in this case (Art. 263, Code of Civil Procedure). See also Shusuke Kakiuchi, 'Contractualisation of Civil Litigation in Japan: Party Autonomy in Procedural Context and its Limits' in Anna Nylund and Antonio Cabral (eds), *Contractualisation of Civil Litigation* (Intersentia 2023) 299-300.

39 As Cabral argues, this is a question of 'the leeway to negotiate, the boundaries within which individuals can legitimately waive their procedural rights, changing the proceedings'. See Cabral (n 29) 371.

40 If the rules of procedural law as a general framework are flawed, it will be a problem requiring legislative reform rather than minor adjustments by agreement.

3.3 *Effectiveness of Litigation Agreements*

3.3.1 Possible Obstacles to the Conclusion of Litigation Agreements

The second challenge is the existence of doubts about the effectiveness of litigation agreements. The fact that an agreement is legally admissible does not necessarily mean that the parties are always ready to enter into such an agreement. In fact, there are several concerns in this regard.

First, although the parties to a dispute usually have a concrete interest in the outcome of the dispute, they do not necessarily have sufficiently precise needs regarding the procedures leading to the outcome. In addition, compared to the needs relating to the outcome, procedural needs may change more easily in the course of the proceedings.

Second, even if the parties have recognised their needs related to the procedure in a sufficiently precise way, there is no guarantee that both parties' needs will match each other. It is not unusual, for example, that the potential plaintiff seeks more expeditious relief while the potential defendant prefers more heavily equipped procedures. If there is such a gap between the needs of the two parties, negotiation to reach an agreement will not always be easy.

To overcome the aforementioned difficulties, it may be necessary to provide some guidelines to reduce negotiation costs and facilitate agreements. Experience in arbitration practice and the procedural rules of various arbitral institutions may be helpful in this regard. Furthermore, it would make sense for the law to offer the parties more or less concrete options in advance. In any event, if no agreement can be reached, the matter will have to be left to the default rule provided by law or to the discretion of the court.[41] Thus, the possibility of a litigation agreement does not diminish the importance of the rules specified by law.

3.3.2 Predictability and Decision-Making Costs

If there are certain limits to the modification of procedural rules by litigation agreements, as discussed earlier, the criteria on what agreements are permissible must be sufficiently clear so that the outcome of their application will be predictable. The problem, however, is that it is not always easy to set out the criteria with sufficient clarity.

As a hypothetical example, is it permissible to agree in advance that the parties appear before the court in turns and that each party makes oral arguments in the absence of the other party? This would be a kind of caucusing, which is sometimes used in mediation proceedings. In fact, this type of private meeting is used quite commonly in Japanese courts for the purpose of settlement discussion: judges call each party separately to hear frankly about its wish regarding settlement, a practice that

---

41 See Section 2.3.1.

has traditionally been popular with Japanese litigants.[42] Although there have been no reports to date of this method's use in formal oral argument proceedings – as only a few authors have discussed this issue to date – the issue has not yet been settled clearly.[43] Thus, one might argue that because the parties have the freedom not to appear before the court, it is within parties' disposition to agree to not to appear during the hearing of the other party.[44] Against such a view, which emphasises party autonomy, it could be objected that the right to be heard in a manner that allows the parties to contradict each other's positions belongs to the minimum procedural guarantees, which neither party can waive in advance. According to the latter view, even if such an agreement exists, it would not be binding and the judge cannot prohibit the presence of the adverse party even if the other party invokes such an agreement. However, which of the two views is correct is not self-evident and may still be open to debate.

The problem here is that the criteria of 'minimum procedural guarantees' are not sufficiently precise or detailed because there is no clear and common understanding of the contents of such guarantees when it comes to specific problems that may be raised by atypical procedural arrangements.

This situation is quite problematic because if the criteria are not clear enough, the incentive to enter into agreements in advance would be considerably undermined, and, for the courts, the burden of determining the validity of each specific agreement will increase, which may cause delays in the proceedings.

Thus, again, to reduce the uncertainty over the validity of the agreement and the associated decision-making costs, it may be useful to develop certain guidelines.[45]

3.4 *Legitimacy of Litigation Agreements*

Another challenge is the question of legitimacy. Although changes in the procedural rules through litigation agreements are justified by the parties' free will and autonomy, for this justification to be valid, it is important that the parties have access to sufficient information when making a decision and that the option of not entering into such an agreement exists as a sufficiently realistic one. From this perspective, even regarding matters for which litigation agreements are generally permitted, whether agreements

42 See for example Shusuke Kakiuchi, 'Règlement des litiges' in Pascale Bloch et al. (eds), *Droit japonais des affaires* (Larcier 2019) 310-311.

43 The literature that exceptionally mentions this point argues that the validity of such agreements should be denied. See Kazuhiko Yamamoto, *Minji Soshô Hô no Gendai teki Kadai* [Contemporary Issues in the Law of Civil Procedure] (Yûhikaku 2016) 328 and Shusuke Kakiuchi, 'Wakai Tetsuzuki Ron [On the Court Settlement Procedure]' in Kôji Shindô (ed), *Jitsumu Minji Soshô Kôza* [Lectures on Civil Litigation Practice] (Vol. 3, Nihon Hyôron Sha 2013) 195.

44 The author once discussed the matter with a Japanese judge, who was inclined to support this view.

45 For this purpose, comparative law would be a useful tool.

should be allowed between parties with disparities in resources will be a sensitive issue. This issue typically emerges with regard to agreements between consumers and businesses.[46]

One solution would be to treat such agreements as null and void or to give the weaker party the right to rescind them, but it may be worth considering whether more flexible adjustments are possible instead of such an all-or-nothing approach. For example, while maintaining the validity of the agreement, its binding force could be relaxed to allow room for adjustments by the court. However, the effects of litigation agreements and the possibility of their posterior adjustment still require further study.

4 Concluding Remarks

The answer to the question that we set out at the beginning of this chapter – whether the hypothesis that increasing complexity creates the need to adapt civil litigation procedures to it and that litigation contracts can be effective tools to achieve this is plausible – is that, yes, the hypothesis is plausible, but with some reservations, as we have seen. Litigation agreements are not magic wands that solve all problems at once; neither do they eliminate the need to improve the law of civil procedure. The extent to which they can fulfil their expected functions depends on how they can handle the various challenges they face, including those pointed out in this chapter, which is left to further study.

46 The conflicting views on whether to permit arbitration clauses between consumers and businesses illustrate well the difficulty of this issue.

Shaping Civil Litigation Using Procedural Agreements: Perspectives and Prospects

Anna Nylund

1 Introduction

This concluding chapter draws on insights from the contributions of this book. First, it revisits the boundaries between procedural contracts and related phenomena (Section 2). Then it situates litigation clauses in their legal-cultural, systemic and regulatory contexts (Section 3). Next, Section 4 examines the limits to procedural agreements put by the principles of the rule of law and public and third-party interests. Section 5 discusses how courts should deal with procedural contracts and how this influences the potential procedural contracts harbour in rendering civil litigation more efficient. The final section (Section 6) offers some remarks on the prospects of procedural contracts.

2 Revisiting the Definition of Procedural Contracts

2.1 Procedural and Substantive Contracts

As this book illustrates, the demarcation between procedural and substantive issues is porous and far from clear.[1] The term 'agreement', or 'contract', suggests that the parties must act jointly. Yet, even situations in which (prospective) parties to litigation make unilateral declarations that they refrain from availing themselves of procedural rights or opportunities, such as the right to appeal,[2] are considered parallel to a procedural agreement.

The word 'procedural' implies that the contract or clause modifies procedural rules. However, some agreements directly related to court proceedings are entangled with substantive law. Litigation cost agreements are one example. The distribution of costs does not alter the procedure other than indirectly. Henrik Bellander argues that

1 Bellander, this volume, Section 2.4; Eichel and Tovar, this volume, Section 2.

2 Vebraite, this volume, Sections 3 and 5.

compensation for litigation costs could be regarded as damages paid by parties who refuse to comply voluntarily with their legal obligations rather than as a procedural tool.[3] Another type of contract that governs substantive law matters firmly interlocked with court proceedings is agreements on the burden of proof, which are considered to belong to the domain of substantive law in many jurisdictions.[4] Thus, the authors have abandoned the conceptual clarity of a delimitation based on formal classifications in favour of a functional approach.[5]

Apart from agreements at the intersection of procedural law and substantive law, this book engages with agreements that govern the commencement and end of court proceedings, such as choice of court and settlement agreements. These agreements, which are widely recognised in commercial cases,[6] have no bearing on access to an adjudicative procedure resulting in an enforceable title, and the course of proceedings remains unaltered. In principle, agreements to use an alternative dispute resolution (ADR) process only postpone access to court, not hinder access.[7] Agreements to end litigation through settlement, or withdrawal, are a manifestation of the principles of adversarial and party proceedings. Since parties have the autonomy to resolve their dispute before bringing an action, they should retain that autonomy during court proceedings.[8] Similarly, because the right to appeal does not impact access to court and a binding and enforceable ruling, many jurisdictions allow waivers of appeal.[9] However, appeals agreements are not universally recognised in contrast to jurisdiction and arbitration agreements.

Most jurisdictions, except notably Brazil and the US, are reluctant to agreements that alter the course of the proceedings, such as agreements waiving oral hearings or selecting a specific track.[10] An important reason for rejecting such contracts seems to be that they interfere with the court's powers, the course of the proceedings, or the determination of facts and law. However, the institution of International Commercial Courts (ICCs) can be regarded as a step towards the 'arbitralisation' of courts because the proceedings are flexible by design to allow the courts to compete with arbitration.[11]

3 Bellander, this volume.

4 Strandberg, this volume, Section 3.

5 For more details, see Cabral, this volume, Sections 2, 3 and 5.

6 Anna Nylund and Antonio Cabral, 'General Report: Contractualisation of Civil Litigation' in Anna Nylund and Antonio Cabral (eds), *Contractualisation of Civil Litigation* (Intersentia 2023) 10-14.

7 Nylund, this volume.

8 Uzelac, this volume, Section 2.3. See also Leo Rosenberg, Karl Heinz Schwab, Peter Gottwald, *Zivilprozessrecht* (18th edn, C.H. Beck 2018) 375-376.

9 Vebraite, this volume, Section 4.

10 Nylund and Cabral (n 6) 10-14; Antonio Cabral and Pedro Henrique Nogueira, 'Contractualisation of Civil Litigation in Brazil'; Helen Herschkoff and Judith Resnik, 'Contractualisation of Civil Litigation in the United States', both in Anna Nylund and Antonio Cabral (eds.), *Contractualisation of Civil Litigation* (Intersentia 2023).

11 Hau, this volume; Uzelac, this volume.

2.2 Contracts, Case Management and Consensualisation

In recent decades, case management and flexible rules have arguably equipped parties with increasing influence over civil litigation. This could be characterised as a 'consensualisation' of civil proceedings. The demarcation between 'contractualisation' and 'consensualisation' is equally blurred as the distinction between substantive contracts and procedural contracts.

As Alan Uzelac remarks, active case management and the flexibilisation of civil litigation have produced a seismic shift in the landscape of civil litigation, thus also palpably transforming the context and potential of procedural contracts.[12] In this novel paradigm, proceedings are flexible by design: the court and the parties cooperate in moulding the proceedings to fit the case at hand. The procedure is subject to negotiation but not necessarily agreements. One reason is that the case-managing judge must strive for the proportionate use of resources, ensuring that the use of resources is appropriate – not too low or high or ill-directed.[13] In this setting, judges must have the power to decide whether to proceed following the wishes of the parties, be they agreements concluded before or during court proceedings or mutual or even unilateral requests.

Moreover, when case management is a tripartite endeavour, and the proceedings are, to some extent, tailored to each case, the origins of an initiative to shape the proceedings are not necessarily significant. Whether the parties agreed on an arrangement before bringing the action, whether one party took the initiative unilaterally and the other party acquiesced, or whether the case-managing judge (or court employee) conceived it, all these questions are unimportant. Moreover, although proceedings are flexible, the number and type of options and permutations are limited and specific principles and aims guide and restrain decision-making. The principle of cooperation, as expressed in the European Rules of Civil Procedure (ERCP) Rules 2 to 4, refers to a duty to act loyally to ensure an expedient procedure but not a right to alter the proceedings. Consequently, flexible, collaborative proceedings are not a matter of contractualisation per se but rather a form of consensualisation of civil proceedings that moulds the space for procedural contracts.

This may narrow the room for procedural agreements in jurisdictions with flexible rules: the procedure is consensual but not contractual because the arrangement is contingent on the court's approval.

---

12 Uzelac, this volume, Section 2.1.

13 John Sorabji, 'The Contractualisation of Civil Litigation in England and Wales: Party Autonomy, Contracts and Procedure'; Anna Nylund, Magne Strandberg and Marit Tjelmeland, 'Contractualisation of Civil Litigation in Norway: Flexibility and Cooperation in a Rule-based Tradition' 334-336, both in Anna Nylund and Antonio Cabral (eds), *Contractualisation of Civil Litigation* (Intersentia 2023).

2.3 *Contract Law or the Law of Procedural Contracts?*

A corollary to the demarcation between substantive law and procedural law is whether procedural contracts should be treated according to the rules of contract or civil procedure law, or perhaps as a sui generis category. Civil procedure doctrine is oriented to the relationship between a party and the court, not between the parties: applications, requests, and motions are directed to the court and not to the opposite party. It lacks the concepts needed for contracts between the parties. Thus, contract law is an initial source of inspiration for the law of procedural contracts.[14] However, exceptions from the general doctrines of contract law must be carved out to comply with the fundamental tenets of civil procedure law and to protect the third party involved, namely, the court. It is unclear whether uniform rules for all procedural contracts should apply or whether granular rules reflecting the variation in such agreements, their variegated content and context, would be better.

Choice of court contracts can be a starting point for developing a comprehensive theory on procedural contracts, which is an amalgamation of contract law and procedural law.[15] In contrast with the absence of coherent regulation of procedural contracts in most countries,[16] there is a doctrine and practice on choice of court contracts in many jurisdictions, and internationally.[17] Rules on the form, conclusion, validity, and interpretation of the contract are particularly important.[18] In international relations, determining the law governing procedural contracts is likely pertinent. Moreover, courts should have the power to disregard or reinterpret agreements that are against important values underpinning the civil procedural system.[19]

An interesting facet of this problem is that procedural agreements are likely to be embedded in a substantive law contract rather than a separate contract. Thus, 'procedural clause' could be a more accurate term than 'procedural agreement' or 'contract'.

The doctrine of separability, which applies to arbitral and choice of court agreements, as Florian Eichel and Rorick Tovar Galván discuss, addresses this issue. According to this doctrine, the validity of the procedural clauses is independent of the validity of the contract that they are part of. Another example is the competence – that is, the competence of the selected court or tribunal; only the court or the tribunal can

14 Rosenberg et al. (n 8) 356 and 377.
15 Eichel and Tovar Galván, this volume, Section 2.3.
16 Nylund and Cabral (n. 6), Section 5.
17 Eichel and Tovar Galván, this volume.
18 Ibid., Section 3.
19 Ibid., Sections 2.2 and 4.

decide whether the clause or contract is valid. A third is that the law applicable to the jurisdiction clause might differ from the law applicable to the rest of the contract.[20]

Consequently, even if the parties disagree on the validity of the agreement's procedural and substantive parts, the selected court (or arbitral tribunal) will hear disputes arising from the contract. If it finds that the choice of court (or arbitration) clause is not valid or is inoperative, the parties may bring an action elsewhere.[21] As explained above, choice of court and arbitration agreements only designate the forum; they do not limit access to the proceedings in general.

Nevertheless, these rules might not be suitable for all procedural contracts.[22] One reason is choice of court clauses do not alter the proceedings of the selected forum. Second, such clauses are mainly tailored for international (commercial) cases and thus are intentionally decontextualised to promote the equal application of the norms across different countries, which the autonomous interpretation of many terms in the Brussels Ibis Regulation manifests. Procedural agreements that alter procedural rules are deeply embedded in the national context.

Third, in (commercial) private international and arbitration law, party autonomy is an axiom which guides the interpretation of such agreements.[23] Translating it into general civil procedure law could be problematic. Party autonomy has traditionally been foreign to traditional civil procedure doctrine and is not mentioned as a principle in standard textbooks on civil procedure in countries such as England, Germany and Norway.[24] Instead, they apply concepts such as the principle of party disposition.[25] As discussed above, party disposition is limited to the commencement and end of litigation and determining the ambit of the disputes, as well as a few selected aspects.[26] It is unclear whether letting language from the world of contract law colonise civil procedure doctrine beyond the choice of court and arbitration clauses is advisable and what implications it would have.

---

20 Ibid., Section 3.

21 E.g., UNCITRAL Model Law on International Commercial Arbitration, Art. 8.

22 See also Nylund, this volume.

23 E.g., Klaus Peter Berger, 'Institutional Arbitration: Harmony, Disharmony and the "Party Autonomy Paradox"' (2018) 34 *Arbitration International*, 473; Alex Mills, 'Rethinking Jurisdiction in International Law' (2104) 84 *British Yearbook of International Law* 187; Alex Mills, 'Conceptualising Party Autonomy in Private International Law' [2019] Revue critique de droit international privé 417.

24 The author has searched indexes of several textbooks from each jurisdiction. In one book, party autonomy was mentioned but explicitly as a private law concept that only had procedural implications for the right of parties to choose whether to bring an action, the scope of the action and ending court proceedings through settlement or withdrawal – see Johann Braun, *Lehrbuch des Zivilprozessrechts* (Mohr Siebeck 2014) 72.

25 E.g., ERCP Rule 21, Comment 1; Rule 24, Comment 1; and Rule 88, Comment 2.

26 E.g., Rosenberg et al. (n 8) 375. ERCP Rule 25, Comment 8; Rule 120, Comment 6; Rule 163, Comment 1; Rule 167, Comment 1; and Rule 189, Comment 2.

Considering the ubiquity of choice of court clauses in commercial cases, parties can be expected to be aware that standard terms and conditions might include such a clause, as the Court of Justice of the European Union (CJEU) argued in the *Tilman* case.[27] The CJEU opined that to establish a valid choice of court clause, a reference to the general terms and conditions used by one party – which could be read and downloaded by clicking on a hypertext link and that stated that English courts had exclusive jurisdiction – sufficed. In contrast, in consumer relations and other relations characterised by a manifest power imbalance, the conclusion is likely to be the opposite.[28]

Without a coherent theory of procedural agreements, the uncertainties relating to the validity, interpretation and effects of such agreements entail considerable risks for current and prospective litigants. While the contributions in this book do not contribute directly to the formation of such theories, particularly aspects drawing on contract law, they shed light on the limits civil procedure law puts on shaping court proceedings contractually.

3 The Context of Procedural Agreements

The context in which procedural agreements operate depends on several factors, including the prevailing perception of the role and functions of civil courts, the relative flexibility and rigidity of court proceedings, the efficiency of court proceedings, and the regulatory principles of aspects of civil procedure.[29] The profound contextual diversity probably affects to which extent and in which areas procedural agreements are considered valuable.

3.1 Ideas Underpinning Courts and Court Proceedings

Arguably, there is a nexus between the proliferation of procedural agreements and the fundamental ideas regarding courts and court proceedings. These foundations are latent, vary between countries and oscillate over time.[30]

The perceptions about the primary functions of court proceedings, whether courts primarily serve private or public interests, are part of these fundaments. The private

27 Case C-358/21 *Tilman SA v. Unilever Supply Chain Company AG* [2022] ECLI:EU:C:2022:923, paras. 56-58.

28 Eichel and Tovar Galván, this volume, Section 4.3.1.; Ancery and Krans, this volume.

29 Bellander, this volume, Section 2.

30 E.g., Anna Nylund, 'Civil Procedure and the Rule of Law in Scandinavia' (2023) 69 Scandinavian Studies in Law.

function can be either dispute resolution as such, or the vindication of rights, seeking justice through the law. Particularly when dispute resolution is accentuated, agreements that improve the service should be welcome, at least if no additional 'production costs' are accrued. However, if court proceedings are considered mainly a public good, a forum for enforcement of legal rights and obligations, and a vehicle for promoting the policies underlying the law as a governance tool, then procedural agreements harbour potentially disruptive forces.[31]

Efficient enforcement of rights, equality before the law, and using court proceedings as a process where 'democratic practices occur'[32] reduce the space for procedural agreements as these could disrupt the process. Moreover, regarding the law as a governance tool is likely to limit the room for procedural agreements, at least when they could be contrary to those policies. Alain Ancery and Bart Krans discuss how the CJEU has taken this view in some consumer law cases.[33] Of course, the use of courts to promote public goods depends on the willingness of individuals to file actions. Thus, at least in complex cases, allowing procedural agreements could turn the tide from arbitration to litigation, which enhances the public functions of courts.[34] These three approaches exist in parallel and are not mutually exclusive. Differences emerge from which of these is the dominating paradigm.

Another facet is for whom courts are accountable. If courts are perceived as Weberian bureaucratic organisations – institutions that derive their legitimacy by pursuing public interests and from a 'rational', 'due' process –[35] then procedural agreements can easily become a disruptive force, sand in the machinery, or a distraction to judges whose task is to administer the production of civil justice. This logic requires limiting variation in proceedings and discretion to be exercised within clear boundaries. In contrast, New Public Management and neoliberalism[36] advance the marketisation of dispute resolution and private ordering,[37] creating fertile ground for procedural agreements. Such agreements are a vehicle for courts to 'compete' with arbitration and ADR, to be

31 E.g., Alexandra Lahav, *In Praise of Litigation* (Oxford University Press 2017).

32 Judith Resnik, 'Constituting a Civil Legal System Called "Just": Law, Money, Power, and Publicity' in Xandra Kramer et al. (eds.), *New Pathways to Civil Justice in Europe* (Springer 2021).

33 Ancery and Krans, this volume.

34 Kakiuchi, this volume, Section 2.3.2.

35 Steven Van de Walle, 'NPM: Restoring the Public Trust through Creating Distrust?' in Tom Christensen and Per Lægreid (eds), *The Ashgate Research Companion to New Public Management* (Taylor and Francis 2016) 298.

36 Ibid.; Jonathan Boston, 'Basic NPM Ideas and Their Development' in Tom Christensen and Per Lægreid (eds), *The Ashgate Research Companion to New Public Management* (Taylor and Francis 2016) 31-33; Simon Springer, *The Discourse of Neoliberalism: An Anatomy of a Powerful Idea* (Rowman & Littlefield Unlimited Model 2016).

37 Ravi Malhotra, 'Neoliberalism, Law, and Its Discontents: Three Recent Interventions' (2020) 23 Left History: An Interdisciplinary Journal of Historical Inquiry and Debate 98-106; Felix Steffek, 'Principled Regulation of Dispute Resolution: Taxonomy, Policy, Topics' in Felix Steffek et al. (eds), *Regulating Dispute Resolution: ADR and Access to Justice at the Crossroads* (Bloomsbury 2014) 43-46. Hazel Genn (*Judging*

accountable to their 'customers'.[38] The enactment of procedural rules that carve out space for flexible norms[39] dilutes the Weberian ideals that have been dominant in many jurisdictions. The emergence of ICCs, the 'caviar courts', illustrates the turn away from traditional ideas.[40]

3.2 *Flexible, Rigid, (In)efficient, and Fragmented Procedural Systems*

The perception of courts as organisations and how well they function will also likely influence the need for procedural agreements and rules regarding them. When courts are (perceived as) inefficient, procedural agreements could be a vehicle for simplifying and expediting the proceedings to reduce their opacity and uncertainty. They could serve to emulate flexible rules. However, procedural agreements could also be counterproductive because they could draw attention away from the need for vital reforms, thus perpetuating inefficiency.[41]

Correspondingly, the more efficient and flexible procedural rules are, the lesser the benefits of procedural agreements. However, even in a flexible, swift system the parties could be interested in agreeing on using an ADR procedure or controlling some parts of the litigation process, such as the venue, litigation costs, appeals, and access to evidence. By emulating selected features of arbitral proceedings, procedural agreements could further enhance the advantages of litigation, such as an appeal waiver which augments the innate expeditious enforcement of outcomes in litigation.[42] Very flexible rules, or judges having broad discretionary powers, could render proceedings less foreseeable, thus making procedural contracts a tool for reducing uncertainty regarding how the proceedings unfold and the case's outcome.

In recent years, court proceedings in many jurisdictions have been fragmented by the creation of new tracks, ICCs,[43] and the emergence of new specialised courts, such as the supranational European Unified Patent Court.[44] Moreover, civil procedure rules are increasingly fragmented. A predominant example of sectoral laws is found

Civil Justice. The Hamlyn Lectures 2008 [Cambridge University Press 2010] 1-26) refers to postmodern values.

38 This is the case in the US, see Herschkoff and Resnik (n 10).

39 E.g., Sławomir Cieślak, Janusz Jankowski and Maciej Muliński, 'Contractualisation of Civil Litigation in Poland: The admissibility of Procedural Agreements in Civil Proceedings'; Petr Navrátil and Tomáš Střeleček, 'Contractualisation of Civil Procedure in the Czech Republic: A Strict Approach', both in Anna Nylund and Antonio Cabral (eds), *Contractualisation of Civil Litigation* (Intersentia 2023).

40 Hau, this volume, Section 7.

41 See also Uzelac, this volume, Section 2.3.

42 Kakiuchi, this volume, Section 2.3.2.

43 Hau, this volume.

44 https://www.unified-patent-court.org/en/court/presentation (accessed 25 January 2024).

in EU law,[45] including special requirements applicable in consumer cases.[46] This is a pendulum swing away from the ideals of unitary rules and the consolidation of courts that underpinned civil procedure reforms of the late 19th and early 20th centuries.[47] Customisation of proceedings through procedural agreements could be a facet of this trend. However, while 'granular' regulation could advance the quality and efficiency of court proceedings, it could also reduce coherence and consistency, thus producing an opaque, unnavigable, and unmanageable justice system. Procedural agreements could be employed to bridge gaps and take advantage of the fragmented system. For instance, parties could have strong incentives to frame their case to fit a specific track or to manage the uncertainty associated with tracks or special rules applicable only to some cases. However, the absence of special rules could also trigger parties to create such rules by contract.

While increased contractualisation of proceedings could render litigation more efficient, it could also have unintended and unforeseeable repercussions. It could also reduce efficiency, particularly in small cases where standardisation is a prerequisite for a smooth, foreseeable process. The opposite could be true for 'singular', complex cases.[48]

Rather than postulating that customisation - be it through contracts or general rules - increases efficiency, we should ask how much, when and which forms of special rules are desirable and assess the combined effects of fragmentation.

3.3 *Variations in Civil Procedure Rules*

The content of existing regulations of civil litigation influences whether and how (potential) litigants might wish to modify procedural rules. Henrik Bellander and Magne Strandberg illustrate these contingencies in this volume by discussing the rules on litigation costs and access to evidence.[49] Default rules that make the losing party liable to pay full compensation of the prevailing party's litigation costs create an incentive to agree on costs to decrease the economic risks of litigation. The same could also be true when the parties bear their own costs or cost-shifting is limited, albeit for different reasons. Similarly, the absence of rules on discovery or disclosure could thrust the parties to create a contractual basis for access to evidence. In contrast, very liberal rules on discovery could propel them to limit access.

45 E.g. Bart Krans and Anna Nylund, 'Comparative Insights on Procedural Autonomy' in Bart Krans and Anna Nylund (eds), *Procedural Autonomy Across Europe* (Intersentia 2020) 234-235.

46 Ancery and Krans, this volume.

47 Peter Colin, 'Einführung: Europäische Entwicklungslinien gerichtlicher und aussergerichtlicher Konfliktlösung im 19. und 20. Jahrhundert' in Peter Collin (ed), *Konfliktlösung im 19. und 20. Jahrhundert* (Springer 2021) 7-9 and 20-31.

48 Kakiuchi, this volume.

49 Bellander, this volume; Strandberg, this volume.

Civil procedural rules form a (relatively) coherent system. Thus, the combined effect of procedural rules, rather than the design of a specific rule, will likely influence what kinds of agreements the parties find useful. If cost-shifting is the default rule, the potential benefits of winning the case by producing costly evidence are more prominent than if each party bears its own costs. This is likely to impact the propensity for and contents of agreements on costs. Similarly, the subject matter of the dispute, such as contract law or tort law, could influence how the parties wish to mould the proceedings. Hence, there may be a nexus between the underlying civil procedure regime and the type of procedural agreements the parties find fruitful.

4 Limits to Procedural Contracts

4.1 *Fair Trial Rights Curbing Procedural Contracts*

Procedural agreements could endanger the rule of law[50] by limiting real and equal access to legal remedies, eroding the legitimacy of courts, and preventing the use of law as a governance tool. Still, the rule of law and democratic principles are not an argument against procedural arrangements en bloc.[51]

Agreements that prevent a disputant from accessing courts and essentially deprive citizens of meaningful remedies will likely violate basic fair trial rights and the rule of law.[52] In a European context, EU law doctrines on effective judicial protection[53] are a key supplement to fair trial rights found in national and supranational law. While ADR procedures are a prime example of ways to hinder access to court, when appropriately designed and regulated, they are an important supplement to courts.[54]

Agreements that limit the core functions of courts – markedly those that would unduly limit the capability of the court to function as a fact-finder, that is a body that seeks to establish the truth or at least arrive at a finding that emulates the truth – are unlikely to be valid. The same applies to agreements that would considerably restrain the power of the courts to apply the law correctly or exercise its core procedural powers.

---

50 Brian Z. Tamanaha, *On the Rule of Law. History, Politics, Theory* (Cambridge University Press 2012) 92-93 and 119; Tom Bingham, *The Rule of Law* (Penguin 2010).

51 See also Ancery and Bart, this volume, Section 1.

52 See also Braun (n. 24) 84; Nylund and Cabral (n 6) 35-36.

53 See, e.g., Giulia Gentile, 'Effective Judicial Protection: Enforcement, Judicial Federalism and the Politics of EU Law' (2022) 2 European Law Open 1-16; Fernando Pastor-Merchante, 'The Overlap Between the Principles of Effectiveness and Effective Judicial Protection in Union Law' in C. Izquierdo-Sans, C. Martínez-Capdevila and M. Nogueira-Guastavino (eds), *Fundamental Rights Challenges: Horizontal Effectiveness, Rule of Law and Margin of National Appreciation* (Springer 2021) 211-228.

54 Nylund, this volume.

While there could be a consensus that fair trial rights and the key functions and roles of courts should restrict procedural agreements, the extent of those restrictions is contested. The considerable variation in attitudes to the right to appeal demonstrates this.[55] Another example is the independence or impartiality of the judge. For instance, while parties have the right to enter into choice of court agreements in accordance with national and supranational rules, these regulations do not contain a framework for selecting a particular chamber at the selected court. Yet, as Wolfgang Hau argues, agreements that specify that an ICC has exclusive jurisdiction, thus vesting jurisdiction on a selected chamber of a larger court, are likely acceptable.[56]

Procedural agreements could also enhance fair trial rights. Agreements limiting appeals, shifting litigation costs, or limiting evidence could increase access to court by lowering or reducing uncertainty regarding litigation costs (and risks).[57] Whether the procedural agreement increases or decreases access to courts depends on the circumstances of the case, the agreement, and the rules governing such agreements. For instance, the combined effect of relatively minor adjustments to the rules of procedure could be a tangible reduction of procedural fairness. Thus, while a waiver of appeal would be acceptable as such, it might not apply if the proceedings in the lower court violated fair trial rights, and the combination of the clauses in an agreement on evidence when applied to the case at hand could be unacceptable even if each clause, when viewed in isolation, is allowed.

4.2 *Guarding Weak Parties and Public, Third-Party, and Diffuse Interests*

In addition to fair trial rights constraining procedural agreements, there are other limits as well. First, because courts are public bodies, agreements that would increase the use of the judiciary's scarce resources are likely to have repercussions for other cases. Procedural contracts should, therefore, be contingent on being resource-neutral. This distinguishes litigation agreements from arbitral tribunals and other privately funded ADR procedures: the amount of work and services that they provide are limited only by the parties' willingness and ability to pay. Allowing the parties to agree to modifications is thus unproblematic.

Second, protecting less powerful and vulnerable parties, such as consumers, employees, and tenants from being tricked into agreements to their detriment is a concern. Alain Ancery and Bart Krans discuss how the CJEU has struck down choice of court contracts between traders and consumers when they prevent the consumer

55 See Vebraite, this volume.

56 Hau, this volume, Section 3.1.

57 Bellander, this volume, Section 2; Strandberg, this volume, Sections 2.1 and 4; Vebraite, this volume, Sections 3 and 5.

from bringing an action close to the place of their domicile.[58] The CJEU has also struck down agreements that shift the burden of proof to the detriment of the consumer.

Third, procedural agreements could adversely affect third-party, collective, and diffuse interests. No coherent doctrine on how to protect these kinds of rights has emerged yet. This raises several questions, such as whether and to what extent and in which ways courts should investigate the existence of such interests. When these interests are manifest, the task is likely to be relatively easy; when these interests are less pronounced, or even latent, courts could face difficulties in rendering efficient protection of them. It is not clear how courts should establish to what extent the agreement jeopardises such interests and what is the threshold for acceptable interference.

In a European context, the CJEU has stepped in to guard public interests. In the *Braathens* case, the Swedish Equality Ombudsman brought an action against Braathens Regional Aviation AS for discriminating against a passenger.[59] The action ended in a settlement in which Braathens Regional Aviation AB agreed to pay the passenger a sum without recognising that discrimination had occurred. The CJEU held that the sanctions for racial discrimination need to be commensurate to the seriousness of the breaches against the Equal Treatment Directive.[60] Because the action was brought by the Equality Ombudsman, the claimant had expressly submitted a request for a finding of discrimination, and, as EU law requires national courts to provide effective protection of rights derived from EU law, the national court was precluded from ending such action by settlement unless the defendant explicitly recognises the discrimination. As with other aspects of EU law, it is unclear to which additional categories of cases the arguments forwarded by the CJEU apply and whether EU Member States are willing to adopt these views and extend them to areas dominated by domestic law.

Fair trial rights and the protection of public interests and weaker parties do not preclude procedural agreements; they only state that freedom of contract does not fully apply to procedural contracts. There is a threshold for how much and in what ways the parties can agree to deviate from the rules of civil procedure.

58 Ancery and Krans, this volume, Section 5. See also Bellander, this volume, Section 2.4; Kakiuchi, this volume, Section 3.4; Strandberg, this volume, Section 3.

59 Case C-30/19 *Diskrimineringsombudsmannen v. Braathens Regional Aviation AB* [2021] ECLI:EU:C:2021:269, paras. 38, 43-44, 49 and 56-57. See also Anna Wallerman Ghavanini, 'Remedies for Non-material Damages: Striking Out in a New Direction? Braathens' (2022) 59 Common Market Law Review 151.

60 Council Directive 2000/43/C implementing the principle of equal treatment between persons irrespective of racial or ethnic origin [2000] OJ L180/22.

5 Procedural Agreements at Trial

One argument for procedural agreements is that they could increase the efficiency of court proceedings by tailoring them to the needs and preferences of parties. However, procedural agreements could also delay proceedings and reduce efficiency for several reasons, such as when the procedural clause generates disputes.

5.1 *Courts Dealing with Procedural Agreements*

From the courts' perspective, procedural agreements could also be costly, particularly in the absence of a regulatory regime. How should courts then proceed when interpreting procedural agreements? Should they apply the usual standards for the interpretation of contracts? Which documents, arguments, and information should they base their interpretation on? Should they assume an active role in investigating the existence and background of procedural clauses?[61] Should courts consider that a party might have entered into the contract under a veil of ignorance or drafted it hastily without proper consideration?[62] Or, that the parties had foreseen very different disputes and circumstances when drafting the clause than what is at hand in the present case?[63] Moreover, agreements on procedure usually only surface if one of the parties does not comply, unless the court has a duty to investigate the existence of such agreements on its own motion. So, if the parties comply with an agreement not to invoke certain circumstances or facts or to exclude or cap certain litigation costs, the court will not know why the parties act as they do. Perhaps courts should investigate the presence of a procedural agreement on their own motion, or perhaps litigants should be obliged to disclose all clauses with direct procedural consequences.[64]

Suppose the court finds that the clause violates some important public policy or interest; should it simply disregard the clause or attempt to reconstruct it to make it compatible with those policies?[65] The standards applicable to the control are, nonetheless, unclear, perhaps except for the choice of court clauses in European consumer contracts. The argumentation of the CJEU in *Tilman*, when contrasted with its ruling in, for

61 Ancery and Krans, this volume, Sections 3 and 5.1.

62 Kakiuchi, this volume, Section 3.3.1; Uzelac, this volume, Section 2.2.

63 Gernard Wagner, 'Dispute Resolution as a Product: Competition between Civil Justice Systems' in Horst Eidenmüller (ed), *Regulatory Competition in Contract Law and Dispute Resolution* (C.H. Beck 2013) 376-385.

64 Ancery and Krans, this volume, Sections 5 and 6; Bellander, this volume, Section 3.2.

65 Ancery and Krans, this volume, Section 4.

instance, *Grupo Oceano*[66] and *Pannon*,[67] tangibly demonstrates that such standards are likely to be very contextual and only apply to a specific group of cases. This seems to suggest that the method of interpretation should consider the subject matter of the case, the parties to the case etc.[68]

How should courts proceed when they encounter imbalanced procedural clauses? How should courts proceed when, for instance, the agreed-upon ADR process is not sufficiently identified or the obligations related to the process are ambiguous? Should courts simply disregard such agreements or reconstruct them? Or should they allow the parties to reformulate the clause? Courts run the risk of procedural contracts increasing their workload and considerably increasing the cost and duration of litigation if procedural agreements beget new disputes or escalate the complexity of dispute resolution.

If procedural clauses are deeply entangled with substantive clauses, then disregarding the clause could render the agreement unbalanced. Simultaneously, allowing the parties to renegotiate the procedural clause could thrust the parties to renegotiate the rest of the contract or to disputes regarding rebalancing. This raises the question of who should bear the risk of a potentially unclear or disallowed procedural clause.[69]

It is also unclear whether courts should enforce procedural agreements as such, as a breach of the agreement by ordering penalty fees and similar contractual sanctions, or not at all. For instance, courts could sanction noncompliance with ADR agreements by penalty fees or by ordering the noncompliant party to bear the costs of proceedings, but only if the sanction is not disproportionately harsh. Enforcing the obligations against weak parties who might not have understood what the ADR clause entails could, in practice, result in denial of access to court and weak parties being forced to use low-quality ADR procedures or settle at unfavourable terms due to lack of real access to court.[70]

What happens if there is a joinder of parties, or third-party intervenors, who are not a party to the litigation agreement? Should the agreement be disregarded, or should it prevent having multiple parties in the case?[71] Especially for (potential) landmark cases, a procedural clause that has the potential to alter the outcome of the case could have adverse consequences for using the case as a source of legal arguments in future cases.

---

66 Joined cases C-240/98-244/98 *Océano Grupo Editorial SA v. Rocio Murciano Quintero and others* [2000] ECLI:EU:C:2000:346.

67 Case C-243/08 *Pannon GSM Zrt. v. Erzsébet Sustikné Győrfi* [2009] ECLI:EU:C:2009:350.

68 Eichel and Tovar Galván, this volume, Section 4.3.2.

69 See also Kakiuchi, this volume, Section 3.3.2.

70 Nylund, this volume, Section 3.2.

71 Hau, this volume, Section 6.

Consequently, while procedural agreements harbour the potential to increase the predictability and efficiency of court proceedings, they could also escalate litigation risks and inefficiency. This applies mainly when the doctrines and regulations are underdeveloped.

5.2 *A Critical Appraisal of Procedural Agreements*

From the parties' perspective, procedural contracts could significantly increase litigation risks if the rules and standards for determining the validity and interpretation of procedural agreements are not sufficiently predictable. Without a clear doctrine for procedural agreements, such agreements could be a source of cost and delay. Unless the procedural contract clause is unequivocal, the parties to the contract also run the chance of disputes arising from the interpretation of the clause. A doctrine of the requirements for procedural agreements is necessary yet insufficient to resolve all legal problems arising from such contracts. Particularly for clauses that could prompt courts to strike down the agreement in the name of public interests, the outcome is hard to predict.[72]

As Alan Uzelac and Wolfgang Hau remind us, parties to arbitration agreements often do not avail themselves of the freedom to tailor the procedure.[73] Most arbitration agreements refer to the rules of a specific arbitral institution and make no amendments to the rules of proceedings because tailoring procedural rules is both time-consuming and not necessarily worth the effort. They could increase uncertainty and consequently also the risks regarding the proceedings. Drafting precise, predictable procedural clauses is often laborious. Furthermore, as Shusuke Kakiuchi observes, an agreement between the parties is a prerequisite for deviating from the standard rules of procedure by contract: unless the parties reach an agreement on specific modifications, the regular rules apply.[74] Thus, the costs of negotiating changes might far exceed the benefits of those changes unless the parties use a 'standard procedural agreement', the consequences of which are easily foreseen. Experience drawn from arbitration seems to indicate a finite demand for procedural agreements in many jurisdictions.[75]

6 THE PROSPECTS OF PROCEDURAL AGREEMENTS

The proper place of, and the perceived need for, procedural agreements depend on many factors, including its relative rigidity or flexibility, perceived efficiency, level of

72 Kakiuchi, this volume, Section 3.3.2.
73 Hau, this volume, Section 4.2; Uzelac, this volume, Section 2.4.
74 Kakiuchi, this volume, Section 3.3.1.
75 Uzelac, this volume, Section 2.4.

fragmentation, and so on. Also, the perception of the ideal balance between private and public functions of civil litigation, as well as the extent to which public considerations are weighted, are likely to impact the attitudes towards procedural agreements. Because civil procedure rules should be treated as a system, procedural agreements should be designed to serve the system to which they are introduced.[76]

Procedural agreements are neither a panacea nor something that should be prohibited. Given the variation in the design of the underlying civil procedure systems and cultures and various policy considerations, there appears to be no single formula which would fit every context. Jurisdictions considering facilitating the use of procedural agreements should carefully consider which purposes the agreements could serve in various types of cases, how they interlock the underlying civil procedure system, and how to balance the endeavours of increasing the efficiency of court proceedings with fundamental values underpinning the rule of law, including equal access to justice and fair trial rights.

Therefore, a balance must be struck between tailor-made proceedings and the need for uniformity to guarantee foreseeability, equal treatment, access to court, and safeguarding the essential functions of courts as a critical institution in the rule of law.[77]

It remains to be seen whether procedural agreements will proliferate, whether the shift towards increasingly flexible court proceedings and active case management will become the preferred avenue for tailoring proceedings,[78] or whether in future the systems may be inclined towards reverting to more unitary rules, or any combination of these alternatives.

76 See also Bellander, this volume, Section 2.2.

77 See also Strandberg, this volume, Section 2.2.

78 Uzelac, this volume, Section 3.

List of Authors

Alain Ancery is Secretary-director of the Supervisory College of the Dutch Bar Association
Henrik Bellander is Senior Lecturer of Law at Uppsala University
Antonio Cabral is Professor of Law and Co-Director of the Center for German and Comparative Law Studies, Rio de Janeiro State University
Florian Eichel is Co-Director of the Institute for Private International Law and Civil Procedure at the University of Bern
Rorick Tovar Galván is former Research Associate and Lecturer at the University of Bern
Wolfgang Hau is Professor of Law at the Ludwig Maximilians University Munich
Shusuke Kakiuchi is Professor of Law at the University of Tokyo
Bart Krans is Professor of Law at Leiden University
Anna Nylund is Professor of Law at the University of Bergen
Magne Strandberg is Professor of Law at the University of Bergen
Alan Uzelac is Professor of Law at the University of Zagreb
Vigita Vėbraitė is Associate Professor of Law at Vilnius University

INDEX

www.ingramcontent.com/pod-product-compliance
Lightning Source LLC
Chambersburg PA
CBHW080939240926
51849CB00004BA/496
9789047302254